OFFICE *US* Manual

Edited by
Eva Franch
Ana Miljački
Carlos Mínguez Carrasco
Jacob Reidel
Ashley Schafer

Lars Müller Publishers
**Storefront for Art
and Architecture**

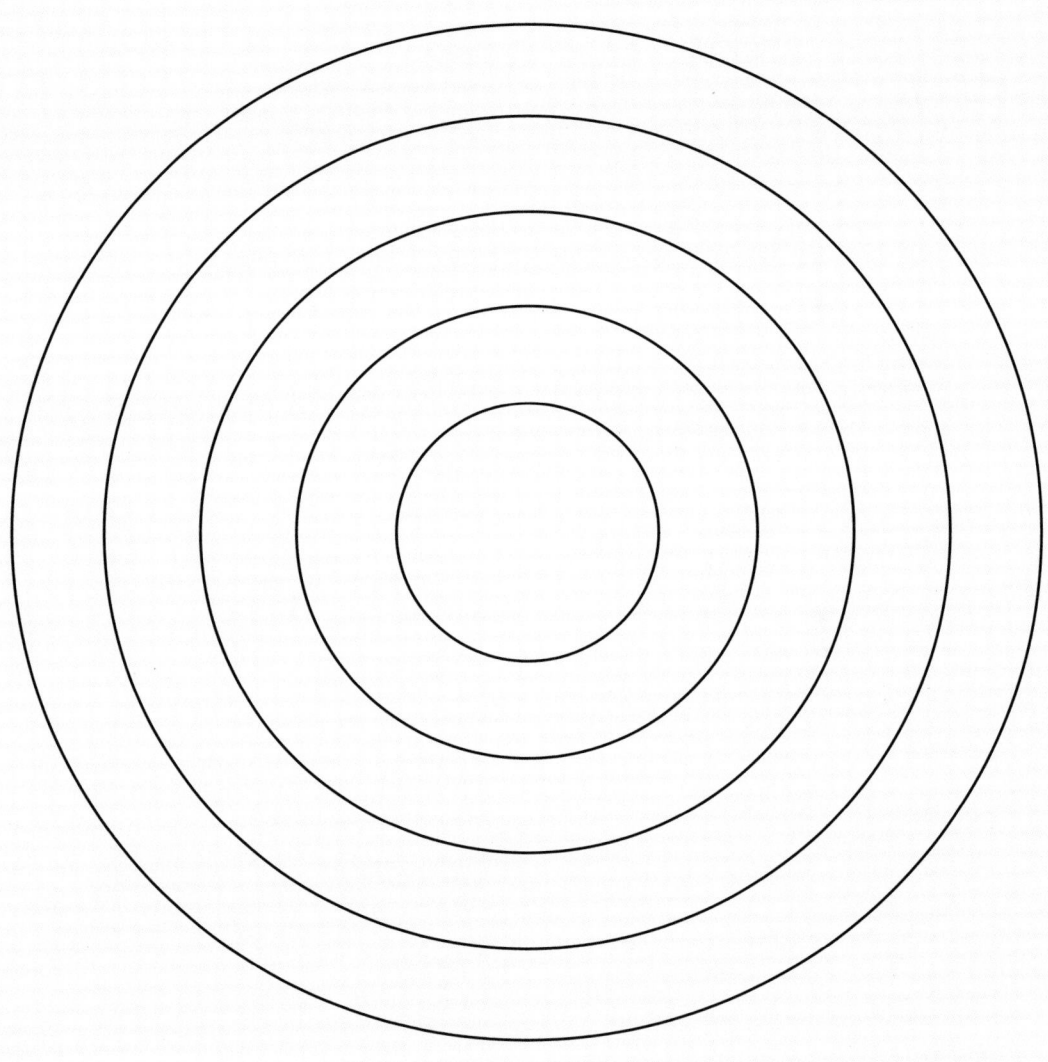

OFFICE*US* Manual

Editors

Eva Franch i Gilabert, Ana Miljački, Carlos Mínguez Carrasco, Jacob Reidel, Ashley Schafer

Images

Amie Siegel, The Architects, 2014. Commissioned by Storefront for Art and Architecture for Office*US*.

Research Assistants

Miriam Abd El Azim, Hanna Ahblad, Amna Ahmed, Carolina Alexander, Victoria Álvarez Calvo, Jordan Marie Anderson, Erika Angel Fernández de Soto, Christina Badal, Kimji Bae, Levi Bedall, Sébastien van den Berg, Viviana Bernal, Alina Bibisheva, Abena Bonna, Livia Calari, Tyrene Calvesbert, Nickolas Castillo, Diandra Cohen, Nerissa Cooney, Ian Costello, Abdelrahman El-Zamly, Sergio Galaz, Carolina Gomez, Susana Holguin-Veras, Ines Klausberg, Katerina Kulanova, Inju Lee, Charlene Liang, Katia Loizou, Jesse McCormick, Natalie Mufson, Maria Paz de Moura Castro, Olivia Paonita, Elise Stella, Michael Signorile, Yuma Shinohara, Caterina Viguera, Demet Yildiz

Special Archives Research

Johnathan Puff

Graphic Analysis Assistants

Megan Armstrong, Adam Feldman, Ana López Sánchez-Vegazo, Ángel Ramos Mombiedro, Sai Rojanapirom, Yuma Shinohara, Darcy Spence, Ann Vaikla, Connie Wang

Copy Editor

Walter Ancarrow

Special Thanks

The students of GSAPP Research Seminar Fall 2013 "Corporate-Avantgarde, Get Yourself Together: Instrumentalization and Disruption in Cultures of Creative Production— Or How to Make the Most Intelligent Architecture Office...Ever." Taught by Eva Franch, Dominic Leong and Chris Leong, Carlos Mínguez Carrasco, and Jacob Reidel

Students: Jordan Anderson, Cecil Barnes, Miles Fujiki, Yasmina Khan, Ryan John King, Ricardo Leon, Nicolo Lewanski, George Louras, Bika Rebek, Karl Roarty, Monica Socorro, Davi Weber

Thank you also to: Lance Brown, Irina Chernyakova, Laura Cheung, Ennead Architects, Michael Kubo, Helene Nguyen, Margery Perlmutter

Storefront Staff

Chialin Chou, Andrew Emmet, Eva Franch, Jinny Khanduja, Max Lauter, Carlos Mínguez Carrasco

Design

Pentagram: Natasha Jen, Jang Hyun Han, Joseph Han, Veronica Hoglund, Maurann Stein, Boqin Peng, Ji Park

Publisher

Lars Müller Publishers
Zürich, Switzerland
www.lars-mueller-publishers.com

Printing

DZA Druckerei zu Altenburg, Germany

Typefaces

Courier, Arial and Times New Roman are the typefaces of the Office*US* project. These three typefaces are among the most mundane and readily available on the market, and as such are frequently used for efficiency by US offices.

ISBN 978-3-03778-439-6

This publication has been made possible through the support of the The Graham Foundation.

TABLE OF CONTENTS

a) Salary plus a monthly bonus. The general salary today for a qualified man being anything from £45 to £75 a month, and bonus of course depending entirely upon his value in the office.

b) Salary from £40 to £60 a month plus a percentage on such parts of the work executed in the office by the Assistant. This, of course, would only apply to a fully qualified Architect, and would bring to such a man anything from £75 to £125 a month if of the right type.

Naturally conditions in South Africa are somewhat different and it would take some months for anybody coming out here to get a grip of the differences and regulations, etc. The American Consulate hold that there would be no difficulty under the present emergency in obtaining a passage and permission to land.

The arrangement naturally would have to be made for suitable accommodation for such Assistants and family, if any.

I would appreciate having your earliest reply if there is any possibility of suitable men being found to come out to this country. The conditions generally in South Africa are reasonably good, but the cost of living is fairly high, as the average European maintains a fairly high standard of living.

Thanking you, Yours faithfully, M. F. Stern

Please address any inquires to the office of the Director of Public and Professional Relations at The Octagon.

AIA Bulletin, American Consulate, 1947

IN SYRIA

WE HAVE BEEN INFORMED by the Minister of Syria that the municipality of Aleppo is desirous of engaging two American architects for city planning and development schemes for that city. The work for this city, some 40 sq. kilometers in area and with a population of some 300,000 will consist of the design of new buildings, the organization of the old existing city, the design of bridges, public market places, etc. Anyone interested should send in his application *in duplicate* to this office. We, in turn, will submit the applications to the Minister of Syria. We quote from the Minister's letter:

"The general conditions on which foreign personnel are engaged by the Government of Syria are as follows
"The monthly salaries ranges from $750.00 to $1,000.00 subject to no allowances. Half of the salary is paid in dollars and half in Syrian pounds.
"The Government pays the travel expenses of the architect from the United States to Syria and back to the United States when the work is completed.
"The contract is for one year, but can be renewed for two more years if the two contracting parties agree to such renewal.
"The above are roughly the general terms on the basis of which contracts have been signed between various Departments of the Government of Syria and foreign experts."

IN AFGHANISTAN

WE HAVE BEEN NOTIFIED by the Royal Afghanistan Legation that the Government of that country is seeking American architects to render full architectural services for a proposed Public Works Program. The Afghan Ministry of Public Works calls our attention to the following requirements:

1) The applicants must be graduates of recognized architectural schools;
2) They must have at least ten years' technical experience in an architect's office;
3) They must be able to plan whole buildings of various types, both simple and elaborate, from the original conception to the last detail;
4) They must be conversant with the estimating of building costs;
5) They must be conversant with modern city planning.

We are further informed that the position offered by the Afghanistan Government will pay about $8,000 per annum, plus allowances and travel expenses. Anyone interested and wishing to apply will please send to the Department of Public and Professional Relations, A.I.A., a resume of his qualifications and experience –
in duplicate.

AIA Bulletin, Government of Syria and Government of Afghanistan, 1947

ARCHITECTURAL DRAFTSMAN

Experienced in working drawings and details with firm specializing in school design in several states. Good opportunity for experience in other phases of office activities. Please state training and salary expected. Warren S. Holmes Company, Architects, 2200 Olds Tower, Lansing, Mich.

Progressive Architecture, Warren S. Holmes Company, 1949

EMPLOYMENT OPPORTUNITY FOR DESIGNER-DRAFTSMAN

The Lambert Landscape Company, Dallas, Texas, needs designer-draftsman with general landscape training, preferably with degree. Work of great variety, expanding through Southwest, with emphasis on private home grounds. Present design and drafting staff comprises eight people, including graduates of Harvard, California, and Michigan.

Starting salary, depending on experience, $250-375 per month.

Apply: Mr. Richard B. Myrick, Lambert Landscape Company, 3800 Northwest Highway, Dallas, Texas.

Landscape Architecture, Lambert Landscape Company, 1950

SPECIFICATION WRITER

Practical man with broad, general experience in building construction work (not mechanical). State qualifications and salary expected. Specification Department, Albert Kahn Associated Architects and Engineers, Inc., 345 New Center Building, Detroit 2, Mich.

Progressive Architecture, Albert Kahn Associated Architects and Engineers Inc., 1951

DESIGNERS AND DRAFTSMEN

A genuine opportunity to work and grow with an expanding progressive architectural organization specializing in contemporary school planning which has gained national recognition. We can offer the security that comes with a permanent position and company benefits in a medium sized office with outstanding facilities for engineering and site planning. Send resume or phone to Warren H. Ashley, Architect, 740 North Main Street, West Hartford, Conn.

Progressive Architecture, Warren H. Ashley Architect, 1957

DESIGNER-ARCHITECTURAL

Minumum 5 years experience. Send resume to Norman N. Giller & Associates, 975 Arthur Godrey Road, Miami Beach, Florida.

Progressive Architecture, Norman N. Giller & Associates, job posting, 1963

OVERSEAS ARCHITECT

French speaking, U.S. citizen, registered architect with 10 to 15 years experience, preferably in school or university type design, for work in Southeast Asia. Send complete resume of technical training, experience, and salary requirements to Box #553, Progresive Architecture.

Progressive Architecture, 1963

ARCHITECTURAL DESIGNER

Experienced architectural designer required by long established firm of Canadian Architects situated in Toronto. Applicant must have proven ability and be capable of presenting his ideas in distinctive renderings. Applications will be treated with strict confidence and should include resume of qualifications and experience. Box #500, Progressive Architecture.

Progressive Architecture, 1963

ARCHITECT'S ESTIMATOR

Wanted for a position in Chicago. Must be experienced estimator with knowledge of building construction cost. Salary open. Skidmore, Owings & Merrill, 30 West Monroe Street, Chicago, Illinois 60603.

Progressive Architecture, Skidmore, Owings & Merrill, 1968

ARCHITECT DESIGNER

Experience preferred. Will consider recent graduate. Medium sized firm. National and international practice. Can offer excellent salary. Associateship, partnership possibilities, competent colleagues, exciting work. City close to hunting, fishing and lake country of Northwestern Ontario. Enquiries to: R.D. Gillmor, No. 10 Architectural Group, 10 Donald Street North, Winnepeg 1, Manitoba.

Progressive Architecture, R.D. Gillmor, No. 10 Architectural Group, 1968

EXCEPTIONAL OPPORTUNITIES FOR ARCHITECTS...AND WE MEAN EXCEPTIONAL!

We are willing to provide the imaginative, ambitious Architect with a diversity of career-broadening challenges only a major architectural firm can offer. Your advancement – both professionally and financially – can parallel the growth of A. Epstein & Sons, Inc., (founded in 1921), a company which has grown significantly in the last five years and continues to move ahead at even more rapid pace... a company large enough to be active in every phase of industrial, commercial and institutional building, yet structured so individual efforts are highly visible and immediately rewarded. Salaries are excellent, benefits plentiful. Exceptional opportunities for GROUP LEADERS & DESIGNERS also.

If you're a graduate architect, registered professional or have solid related experience, contact: Ron Jankowski, Personnel Manager.

A. EPSTEIN AND SONS, INC.
2011 W. Pershing Rd. Chicago, Illinois 60609
Phone: (312) 847-6000
An Equal Opportunity Employer

Progressive Architecture, A. Epstein & Sons Inc., job posting, 1968

ARCHITECTURAL DESIGNER

Design oriented, West Coast Architectural and planning firm has opening for a creative designer to develop concepts, work with clients, and control design development through production phases. Diversified and expanding nationwide practice. Send confidential resume including salary requirements to: Walter Richardson Associates A.I.A., 230 E. 17th Street, Suite 200, Costa Mesa, California, 92627.

Progressive Architecture, A. Epstein and Sons Inc., 1968

POSITION OPEN FOR DIRECTOR OF DESIGN

Applicant must have a masters degree in Landscape Architecture (Harvard Graduate preferred), be of proven design ability with a minimum of three years experience in a professional office in planning and project work, be capable to assuming total responsibility for this growing firm's design effort.

Salary is from $15,000 to $18,000 dependent on ability and available time (if applicant is teaching), plus profit sharing and fringe benefits.

Interested individuals may contact Mr. Donald Brinkerhoff, President, Lifescapes, Inc., Landscape Architects & Planners, 2800 So. Main Street, Santa Ana, California 92707, (714) 540-7422.

Landscape Architecture, Lifescapes, Inc., Landscape Architects and Planners, 1972

LANDSCAPE ARCHITECT / ASSOCIATE

Small landscape architecture firm needs graduate landscape architect as associate and design manager. Associate will work with clients and be responsible for some promotion.

Experience is not as important as the ability to work effectively with clients.

Unique opportunity for aggressive person tired of large design corporations to advance and grow with our progressive management.

Send complete reume to:

PCA Associates #104
6535 Golden Valley Road
Minneapolis, Minnesota 55427

Men over 35 need not apply.

Landscape Architecture, PCA Associates, 1972

ARCHITECT – PERMANENT POSITIONS OPEN

Graduate Architects with outstanding Design ability and minimum 3 years Planning/Design experience on major projects. Experience in the Health Facilities desirable but not mandatory. Outstanding opportunity for advancement and growth as key members of interdisciplinary teams, working on national/international projects. Company paid benefits. Submit resume, salary requirements: The Drake Partnership, Architects, 10425 Old Olive Street Road, St. Louis, Mo. 63141.

Architectural Record, The Drake Partnership, Architects, 1975

SYSTEM ANALYST / PROGRAMMER

To work on computer applications to architecture. Emphasis on data-base systems. Architectural degree, and experience developing computer systems, required. Send complete resume and salary requirements to: Barry Milliken, Skidmore, Owings and Merrill, 400 Park Ave., New York, NY 10022

ARCHITECTURAL OPENINGS

Bernard Johnson Inc. An Architectural & Engineering Consulting firm in the ENR Top 100, has immediate openings for:

PROJECT MANAGER
BA/BS in Architecture with registration required. Minimum of 8 years Architectural experience including at least 3 years in Project Management. Background in schools, labs and hospitals preferred.

PROJECT ARCHITECT
Degree with registration and 5 to 10 years experience in Architectural Design/Production and Specifications. Experience as Job Captain or Project Architect with direct responsibility for producing and coordinating architectural projects required.

ARCHITECT
Degree with 1 to 2 years experience in Architectural Design/Production & Specifications.

For confidential consideration send resume with salary history to:

BERNARD JOHNSON INCORPORATED
Architects – Engineers – Planners
5050 Westheimer
Houston, Texas 77056
Attn: Dave Blascke
An Equal Opportunity Employer M/F

CHIEF OF PROJECT (ENERGY CONSERVATION):

East Africa; start 3/85 for 18 mths. -2 yrs. Required: Advanced architectural or engineering degree. Experience in energy conservation in building sector, passive solar construction, some familiarity with solar/wind technologies. Good French. Desired: previous project management experience; previous LDC living experience (prefer Africa). Send CV to D. Read, VITA, P.O. Box 12438, Arlington, Va. 22209 or call (703) 276-1800.

GROWING SAN FRANCISCO DESIGN FIRM SEARCHING

For highly motivated individual to oversee construction administration. Qualified person must heave 5+ years experience. Architectural registration not essential. Salary commensurate with experience. Send resume, references and salary history to: George Miers & Associates, 2 Bryant St., San Francisco, CA 94105.

PROJECT ARCHITECTS STRUCTURED FOR SUCCESS

Be a part of the team that is building the future in health care service, and share our success as the nation's largest HMO. Kaiser Permanente seeks qualified Project Architects for challenging and rewarding assignments.

Interfacing with top-level management at our Los Angeles Regional Headquarters, you'll be managing the planning, design, development and remodeling of new and existing facilities in Southern California including San Diego.

To qualify you must have a BS in Architecture or equivalent degree and a California Architectural license. Preferred candidates will possess 7 years project management experience and 1-3 years hospital project experience.

We offter a company paid family health and dental plan, life insurance, retirement benefits, long term disability, and more.

If you are looking for a challenging career opportunity with an established expanding organization, send your resume to:

Regional Personnel
Dept. 5287AR
4725 Sunset Blvd.
Los Angeles, CA 90027

KAISER PERMANENTE
Equal Opportunity Employer

ARCHITECTS

We are a growth oriented, state-of-the-art consulting design firm. Opportunity for ownership, bonuses, excellent salary and fringe benefits are only a few reasons for your consideration to join us.

FACILITIES ARCHITECT
Requires 5 years' experience in plant engineering with excellent interpersonal skills. Must be motivated towards achievement and accuracy.

PROJECT MANAGER/ARCHITECT
Registered, with 10 years' experience; responsible for coordinating to work all disciplines through leadership and interpersonal skills.

Send resume and salary history, in confidence, to:

SEAR-BROWN
85 Metro Park
Rochester, NY 14623

An Equal Opportunity Employer M/F

CLEVELAND, OHIO

Landscape Architect, small, progressive Landscape Architecture Firm seeking project manager for large scale recreational and housing projects, immediate need. Minimum of 3 to 5 years experience. Projects throughout the country involving all phases of project development, master planning, site design and construction documents. Send resume to Greg Copeland, Schmidt Copeland and Associates, 1220 W. 6, Cleveland, Ohio 44113

OPPORTUNITIES TO BUILD A FUTURE!!!

Russell Gibson von Dohlen is a growing, multi-disciplined architecture firm located in Farmington, CT, a suburb of Hartford. As a result of acquiring some exciting new projects, we are currently seeking creative, dynamic, top caliber architectural professionals for the following positions:

PROJECT LANDSCAPE ARCHITECT
5 years' progressive experience with a broad range of projects. Knowledge of state and federal regulations, codes and procedures effecting land development. Excellent presentation in marketing skills a must. Bachelor of Landscape Architecture and Licensing required.

ASSISTANT LANDSCAPE ARCHITECT

ASSISTANT LANDSCAPE ARCHITECT

1 to 3 years' experience with basic technical knowledge and design skills to meet specific project requirements. Bachelor of Landscape Architecture or equivalent experience required.

We offer competitive salary, an excellent benefits package, and a pleasant working environment. If you are self motivated and ready for an exciting challenge, please call or send resume and salary history to:

Carol Kardas
Human Resources Manager

Russell Gibson von Dohlen
281 Farmington Avenue
Farmington, CT 06034

An Equal Opportunity Employer

Landscape Architecture,
Russell Gibson von Dohlen, 1988

SPECIFICATION WRITER

For progressive 50-person arch./int./planning firm. Ability to interact with design disciplines essential; min. 10 yrs. exp. in research and spec writing; familiar with AIA MASTERSPEC and CSI format. Send resume and sal. req. to Jack Hodell, Baxter Hodell Donnelly Preston, Inc., 3500 Red Bank Road, Cincinnati, OH 45227, (513) 271-1634. EQE/M/F.

AIA MEMO, Jack Hodell, Baxter Hodell, Donnelly
Preston, Inc., 1991

MCCARTY ARCHITECTS-TUPELO

MS-Front page of the Wall Street Journal March 3, 1994, has recognized Tupelo, Mississippi's strong economic growth and excellent quality of life. Opportunities exist to join an established progressive firm expanding to meet this growth. We have openings for aggressive, innovative team players with 8+ years of solid experience in healthcare/commercial/industrial projects: Lead Architect-project design/ management, Staff Architect-building technology/CADD production, Staff Architect-CA, Construction Manager-complex healthcare projects, Construction Project Manager/Estimator-computerized estimating & accounting for design/build. Send resumes: Barbara Basinger, McCarty Architects, 533 West Main St., Tupelo, MS 38801.

Architectural Record, McCarty Architects, 1994

BILINGUAL INTERN ARCHITECT, 40HRS/WK.,

9am-5pm, $18,000/year. Translate construction documentation, building codes, and terminology for architectural projects in the People's Republic of China. Assist in the preparation of design development drawings. General drafting of construction documents. Tools: Drawbase (Computer-aided design and drafting software); Twin Bridge. Bachelor of Architecture as well as two years of experience as a Bilingual Intern Architect or Assistant Architect required. Must speak, read and write Mandarin Chinese. Must have proof of legal authority to work permanently in the U.S. Send two copies of resume to: Illinois Department of Employment Security, 401 South State Street – 3 South, Chicago, IL 60605, Attention: Jean Woodson, Reference #V-IL-11325-W. No calls. An Employer Paid Ad.

Architectural Record, 1994

GGLO IS FORGING INNOVATIVE SOLUTIONS THAT ELEVATE THE QUALITY AND SPIRIT OF LIFE!

GGLO Architecture and Interior Design, a dynamic,

growth-oriented, multi-disciplinary Seattle design firm seeks talented individuals to join our team. GGLO offers a competitive salary, an attractive benefits package, and a friendly, team-oriented office culture.

We are currently hiring:
PROJECT MANAGERS, PROJECT ARCHITECTS, INTERIOR DESIGNERS, SPACE PLANNERS, INTERN ARCHITECTS

Our clients and work are focused in Landscape Architecture, Master-planning, Retail, Hospitality, Office, Corporate Interiors, Single-family Residential and Multi-family Housing. Successful candidates will be creative, energetic, service-oriented professionals. They will have collaborative design skills and good organization and communication skills. AutoCAD 14 and Windows proficiency are also required.

EOE. Send cover letter and resume to: GGLO, Attn: Sarah Hall, 1191 Second Ave., Ste. 1650, Seattle, WA 98101-3426, fax to (206) 467-0627, or e-mail to shall@ gglo.com.

See one of GGLO's projects featured on page 150.

Architectural Record, GGLO, 2000

SENIOR DESIGNERS

Senior Designer positions in Washington, D.C. Requires: Master's degree in Architecture or City Planning/Urban Design with 6 years experience as a Designer working on projects that include housing, large-scale residential subdivisions, offices, and commercial properties. EEO/AAP Employer. Send resume to: Jeannette Merino, Gensler, 2020 K Street, NW, Washington D.C. 20006. Refer to job #002 when responding to this ad.

Architectural Record, Gensler, 2001

SENIOR PROJECT DESIGNER

WPB, FL – Senior Project Designer for hospitality design firm. B.A. in Architecture +5 yrs exp. in job offered. Formulate basic design concepts for interiors of hotels & international hospitality projects. Consult w/clients, prep info re. designs, specs, materials, cost estimates in connection w/design/construction projects in Europe & Far East. Must have exp. in Asia & Europe projects. Comp salary. Fax resume to (561) 650-7000

Architectural Record, 2002

ARCHITECTURAL SPECIFICATION WRITER

Min. 10 years experience utilizing masterspec. Full-time position in our main office in West Palm Beach. Send resumes only to STH Architectural Group, 515 N. Flagler Dr., Suite 1400, W. Palm Beach, Fl. 33401 or Fax 561-655-4828 or mrossin@sth-arch.com

Architectural Record, STH Architectural Group
2005

ARCHITECTURAL INTERN

Arch Firm sks Arch Intern. Resrch, plan & dsgn. Using Auto Cad R14 & ADT. Speak w/ Korean clients. Req: BS/BA in Arch, Arch Eng or equiv & 2 yrs exp. Send res to Palisades Dsgn Grp Architects, 5 E. Palisades Ave, Englewood, NJ 07631

Architectural Record, Palisades Design Group
Architects, 2003

PROJECT ARCHITECT

Stamford, CT, sought by Perkins Eastman Architects PC

to design & develop concepts for laboratory buildings & golf course club houses. Must have Master in Arch. Must be licensed in CT. Send resumes to: 115 Fifth Avenue, 3rd Floor, NY, NY 10003 Attn: Doreen Carbone

Architecture Magazine, Perkins Eastman Architects PC, 2006

ARCHITECTURAL & URBAN DESIGNER (NYC)

Prep/review/present plans for conceptual dsgn (incl 2D&3D dwgs) for pub spaces & lg scale complex proj. Exp w/leading dsgn teams, innovative space dsgn & lg projs. Exp w/dsgng in India, Korea & China. Knowl of AutoCAD, 3D Max, Sketch-up, Rhino, Adobe Illustrator & Photoshop. Min Masters of Arch Dsgn & 2 yrs exp. Mail resume to:

Ehrenkrantz Eckstut & Kuhn Architects, Job: 0807, 161 Ave of the Americas, 3rd Fl, NY, NY 10013.

Architectural Record, Ehrenkrantz Eckstut & Kuhn Architects, 2009

PROJECT DESIGNER

Page Southerland Page, LLP in Houston, TX seeks Project Designer to execute the design effort on projects including commercial, healthcare, hospitality, institutional, science, and technology and residential facilities. Qualified applicants will possess an MS in Architecture or related field and 1 year of experience in architectural design, experience in computer modeling and rendering including Photoshop, InDesign, 3D Max, and VRay. Must have 1 year of experience with REVIT. In lieu, would accept a BS in Architecture or related field and 5 years of experience in architectural design, experience in computer modeling and rendering including Photoshop, InDesign, 3D Max, and VRay. Must have 1 year of experience with REVIT. E-mail resume to resumes@pspaec. com. Must put job code 2677627 on resume.

Architectural Record, Page Southerland Page, LLP, 2013

INTERMEDIATE ARCHITECT

Diller Scofidio + Renfro is an interdisciplinary design studio that integrates architecture, the visual arts, and the performing arts. Based in New York City, Diller Scofidio + Renfro is led by four partners who work collaboratively with a staff of 100 architects, artists and administrators.

We are currently seeking experienced intermediate design leaders to support significant architectural projects. Candidates will have the following qualifications:

- Professional Degree, Master's Preferred
- 6-12 years experience in Architectural Practice, Registered Architects preferred
- Previous work on internationally significant buildings
- Strong Skills In Conceptual Design, Building Planning, Detailing, and Presentation
- Focus on Institutional Buildings, particularly Museum, Performing Arts, and Education types
- Previous Full Construction Phase Experience
- Demonstrated Leadership of Design Competitions
- Skills in 3Dmax and/or Rhino

A cover letter, resume, and minimum of 3 references with contact information in PDF format of a maximum 10MB should be submitted by email to employment@dsrny.com. Be sure to indicate your specific roles and responsibility in your relevant work experience. Please include the position title "Intermediate Architect" in the subject line.

Please limit correspondence to email at this time.

Diller Scofidio + Renfro is an equal opportunity em-

Diller Scofidio + Renfro is an equal opportunity employer and considers applicants for all positions without regard to race, color, religion, creed, gender, national origin, age, disability, marital or veteran status, sexual orientation, or any other legally protected status.

archinect.com, Diller Scofidio + Renfro, 2016

SENIOR DESIGNER/ARCHITECT

BIG is a young architectural company, characterized by an entrepreneurial spirit, true team-work across areas of expertise and new ways of approaching conventional tasks. We have an informal work environment where camaraderie and collegial support are highly valued and where ambition, very high work morale and dedication to being the innovators of our field unify the staff. Our firm is characterized by creativity, high energy and a unifying team spirit. We are dedicated to creating and maintaining a cool and enjoyable workplace and we continuously work at becoming better and better at what we do. Our headquarters are located in Copenhagen and our New York office has been open since 2010. We are a company in steady growth and over the last few years, we have worked intensely on the professionalization of our business. BIG Architecture seeks several Senior Designer/Architects to join us in our NYC office.

DUTIES MAY INCLUDE
- Reporting to the Partner-in-Charge
- Communication with client & consultant team
- Technical production of drawing sets
- Management of junior team members

ESSENTIAL SKILLS
- Fluent in English, spoken and written (2nd language is an asset)
- Strong conceptual and design skills
- Client management & project coordination skills
- Technical detailing & construction administration
- Software skills required: Revit, AutoCAD, Rhino, Adobe Suite
- Ability to work under pressure, meet deadlines and budget your time
- Ability to take initiative in response to direction or instruction
- A flexible and open attitude towards new ways of working
- Great interpersonal communication skills
- Knowledge of construction methods

EXPERIENCE & QUALIFICATIONS
- Professional degree in Architecture
- New York State licensure is required
- Minimum 8 years of experience as an Architect/Designer on built and published references
- Experience in filing construction documents and construction administration in N. America
- Experience from a leading American or International architecture office
- Licensure and/or LEED certification are assets

This job description reflects the core activities of the role although there will be changes in the emphasis of duties as required from time to time. There is a requirement for the post holder to recognize this and adopt a flexible approach to work.

All applicants will receive consideration for employment without regard to race, color, religion, age, creed, sex, citizenship status, gender, mental or physical disability, marital status, sexual orientation, national origin, or any other protected characteristic. BIG Architecture DPC is obligated under the law and committed to take affirmative action to employ and advance in employment qualified employees and applicants who are disabled veterans, recently separated veterans, Armed Forces service medal veterans, and other protected veterans. BIG Architecture DPC is obligated under the law and committed to take affirmative action to employ and advance in employment qualified individuals with disabilities.

All suitably qualified applicants should submit their

INTRODUCTION
00

0 — 1 INTRODUCTION

During the first few years of practice the absence of a system entails but little inconvenience; but as the work grows, a time will come when the methodless man will begin to tell his friends that it is not work but worry that is wearing him out, while the methodical man will welcome the expansion which enables him to make his organization more complete, and thus to keep his own personal share of work within reasonable limits, while at the same time he can feel confident that nothing is neglected.

The following instructions for the carrying on of office business are intended as a guide and incentive to intelligent systematization of the work to the end that artistic satisfaction in an attained result is not blunted in effect by the certainty of embarrassment and discredit naturally begotten of poor or unbusiness-like administration.

The purpose of this manual is to supply and provide information and help to new employees entering this organization, and to present members desiring information in regard to procedure. It is not intended as a document of rigid law but more as an elastic guide to office procedure, and is subject to revision from time to time.

Employees are to be given an introduction to the office and shown the basic office layout, where things are located, which machine is which, where supplies are kept, then an introduction to the product, the office procedures manual, overlay drafting cut and paste, and shown examples of how to use. Then they are "assigned" to a project architect who is responsible for reviewing their performance and giving them guidance.

This Handbook is prepared to acquaint you with the general policies and procedures of the company. We encourage you to contact the Corporate Personnel Department for assistance regarding any questions you may have. This employee handbook is not intended to create any contractual rights in favor of you or the company. The company reserves the right to change the terms of this handbook at any time. Your ideas and comments on these policies are welcomed and should be directed to the Corporate Personnel Department.

We are glad you have joined us. We look forward to working with you and wish you much success in your employment.

0 — 1 INTRODUCTION

Welcome to OfficeUS. This manual has been created with us—all architects—in mind.

Contemporary architectural practice is a form of collective production embedded within a physical, social, and technological space. This manual provides a series of references to speculate upon the *eternal play of repetition* embedded within the protocols and procedures that govern the "human edifices" (aka workers) that sustain the production of architecture.

Also known as the employee handbook, office guidelines, personnel policy, etc., the office manual explicitly sets down in writing *how things are done*. Addressing topics including hours of operation, file-naming conventions, the reception of visitors, conference room use, overtime, and others, the office manual attempts both to inform design philosophy/identity and to manage processes and people, even if few ever read the document in its entirety. Thus, although it is rarely shared with outsiders—or precisely because of that fact—the office manual illustrates the underlying organizational ideology of an architectural practice in the same way that drawings and models embody an office's design ethos.

This manual will help you become familiar with some of the privileges and responsibilities inherent in creating architecture. Providing both historical perspective and critical distance, the following pages have been assembled to assist you in charting your own path towards the design of alternative forms of practice.

OfficeUS Manual is organized into seventy-one topics (or "Policies") that reflect the most common subjects found in US architecture office manuals over the last century. Each Policy is comprised of two complementary halves. The first half consists of statements spanning the last one hundred years, excerpted from office manuals, office management guides, and professional practice publications. In some cases, sources have been marked as ███████ to maintain confidentiality. The second half of each Policy offers a new statement written by a contemporary contributor. These contributors, some of whom have never encountered an office manual before, include architects, designers, philosophers, historians, critics, and lawyers. Images from the film *The Architects* by Amie Siegel, commissioned for OfficeUS, bridge the two halves of each Policy.

By looking at the most quotidian aspects of office work, this book offers a starting point to critically examine day-to-day architectural practice and its relationship to design and society as a whole. Ultimately, the *Manual* invites us to reflect on the structures and politics ingrained in architecture's business, labor, and conceptual models.

Now, how to build a better practice—and world—is up to *us*. Eva Franch, Carlos Minguez Carrasco, Jacob Reidel

It is as a fine art that architecture has established itself in the hearts of men. If it had been merely the science of building or even of building well, its appeal would not have brought to it minds such as those of Ictinus and Michael Angelo. To good building, architecture adds high qualities of the imagination. It disposes of masses and details in ways that arouse us by their beauty, power or dignity. It writes the record of civilization. But to treat architecture as an art, this Handbook does not aspire.

To young men in architecture upon whose shoulders must fall the task of restoring the profession to its proper position of leadership, as much through the exercise of sound common sense in good business practice as through order and beauty in the design of their buildings.

As the basis of our architectural endeavor, we believe: 1. That a clear and articulate philosophy is the source of, and basic to, a creative architectural practice. 2. That basic to an articulate philosophy is a clear understanding of the nature and purpose of Architecture itself, i.e., What is Architecture?, What is its purpose? 3. That the above questions must ever be re-stated and evaluated with respect to social and technical change. 4. That Architecture is the creative expression of feeling through total ordered environment in terms of human values for social purpose. Values which have their roots in a continuity with the past. "We must feel it under our feet because we have raised ourselves upon it!" 5. That inherent in architectural expression is ordered diversity in harmony and unity with clarity of purpose. 6. That the goal of our professional practice is to provide the highest quality of total services which our capabilities can achieve.

The Company's Objectives are the conscientious, profitable performance of the services contracted to Owners, and the Company's management is responsible to its Board of Directors and in turn its Stockholders. It must remain highly competitive through smooth and efficient operations. Outstanding sales efforts and client relations are an integral part.

The practice of architecture is inherently optimistic—it's a belief in the power of design to enhance our daily lives and in the architect's unique ability to choreograph the human experience. That optimism is what motivates us.

We believe that architecture has a unique power to influence our world. As architects, we must recognize and respect our role in shaping civic life. We strive to create designs that aid society, advance technology, sustain the environment and inspire those around us to improve the world.

We believe that ▮▮▮▮▮▮▮ is a special kind of architectural practice which aspires to a high level of design quality and design innovation. We attempt to balance this goal with the goals of maintaining a viable business that can grow and be profitable for all members of the studio.

▮▮▮▮ is a global architecture, planning and design practice committed to enriching lives and designing solutions to the complex issues of our time. We add value to our clients' businesses by success-fully responding to marketplace and design challenges as well as issues of culture and environmental stewardship.

1 — 1 MISSION

It is no small task to commit to writing a mission statement as architects or as instigators of architectural discourse. Sure, the historical examples of the genre (think Ulrich Conrad's *Programs and Manifestoes on 20th Century Architecture*) are fun to read. Perhaps less so, adjusted for their contemporary internet PR function, where promises of "intelligence," responsiveness to client needs, and professional agility abound, at the expense of political urgency and historical awareness. But who wants to sound as zealous and authoritarian as our politicians do today (in almost every corner of the world), or who is as naïve about their own efficacy as modernist architects willed themselves to be? And yet, at their best, mission statements are contracts with the future; that alone should trump vanity. They allow us to consider the usefulness of even our smallest organizational, cultural, technical, or aesthetic offerings within a context that is bigger than our own pet projects and personal life stories.

It seemed until very recently that lateral tactics were most effective, that tricksters and surfers of historical forces were so much more graceful (and viable) than the foolhardy head-on collision with the wall. But then that smooth construction of synchronized movements of the corporate, national, military, and extra state interests began to burst at all of its various seams simultaneously, seeping toxic matter, fascisms of every shade, and devastated lives by the millions. The contemporary events have to be felt as undeniably historical (again). And when history is palpable and the future uncertain, mission statements just might have collective purchase again.

Read this one then as an invitation to write others, others that will challenge both the kinds of fascism that mobilize and use the desire of the masses, and the everyday fascism crouching deep in all of us, described famously by Michel Foucault as the love of power that inspires us to desire the very thing that dominates and exploits us. "What would that look like?" you might ask. Do we prepare for what might happen after the madness passes, after the deluge? Do we learn books (and buildings) by heart like contemporary versions of Ray Bradbury's fireman turned rebel, Montag? (*Fahrenheit 451*, 1953). Or do we will a future we want to inherit by acting as if we lived in its past already? Office*US* opted for both of these strategies together: preservation and projection. There are others worth trying as well. The archive is full of them. From resistance to détournement, from mass production to non-solicited, they can all be repurposed for our age, one by one, or all at once. There is no guarantee anything will work as planned, but as architects, critics, and citizens, our contemporary imperative must be to act such that the future we build makes other futures—the future itself—possible. Eva Franch, Ana Miljački, Ashley Schafer

INTERNAL MEMOS
AND GUIDELINES

1929
Albert C. Martin, Architect
Office Reorganization Memo

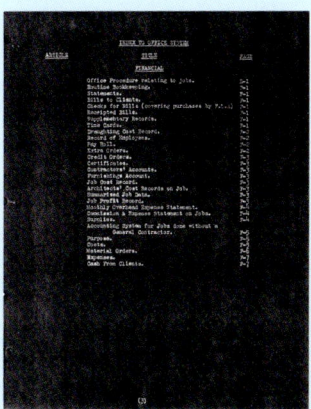

A
Manual of Office
Practice

Compiled for Use in The Office

of

McKIM, MEAD & WHITE
ARCHITECTS

By
F. J. ADAMS
1922

1922
F.J. Adams
*A Manual of Office Practice
Compiled for Use in the Office
of McKim, Mead & White*

1957
Atlee B. and Robert M. Ayres
Office Rules

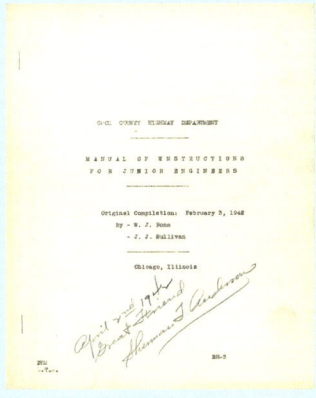

MANUAL OF INSTRUCTIONS
FOR JUNIOR ENGINEERS

Original Compilation: February 3, 1942
by H. J. Rone
J. J. Sullivan

Chicago, Illinois

1942
McNally and Quinn Associates
Manual of Instructions for Junior Engineers

1961
Daggett, Naegele &
Associates, Inc.
*Statement Concerning
Company Policies*

1926
Frederick L. Ackerman
Office Policy Manual

FREDERICK G. FROST, JR. & ASSOCIATES, ARCHITECTS

OFFICE MANUAL

1948
Frederick G. Frost Jr. &
Associates Architects
Office Manual

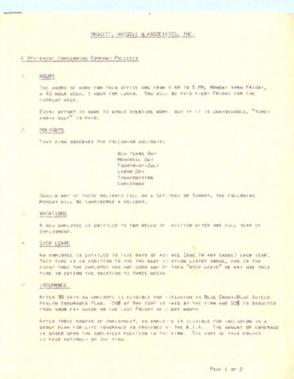

1962
Richard J. Neutra Office
Rules for Apprentices

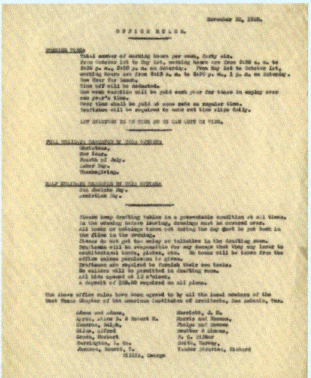

1928
Atlee B. and Robert M. Ayres
Office Rules

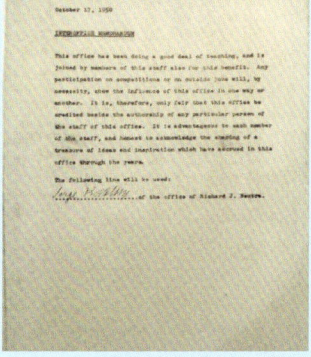

1950
Richard J. Neutra Office
Interoffice Memorandum

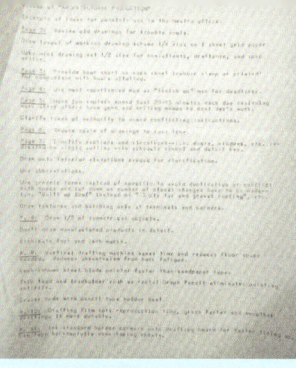

1963
Broad and Nelson
Office Manual

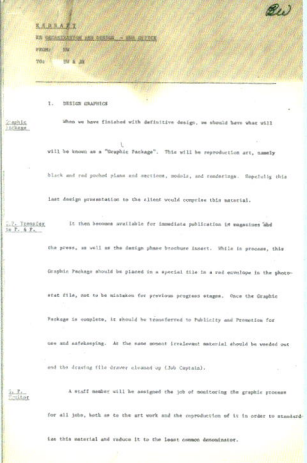

1967
Bertrand Goldberg Associates
Office Procedures

1968
Harry Weese and Associates
Design Standards

1969
Ernest J. Kump Associates Architects,
Organization for Architectural Practice

1969
Richard J. Neutra Office
Excerpts from *Ideas for Possible Use in The Neutra Office*

1974
Venturi and Rauch
Handbook

Assignment:
SAUDI ARABIA

1976
Bechtel
Saudi Arabia Handbook

1979
Ibsen Nelsen and Associates
Office Personnel Guidelines

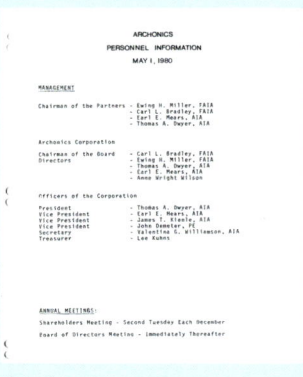

1980
Archonics
Personnel Information

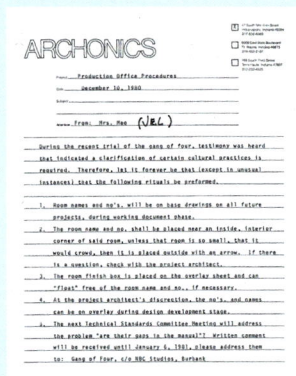

1980
Archonics
Production Office Procedures

1982
Smithey & Boynton
Architects & Engineers
Operating Manual

A. PURPOSE

DRAFT   6/2/83

1983
Smithey & Boynton
Architects & Engineers Manual

January 2, 1985

OBJECTIVE

1985
Ibsen Nelsen & Associates
Office Personnel Guidelines

M E M O R A N D U M
23 March 1984

To: Ibsen Nelsen
From: Ray Freeman
Reference: Status Reports / All projects

1984
Ibsen Nelsen & Associates
Memorandum

THE SOCIETY OF ARCHITECTURAL ADMINISTRATORS
An Affiliate of The American Institute of Architects

1986
The Society of Architectural Administrators
Handbook for Architectural Administrators

ARCHONICS

MEMO

From: Eugene C. Brown
To: File
Re: Production Meeting, 9-24-84
Distribution: All Management and Technical Personnel.

1984
Archonics
Office Manual

THE GUIDELINES ERRORS AND OMISSIONS BULLETIN
VOLUME II, ISSUE FOUR

TABLE OF CONTENTS

© Copyright Guidelines, 1987. All rights reserved.
Guidelines, Box 456, Orinda, CA 94563.

1987
Archonics
The Guidelines Errors and Omissions Bulletin

B E R T R A N D   G O L D B E R G   A S S O C I A T E S ,   I N C .

DATE: 8/19/85
TO: ALL PERSONNEL
FROM: BOB CUNOV
RE: OFFICE MANUAL

Attached are the first pages of our "Office Manual".

Please read and retain, as supplementary pages will be forthcoming.

1985
Bertrand Goldberg Associates
Office Manual

Emery Roth & Sons, P.C.
Architects

REVISED AUGUST 1988

OFFICE GUIDELINES

The regulations outlined herein govern our general
office procedures. It is impossible to cover every
contingency, but it is hoped that the following
covers the major and usual questions that arise.

WORK WEEK: The normal work week is 37½ hours, Monday
through Friday.

LUNCH HOUR: One hour from 12:00 to 1:00 P.M. for all
personnel, and from 11:45 A.M. to 1:00 P.M. on
Wednesday for check cashing. Any variation in this
time shall be an exception and not the rule and shall
be approved by Management.

Wednesday for check cashing. Any variation in this
time shall be an exception and not the rule and shall
be approved by Management.

1988
Emery Roth & Sons Architects
Office Guidelines

OFFICE MANUAL

PERSONNEL PRACTICES
DRAFTING ROOM STANDARDS
GENERAL OFFICE INFORMATION
STANDARD OFFICE FORMS

SLR/ARCHITECTS   1955 University Avenue East Palo Alto, CA 94303

1991
SLR Architects
Office Manual

DAVIS BRODY BOND LLP
315 HUDSON STREET
NEW YORK, NEW YORK 10013

EMPLOYEE POLICY MANUAL

2004
Davis Brody Bond
Employee Policy Manual

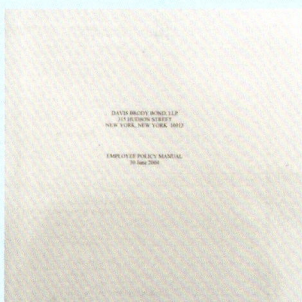

Höweler + Yoon Architecture, LLP

POLICY MANUAL
Rev: JUNE 2008

Welcome to Höweler + Yoon Architecture / MY Studio. Every member of the studio is considered
a valuable contributor to the studio and the following manual is to serve as a guideline to making
sure that the studio is not only an enjoyable place to work but a creative and productive
enterprise.

Space

2008
Höweler + Yoon Architecture
Policy Manual

2014
Snøhetta
Snøhetta Guide

Prepared by Case and Company, Inc. Management Consultants
for

THE AMERICAN INSTITUTE OF ARCHITECTS
Washington, D. C.

1968
The American Institute of
Architects, *The Economics of
Architectural Practice*

PUBLISHED BOOKS

WELD COXE
Management Consultant

Marketing
Architectural
and Engineering
Services

VAN NOSTRAND REINHOLD COMPANY
NEW YORK CINCINNATI TORONTO LONDON MELBOURNE

1971
Weld Coxe
*Marketing Architectural and
Engineering Services*

THE
ARCHITECT'S
GUIDE TO
RUNNING
A JOB

SIXTH EDITION

RONALD GREEN

1962
Ronald Green
*The Architect's Guide to
Running a Job*

OFFICE MANAGEMENT

A HANDBOOK FOR
ARCHITECTS AND CIVIL ENGINEERS

BY
W. KAYE PARRY

London:
E. & F. N. SPON, LTD., 125 STRAND
New York:
SPON & CHAMBERLAIN, 12 CORTLANDT STREET
1901

1901
Kaye W. Perry
*Office Management; A Handbook
for Architects and
Civil Engineers*

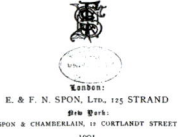

Manual of the
Historic American Buildings Survey

PART IX
MEASURED DRAWINGS
Revised illustrated draft: 300-cy 10/61
compiled by HARLEY J. McKEE architect

eastern office/division of design & construction/national park service

1961
National Park Service
*Manual of the Historic American
Buildings Survey*

RECORDS IN ARCHITECTURAL OFFICES

mass COPAR

SUGGESTIONS FOR THE PROPER ORGANIZATION, STORAGE, AND
CONSERVATION OF ARCHITECTURAL OFFICE ARCHIVES

REPORT OF A SURVEY OF ARCHITECTURAL FIRMS
IN GREATER BOSTON

NANCY CARLSON SCHROCK, PROJECT DIRECTOR

MASSACHUSETTS COMMITTEE FOR THE PRESERVATION
OF ARCHITECTURAL RECORDS

SECOND EDITION
SEPTEMBER, 1981

1981
MASS COPAR
Records in Architectural Office

THIS BUSINESS
OF
ARCHITECTURE

BY
ROYAL BARRY WILLS
WITH THE COLLABORATION OF
LEON KEACH

COLUMBIA
UNIVERSITY
AVERY
LIBRARY
NEW YORK
REINHOLD PUBLISHING CORPORATION
1941

1941
Royal Barry Wills
This Business of Architecture

architecture:

A PROFESSION AND
A BUSINESS

MORRIS LAPIDUS

REINHOLD PUBLISHING CORPORATION
A SUBSIDIARY OF CHAPMAN-REINHOLD, INC.
NEW YORK

1967
Morris Lapidus
*Architecture: a Profession and
a Business*

The
Economics
of
Architectural
Practice

Published on Behalf of
THE AMERICAN INSTITUTE OF ARCHITECTS

1735 New York Avenue, N.W.
Washington, D.C. 20006

Copyright ©1981
All Rights Reserved
Architectural
1735 S.W. 29th Street
Topeka, Kansas 66611

ISSN 0271-6046
ISBN 0-913962-53-6
Made in the United States of America

1981
The American Institute of
Architects, *International
Directory of AIA*

1984
Van Nostrand Reinhold Company
*The Architect's Guide to
Law and Practice*

**NEGOTIATING HIGHER
DESIGN FEES**

by Frank A. Stasiowski, AIA

WHITNEY LIBRARY OF DESIGN
an imprint of Watson-Guptill Publications/New York

1985
Frank A. Stasiowski, AIA
Negotiating Higher Design Fees

The Business of
Architectural Practice

Derek Sharp
DipArch(Hons), FRIBA, FBIM, FCIArb

COLLINS
8 Grafton Street, London W1

1986
Derek Sharp
*The Business of Architectural
Practice*

ACHIEVING
EXCELLENCE
IN YOUR
DESIGN
PRACTICE

IN YOUR
DESIGN
PRACTICE

STUART W. ROSE

WHITNEY LIBRARY OF DESIGN
an imprint of Watson-Guptill Publications
New York

1987
Stuart W. Rose
*Achieving Excellence in Your
Design Practice*

**Designing
Your Practice**

A Principal's Guide
to Creating and Managing
a Design Practice

Norman Kaderlan

McGraw-Hill, Inc.

New York St. Louis San Francisco Auckland Bogotá
Caracas Hamburg Lisbon London Madrid
Mexico Milan Montreal New Delhi Paris
San Juan São Paulo Singapore
Sydney Tokyo Toronto

1991
Norman Kaderlan
Designing Your Practice

AIA

International Committee

**International Design
and Practice: Europe**

**Challenge and
Opportunities
for the '90s**

Conference Report
Washington, D.C.
May 16-17, 1991

The American Institute of Architects
1735 New York Avenue, NW
Washington, DC 20006
(202) 626-7300

1991
AIA
*International Design and
Practice: Europe*

Building Overseas

Butterworth Architecture Management Guide

Francis Baden-Powell
RMJM

1993
Francis Baden-Powell RMJM
Building Overseas

**International
Practice
Checklist**

© 1993 The American Institute of Architects

1993
AIA
*International Practice
Checklist*

**Architectural Office
Standards and
Practices:
A Practical Users Guide**

Office Practice Committee
Denver Chapter
American Institute of Architects

Larry D. Jenks
Chair, Office Practice Committee
Principal, Klipp Colussy Jenks DuBois Architects, P.C.
Denver, Colorado

McGraw-Hill, Inc.

New York San Francisco Washington, D.C. Auckland Bogotá
Caracas Lisbon London Madrid Mexico City Milan
Montreal New Delhi San Juan Singapore
Sydney Tokyo Toronto

1995
Larry D. Jenks
*Architectural Office Standards
and Practices: A Practical
Users Guide*

1996
Charles Nelson
*TQM and ISO 9000 for Architects
and Designers*

The Architect's Handbook of Professional Practice

Fourteenth Edition

Joseph A. Damkin, AIA, Executive Editor

John Wiley & Sons, Inc.

2008
AIA
The Architect's Handbook of Professional Practice, 14th Edition

PUBLISHED ARTICLES

1890
"The Organization of an Architect's Office"
Engineering and Building Record

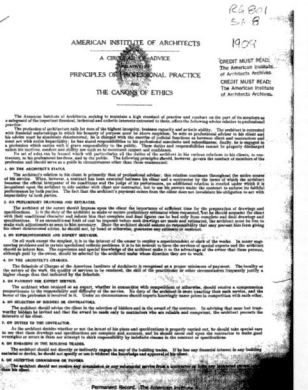

1909
American Institute of Architects
A Circular of Advice Related to Principles of Professional Practice and The Canons of Ethics

1920
Howard Dwight Smith
"The 'Business' of Architecture, The Drafting Room, Engineering and Inspection"
The Architectural Review

1928
Robert Maurice Trimble
"Office and Drafting Room Practice" *The Pencil Points Service Bulletin*

Architecture as a profession is
ALL WRONG
By FRANK LLOYD WRIGHT

1930
Frank Lloyd Wright
"Architecture as a Profession is All Wrong"
The American Architect

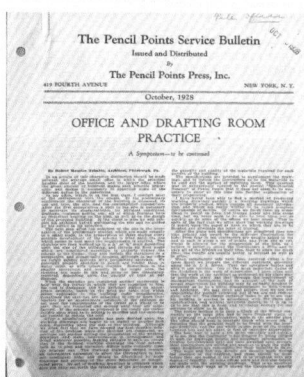

1931
John Russell Pope
"Office Manual of John Russell Pope, Architect, Routine and Procedure" *The Architectural Record*

1931
Edwin Bergstrom
"The Architect's Responsibility"
The Octagon, A Journal of The American Institute of Architects

1949
Henry F. Stanton
"Architecture—a Profession or a Business" *The Octagon, A Journal of The American Institute of Architects*

1916
Daniel Paul Higgins
"The 'Business'
of Architecture.
Part I: Introduction"
The Architectural Review

A young man of my acquaintance graduated from one of the leading American schools of architecture, and was later engaged in a number of prominent offices in this country, worked in important monumental and residential work, and was freely acknowledged to be a man of great capacity. He later won a traveling scholarship and traveled abroad, attended the École des Beaux Arts, and finally returned to this country, feeling that his training and the knowledge he had acquired enabled him to engage in business as a practicing architect. After commencing practice he soon found that he was obliged to do small houses for speculative builders, and owing to his lack of business method he was unable to do even this kind of work efficiently. His discouragement was keen when he considered the time, effort, and money he had spent educating himself, only to the result of being a failure as an architect. He has now again returned to the draughting-board, and works in such offices as required his services in that capacity.

1941
Royal Barry Wills,
Leon Keach
This Business of Architecture

There is no early test for future architectural preeminence, though there is every reason to believe that the average youngster may be directed towards gaining an adequate and pleasant livelihood through its practice. The contributing influences are an early bent for delineation, a family tradition, or the belief that it is a genteel and not too vigorous occupation for an artistic man of means.

1967
Morris Lapidus
*Architecture: A Profession
and a Business*

At last you are ready. You have decided to open an office for the practice of architecture—or shall I say, the "pursuit" of architecture. The word "practice" implies the constant seeking after perfection—"pursuit" means, to be exact, an occupation or the act of chasing—according to Webster. Let us agree that ours is an occupation and a constant search for better clients. By "better work" we mean finer architectural quality and more remunerative fees. Whichever term you prefer, you are preparing to open an office.

1986
Derek Sharp
*The Business of
Architectural Practice*

When I started in practice, I had recently married, moved into a flat, and the spare bedroom was designated the new architect's office. It was big enough for a drawing board and a desk with a telephone. There were no plan chest or storage files because no work had yet been obtained.

1993
Butterworth Architecture
Management Guide
Building Overseas

Before any overseas assignment, your physician will give you vaccinations and inoculations to protect from a variety of ills. There is one disease for which there is no immunization and for which we would like to try to prepare you. This illness, for lack of a better term, is called "culture shock." Culture shock is a very real malady with very real symptoms: growing irritability, depression, frustration, and an increasing need to speak out about the shortcomings and faults of the country in which you find yourself.

2001
The American
Institute of Architects
*The Handbook of
Architectural Practice,*
13th Edition

Starting a business is like getting married. There is no good time and no bad time. Sometimes it is a long-held ambition for an architect to open his or her own firm. Sometimes the decision to start up on one's own is spurred by downsizing by an employer or frustration with the course of one's career path. While the reasons to start a new

...

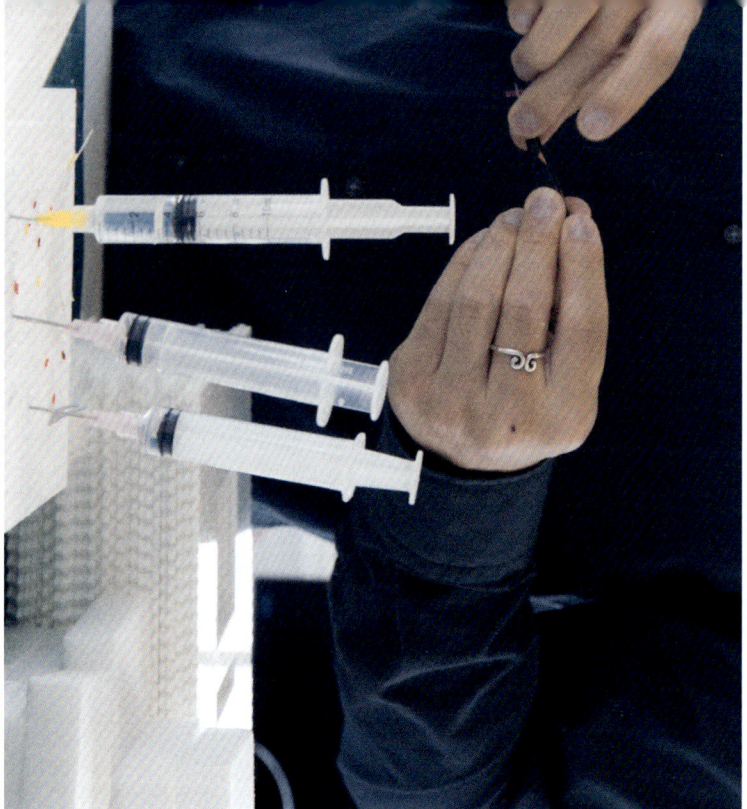

architecture firm can be as varied as the people who start them, architects of all ages and at most stages of their professional careers are
setting up shop.

2008
The American
Institute of Architects
*The Architect's Handbook
of Professional Practice,*
14th Edition

To run a firm, you—or a partner—will need to have or acquire
basic business skills. To obtain work, you need to market your services,
negotiate contracts, and reach agreements. Someone needs to build
relationships with clients and maintain their trust. To grow, you must
hire staff and consultants and then work effectively with contractors
and consultants.

2001

2008

2 — 1 GETTING STARTED

"Emerging practice" is a label currently on everyone's lips. Merely by mentioning it, we are proclaiming that something is changing in the way archtecture offices work. This intuition may be verified at all scales of practice: from the big corporate office that must sacrifice its traditional power, authority, and pragmatism to a more flexible, participative, contextualized, and sustainable system; down to the small office, born in unstable, nomadic, and collective circumstances and observing how the doors of other architectures open— including some fields not clearly linked to traditional practice—in which their performance may be insuperable thanks to their ability to operate in complex environments where the most skillful detect extraordinary opportunities.

This sensitivity on the part of the smaller offices constitutes an excellent field of opportunities for the youngest architects, who find a space in which small practices and young architects for once do not have to face competition from their big counterparts and elders. They are capable of exploring the scenarios of globalization through new sensitivities that foster a capacity for action beyond the scope of the big corporate pachyderms. They are offices that think globally but act locally, offices that by addressing different contexts from the "outsider's" point of view unveil realities otherwise invisible to the locals.

This kind of global practice constitutes the ideal space in which to set off today on a professional career. The protagonists of the phenomenon are the "native" inhabitants of the digital communication and design media, a medium in which web platforms, publications, fanzines, and festivals have generated a world of shared information and quests from which the most firmly established practices are excluded. They are accustomed to dialogue, to citizen involve-ment, and to the empowerment of opinion groups. In those countries immersed in recent economic recessions we have seen these young architects adapting to the demands of austerity by transforming difficulties into instruments with which to invent their own commissions and attain freedom from the power struc-tures that governed their predecessors' careers. These young architects are generating their own publications and maintaining strong links to the academy, demonstrating that it is the most open, diverse, experimental, and critical medium currently available to our discipline.

A new generation of architecture offices is being consolidated. These offices are capable of winning international competitions, of leading diverse and highly-specialized international consultant teams, and of assuming the overall complexity of the contemporary project. Although they may take on only a hand-ful of projects, they do so with ambitious conceptual and technical approaches, realized with both the love of an artisan and with the pragmatism of a globally oriented practice. And eventually, after having become absolutely global, they are able to look back to their city or country of origin and observe it without any previous judgment or archetypical description, almost as if they were travelers coming home after a long journey, reading the landscape with a feeling that allows them to endow something with value that had previously been valueless. Juan Herreros

The business administration of the architect's office today is of vast importance, and until recently it has been the single one of the many sides of his profession that has been most neglected. But with the rapid growth of the business of building in America, and the enormous sums involved, a demand has been created for the architect possessing a thorough knowledge and appreciation of proper business organization and method, combined with the many other qualifications necessary for the successful practice of architecture. The necessity for this new and better organization is being recognized by all progressive and successful architects; and one need not go beyond their offices' entrances to see the result.

We know who runs the business, but, unless un-popularly curious, we no longer know who makes the designs.

The individual architect serves the busiest as best he can or the business will use his name and "lay him off"—unless the undertaker comes along, in time, to "lay him out".

So, Be "Businesslike or Bust" is no idle threat.

Every architect and draftsman whose livelihood really depends on the profession of architecture knows that an office must be run so as to make a reasonable profit, as is any sound business. Furthermore that no amount of wishful thinking or other dodging of realities will lessen the fact that any and all costs entering into the practice must be reckoned with. It is utterly impractical to conduct an office without knowing overhead, both as a running average and as a particular case.

Whoever introduces assignments shall receive what commercially would be called a "finder's fee" but what in reality constitutes an inducement to missionary work for a good cause. For associates this finder's fee might be 50% more than it would for associate aspirants who have not made yet their formal pledges in favor of continuity.

Architects lose money on one out of four projects they undertake. Losses are more likely to occur on projects such as custom residences, churches, banks, theaters, hospitals, clinics and libraries than for other building types. The amount of the losses on individual projects are relatively small and are offset over the year by profits earned on other projects.

The Principals in the firm are responsible for developing new projects for the firm. All members of the staff are encouraged to be alert for new business opportunities and report them to the Principals. Our continued growth depends on how the staff represents the firm to our clients and the public; this will increase opportunities for all members of the staff.

The firm of Smithey & Boynton is organized as a professional corporation according to Chapter 7 in Title 13.1 of the 1950 Code of Virginia, as amended. The stockholding employees provided the funds for working capital thru purchase of stock and share in the earnings and losses. Stock holding employees serving as members of the Board of

...

Directors are responsible for setting up the organization; providing physical facilities, and establishing policy. The Board of Directors meets as necessary to review the status of commissions and prospects and to establish policy as appropriate and necessary for the most effective operation of the firm.

2 — 2 BUSINESS MODEL

Consider what you know. Forget it. Think of the world. Think harder. Imagine every part. Visualize every system. Picture how each fits together as one. Do not fear. Feel the complexity. Accept it in your bones. Be humble.

Consider what you have learned. Doubt it. Look at the world. Look again. Examine every part. Research every system. See where each is broken. Do not turn away. Embrace the complexity. Revel in it together. Be brave.

Consider what you hear. Respect it. Listen to the world. Listen well. Value every part. Weigh every system. Find what each lacks. Do not wait. Replicate the complexity. Match it in your Team. Be generous.

Consider what you believe. Trust it. Tell it to the world. Tell it clearly. Share every part. Explain every system. Describe how each can change. Do not leave the good stuff out. Inhabit the complexity. Invite it into your Office. Be bold.

Consider what you will do. Do it. Build the world. Build better. Draw every part. Fix every system. Test each against an ideal. Do not be gentle. Become the complexity. Model it in your Practice. Be human. SHoP Architects

2 — 3 OFFICE STRUCTURE

1929
Arthur Brown Jr.
Office Reorganization Memo

As the business is now managed we have Mr. Brown, the head of the business and referred to in the following as the Chief; his four associates referred as the etat-major; the specification man; secretarial staff; and the draftsmen.

1966
Victor Gruen International, Ltd.
Articles of Incorporation

The officers of the corporation shall be a president, one or more vice presidents, a secretary, a treasurer, and one or more assistant secretaries and assistant treasurers and such other officers as may be appointed by the Board. Officers may be but need not be directors. One person may hold two or more offices, except the offices of president and secretary may not be held by the same person.

2006
The American
Institute of Architects
*Legal Structure of
Architecture Firms*

SOLE PROPRIETORSHIP
The principal disadvantage of a sole proprietorship is that generally the proprietor may be personally at risk of general business liabilities.

PARTNERSHIP
Like a sole proprietorship, a partnership is an unincorporated business that traditionally has been legally indistinguishable from the partners.

CORPORATIONS
The principal advantage of a corporate legal structure is that, unlike a proprietorship or a partnership, the personal assets of the shareholders generally cannot be reached to satisfy the liabilities or obligations of the company.

LIMITED LIABILITY COMPANIES OR PARTNERSHIPS
An LLC or LLP is a distinct legal entity that usually combines the limited liability protection of a corporation with the profit/loss pass-through tax features of a partnership or Subchapter S corporation. LLCs or LLPs also are generally allowed more flexibility than general business or professional corporations in terms of management structure, which the shareholders may find advantageous.

1929

1966

2006

2 — 3 OFFICE STRUCTURE

The growth of the large-scale architectural practice was associated with new demands of the growing metropolises of the nineteenth and twentieth century, in which new building types and urban-scale projects required complex architectural and engineering skills. The growth of professionalized design services was increasingly driven by the private sector rather than by government-commissions (Francis Duffy, *Architectural Knowledge*, 1999) and supported by the elaboration of rigorous architectural education standards and careful monitoring of professional qualifications through bodies such as the AIA or RIBA.

In the late twentieth century, the increasing liberalization of market economies challenged knowledge-based professions. There was a conflict between the need for professional knowledge built up over many years of education and practice versus unpredictable swings in the market's demand for architectural services. Today, however, the architectural office no longer contains the entire work of the practice. Work is distributed widely among other contributors through a virtual system integrated with new software and tools. Armed with these tools—and a virtual labor force that may be multinational in scope—the architectural practice today is redefined in time and space. Architecture has increasingly become a practice of assembling or amalgamating components (Rem Koolhaas, *Fundamentals*, 2014).

However, the same information technology that enables the practice to be distributed and fragmented in time and space is also empowering clients—and end users—to program, co-design, and obtain space as needed. Utilizing models of collaborative consumption, for example, the end user takes over as the client, using applications to get space as needed, ultimately bypassing old supply chains in which the architect was previously embedded (see www. Liquidspace.com for example). As the definition and ownership of "the project" becomes more fluid, the role of the architect risks being displaced and must be reinvented.

The disintermediation of the actors in the collaborative consumption economy also indicates new models that may replace the hierarchical operations of the conventional supply chain of architectural design. Open source digital design processes allow more participatory design (Carlo Ratti with Matthew Claudel, *w*, 2015). The era of the individual architect as primary author may be ending. The open sourced design processes are coincident with other destabilizing factors in the design supply chain: new forms of crowd sourcing or micro-funding and new techniques of digital fabrication, prototyping, and production. Parametric design enables users to interact with and modify virtual design.

Does the architectural practice assume a new role as an "integrator" of these citizen-centered design processes? Or is the role of the architectural office usurped by the citizen or by tribes of individual architect freelancers alongside many other professional and lay contributors to design? For the architect and architectural practice to remain in a professional leadership role, the architect must be the owner and facilitator of the knowledge and purpose of design, and of the emerging organizational structures and processes through which design will be created and delivered. The idea of the architectural profession may have to be reinvented within the context of an entirely new kind of organizational and technological framework for design practice. [Andrew Laing]

1901
Kaye W. Perry
Office Management; A Handbook for Architects and Civil Engineers

MANAGER

1. To take entire charge of the drawing office.
2. To assist in the preparation of, prepare, or to see that the other draughtsman prepare, all original drawings and copies.
3. To see that the Drawing Register is properly kept, and an entry made in it of every drawing and sketch turned out.
4. To see that every drawing is properly turned out, and that it is provided with its Register Number.
5. To see that all drawings are kept in their proper places

1928
Robert Maurice Trimble
Office and Drafting Room Practice

The General Manager. He is the clearinghouse through which all the wishes of the client are transmitted to the various departments through to the finished product. The architect gives all his instructions to him and it is his responsibility to see that the ball does not fall between the fielders.

1931
John Russell Pope
"Office Manual, Architect Routine and Procedure"
The Architecture Record

In general it will be the responsibility of the job captain to handle the production of the working drawings and details with economy and with no unnecessary loss of time. Both in regard to plan arrangement and aesthetic design he should coach his men not to accept the first solution but to set up one or two alternates and quickly come to a decision in regard to the most acceptable scheme.

1971
Abbott, Merkt & Company
Procedural Manual

The Secretary's first responsibility is to her superior (or superiors). As she becomes more familiar with her job, she can lighten his workload by assuming as much responsibility as possible. Arranging his mail, passing on copies of correspondence to those who may be concerned, researching data and information he will need for replying to correspondence, are only a few of the ways a secretary can be of assistance.

1983
Smithey & Boynton
Architects and Engineers
Operating Manual

– **President. Accountable to: Board of Directors**
– **Administration Officers. Executive Vice-President and Treasurer. Accountable to: President**
– **Vice President for Physical Plant. Accountable to: Executive Vice President and Treasurer**
– **Operation. Vice President for Production. Accountable to: President**
– **Project Manager. Accountable to: Vice President for Production**
– **Section Heads. Accountable to: Vice President for Production**
– **Job Captain. Accountable to : Section Head and Project Manager**
– **Specification Writer. Accountable to: Vice President for Production and Project Manager**
– **Technical Consultant. Accountable to: Vice President for Production**
– **Construction Contract Administrator. Accountable to: Vice President for Production**
– **Vice President for Design. Accountable to: President**
– **Design Architect. Accountable to: Vice President for Design**
– **Vice President for Business Development. Accountable to: President**

1901

1928
1931

1971

1983

2005
The American
Institute of Architects
Definition of
Architects Positions

SENIOR PRINCIPAL / PARTNER
Typically an owner or majority shareholder of the firm; may be the
founder; titles may include president, chief executive officer, or
managing principal/partner.
...

ENTRY-LEVEL INTERN
Unlicensed architecture school graduate in first year of internship.

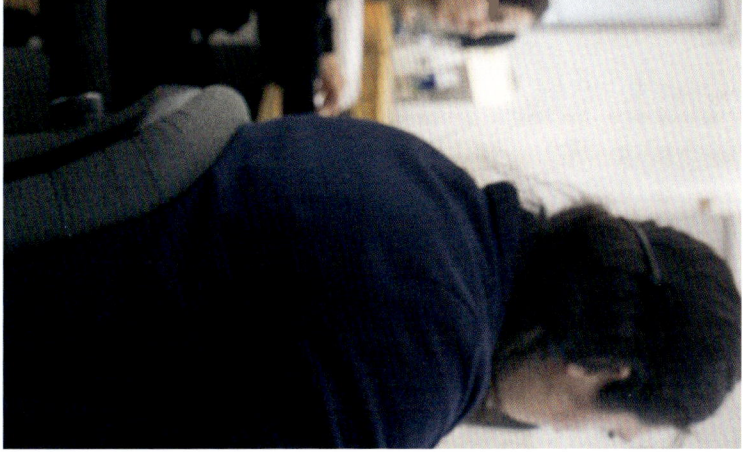

2 — 4 POSITIONS

Welcome. Your position is not assured. Whereas manual protocols are determinate, your position is multiple and indeterminate. Your positions will advance agendas, outlooks, and territorial claims. Please remember that these positions are only partly yours. Think of your positions like study models. They are entries within an ultra-material archive. Together they represent an accrued history of reckoning, challenge, and anxiety. They are paths and mysteries. They are subject to violation and revision. Choose carefully and choose often:

1. We are a process.
2. Leadership is structured.
3. Your environment is not yours.
4. Fictions build futures.
5. Blind spots are opportunities.
6. Community is not decided.
7. Social impact is inevitable.
8. Visualization builds shared fluencies.
9. Systems are rarely closed.
10. Crisis is catalytic.
11. Potential expires.
12. You are already armed.
13. Catastrophe can be avoided.
14. The commons will grow.
15. Dots will connect one way or another.
16. Scales are not to be ignored.
17. Waste is failure.
18. Communication organizes space.
19. Institutions are entrenched.
20. Data creates ghosts.
21. Collaboration is a social competency.
22. A public is an extended reach.
23. Inexperience is an asset.
24. Profits and losses: same topic.
25. Practice is appropriate only for low stakes.
26. Primary objectives can be secondary questions.
27. Consortia are possible.
28. Independence isn't an option.
29. Conservation is an enabler.
30. Positions are exchangeable.
31. Supervision is a luxury.
32. Social capital is plastic.
33. Inertia is an aberration.
34. Conflict is germane.
35. Silos are to be expected.
36. Platforms are not personalities.
37. Accountability is a metric.
38. Behavior is suppressed or released.
39. Resources intensify relationships.
40. Upheaval can be formalized.
41. Relevance isn't assured.
42. Challenges are entangled challenges.
43. Theories are welcomed.
44. The weather will decide.
45. Rebuilding isn't an option.
46. Inclusiveness is a civic defense.
47. Image and visualization live separate lives.
48. Reprogram from within.
49. Narratives form new links.

...

50. Policy is craftwork.
51. Stakeholders are pervasive.
52. Death won't stop.
53. Experts are neatly positioned.
54. Not everyone will participate.
55. Unfinished is accessible.
56. Theories are unlimited.
57. Distance still matters.
58. Small inputs instantiate larger ones.
59. New metaphors are needed.
60. Others will fill gaps if you don't.
61. Scarcity is not inevitable.
62. Volatility is assured.
63. Projection is a guess.
64. The business model is a mess.
65. Building is a by-product.
66. Enable positive social contracts.
67. Limitations will be embraced.
68. Viable futures are produced.
69. Timelines are shared space.
70. We are educated in errors.
71. Commonality and difference are equally justified goals.
72. The Superman/woman.
73. High stakes praxis.
74. Democracy is simply operative.
75. Practice has a character.
76. Produce directionality.
77. Institutional architectures will be exposed.
78. To confront what we are.
79. Political agency will be identified.
80. Daily life has a grain.
81. Systems and services fail.
82. It is to be done for real.
83. Confront resistance.
84. A commitment to time.
85. Innovation and invention are not the same thing.
86. You are a complex system.
87. There are few truths.
88. Models are not always discarded.
89. Stability is affected upstream.
90. Impact will be uneven.
91. Bonds will ebb and flow.
92. Information can hide.
93. Communities accumulate knowledge.
94. Organizations are experiments.
95. The project will end.
96. It must be done in public.
97. Produce more than is consumed.
98. History is a material resource.
99. Systemic challenges have a local nature.
100. Limits are a practiced craft.
101. [...]
102. [...]

Landon Brown

HIERARCHY

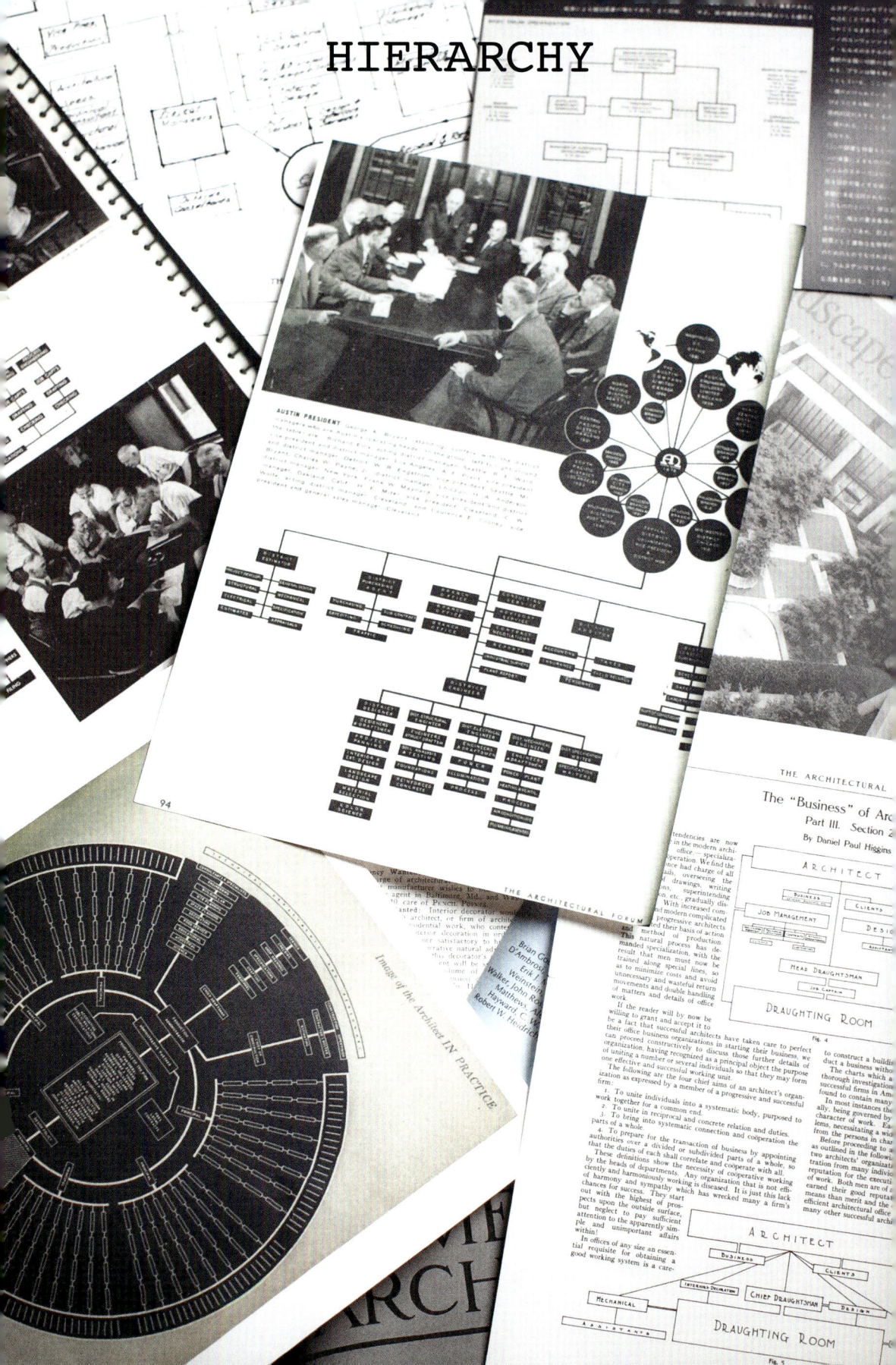

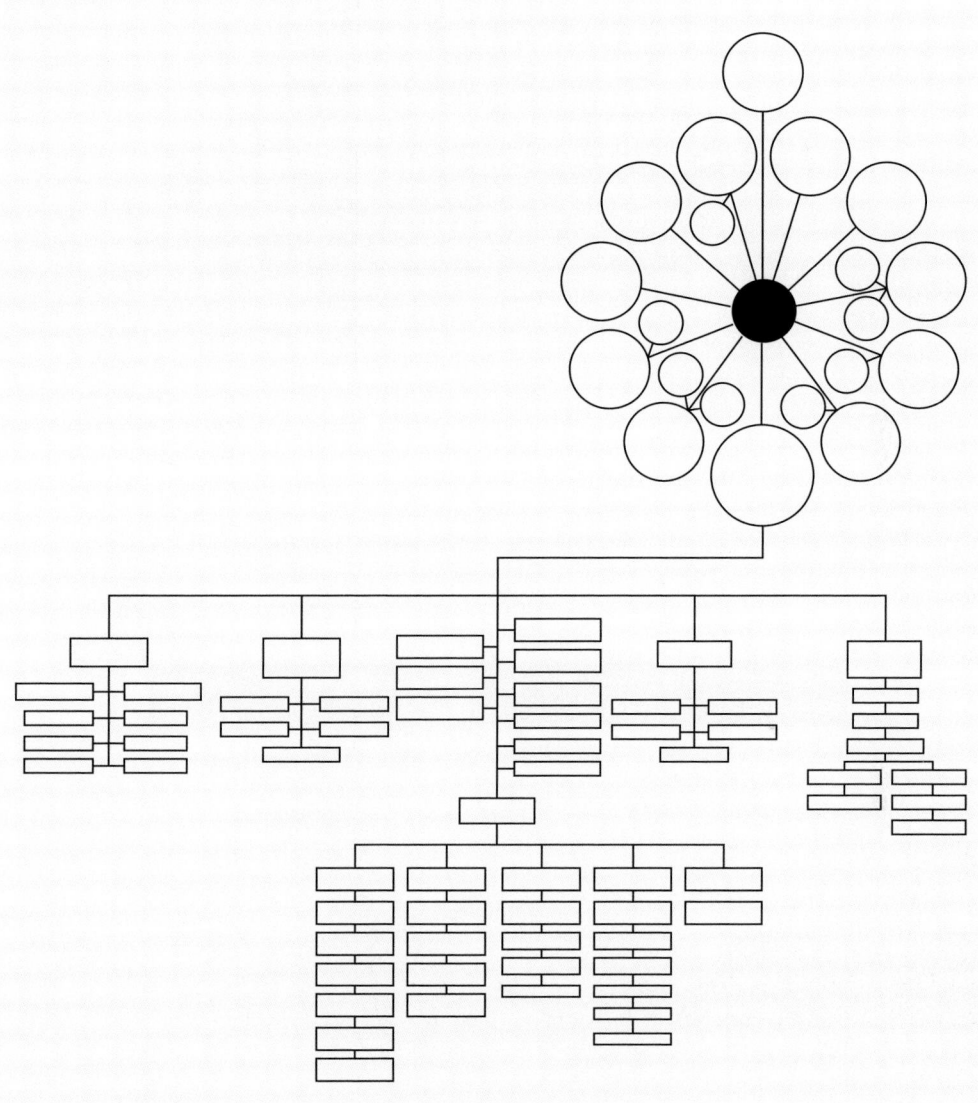

1878
The Austin Company

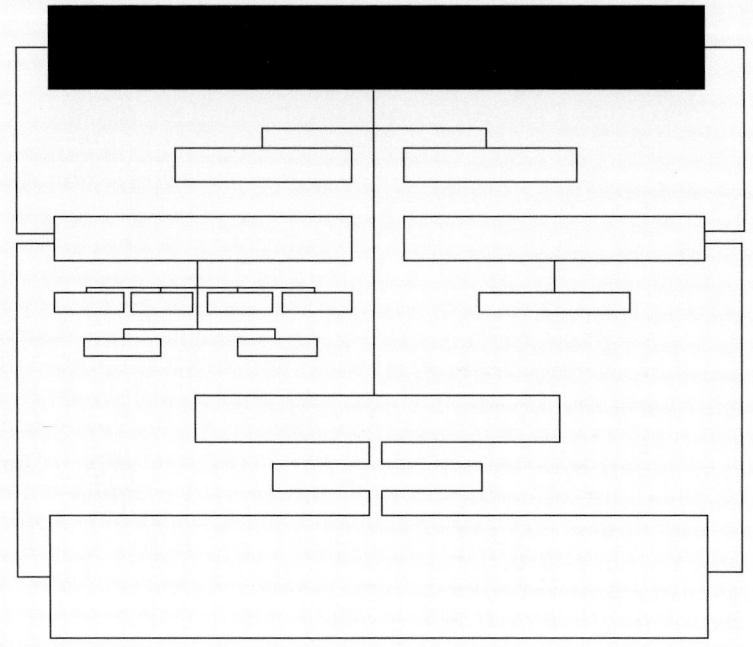

1918
"The 'Business' of Architecture"
Daniel Paul Higgins

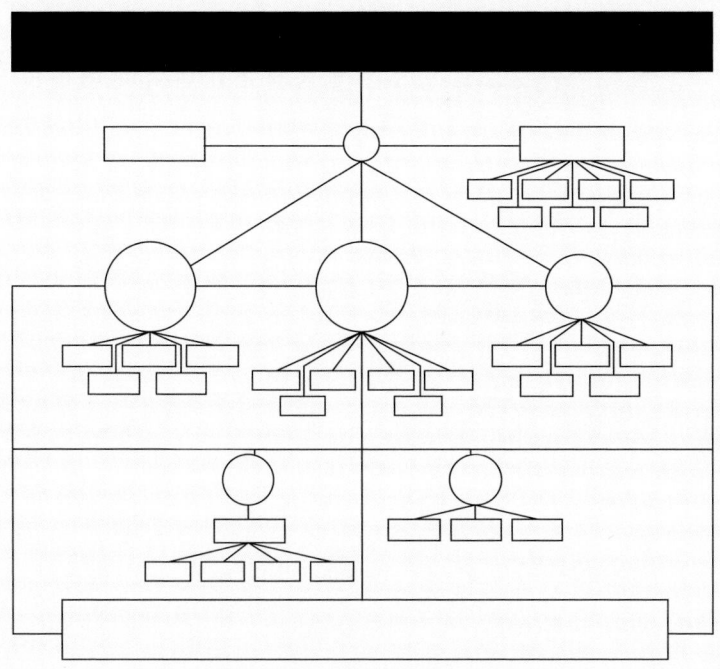

1918
"The 'Business' of Architecture"
Daniel Paul Higgins

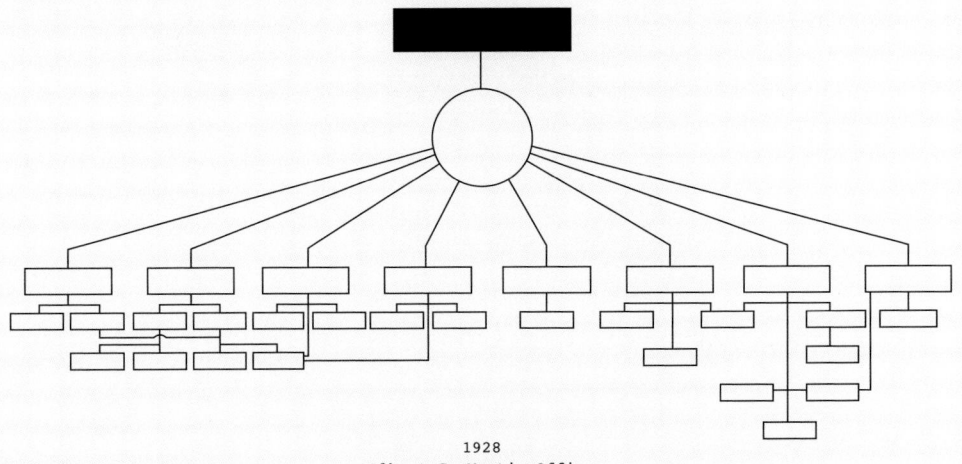

1928
Albert C. Martin Office

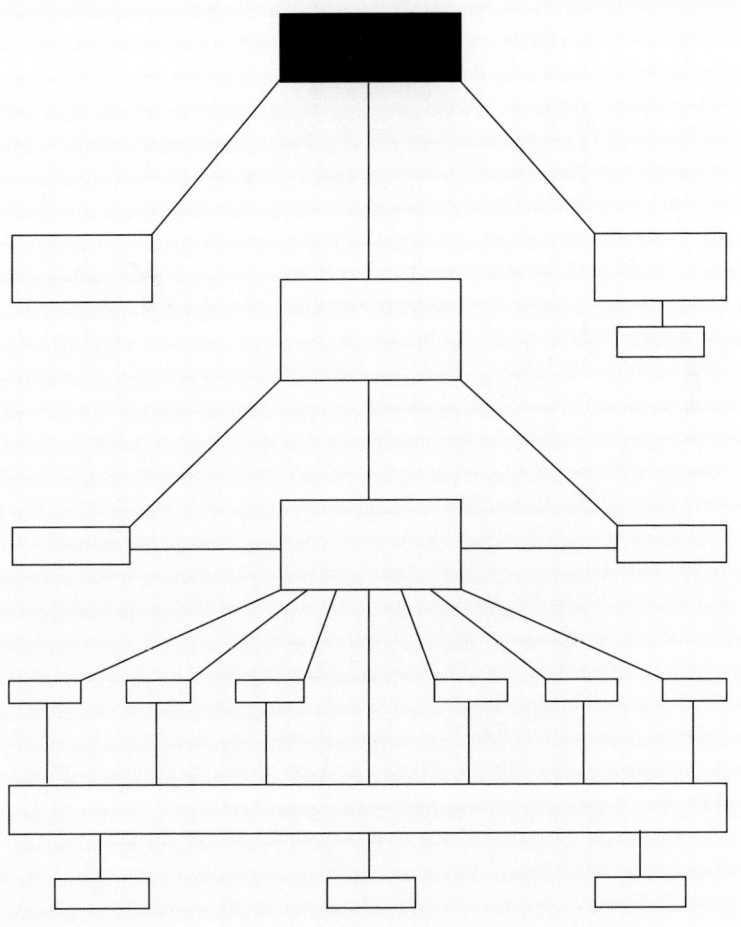

1931
John Russell Pope

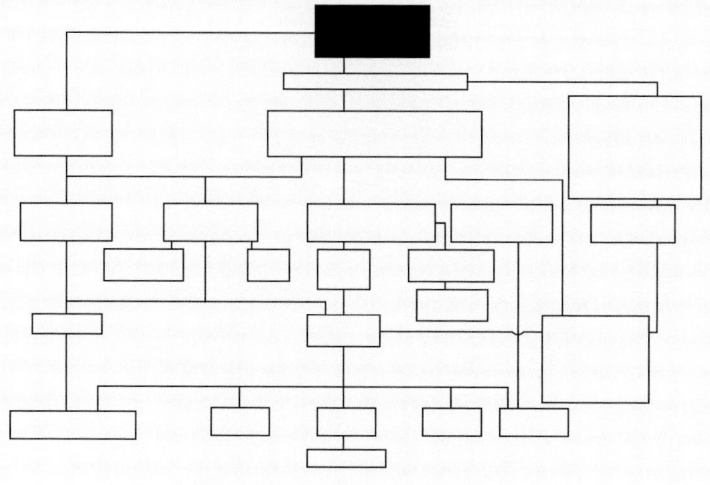

1937
Eggers and Higgins Architects

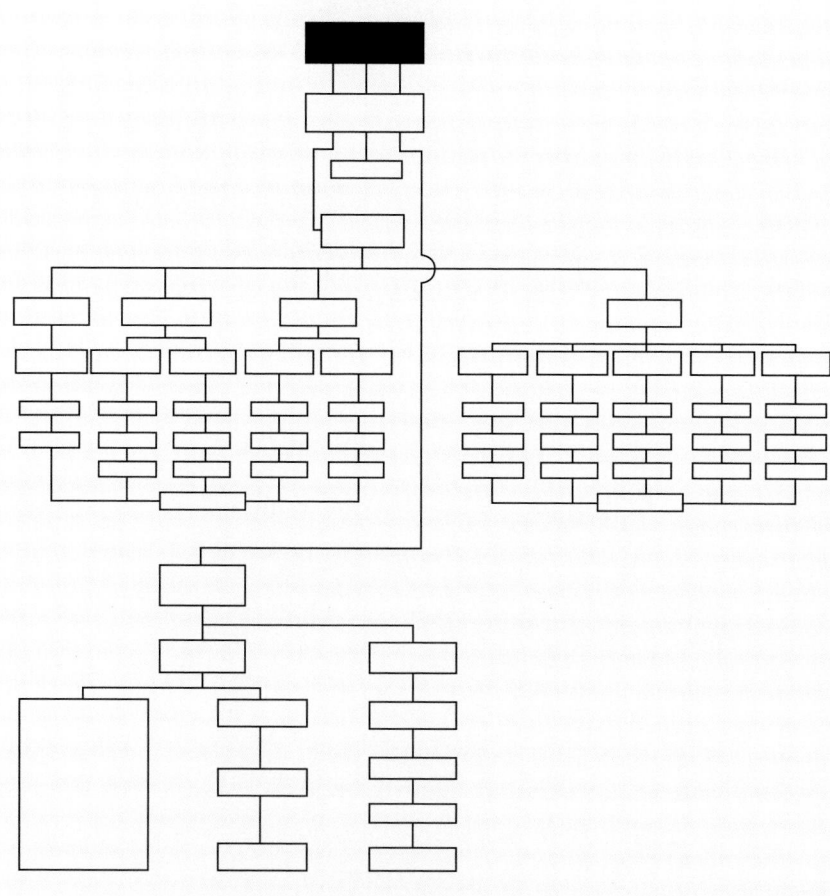

1938
Albert Kahn Associates

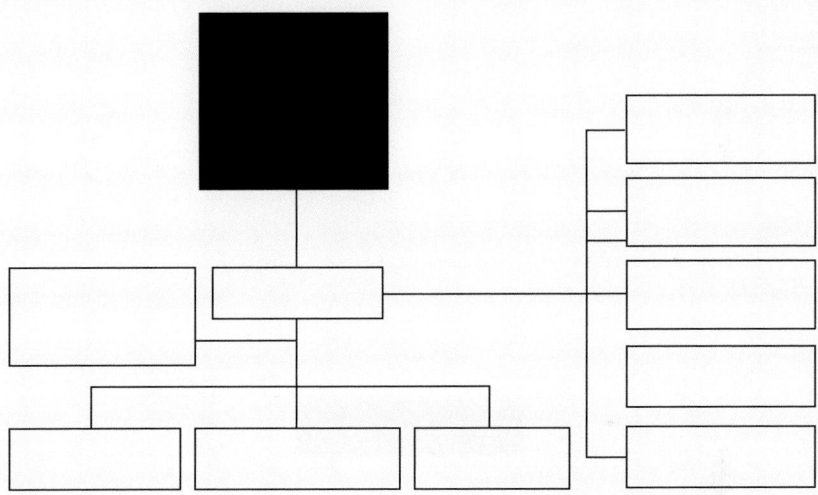

1946
Daniel, Mann, Johnson & Mendenhall

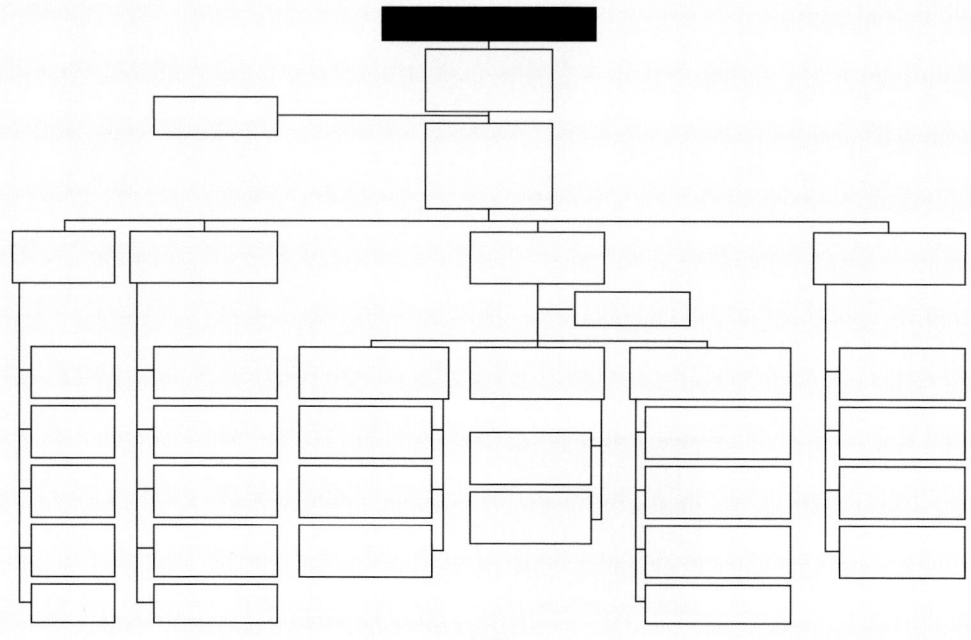

1957
Skidmore, Owings & Merrill

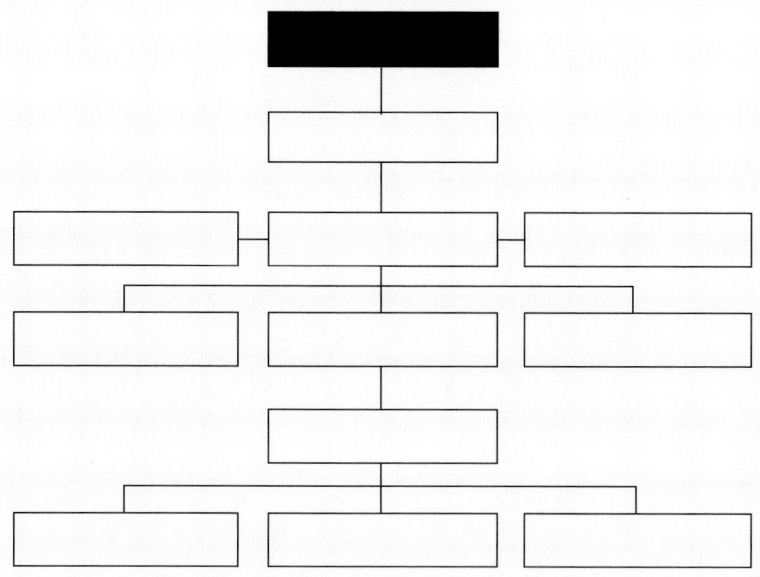

1969
Ernest J. Kump Associates

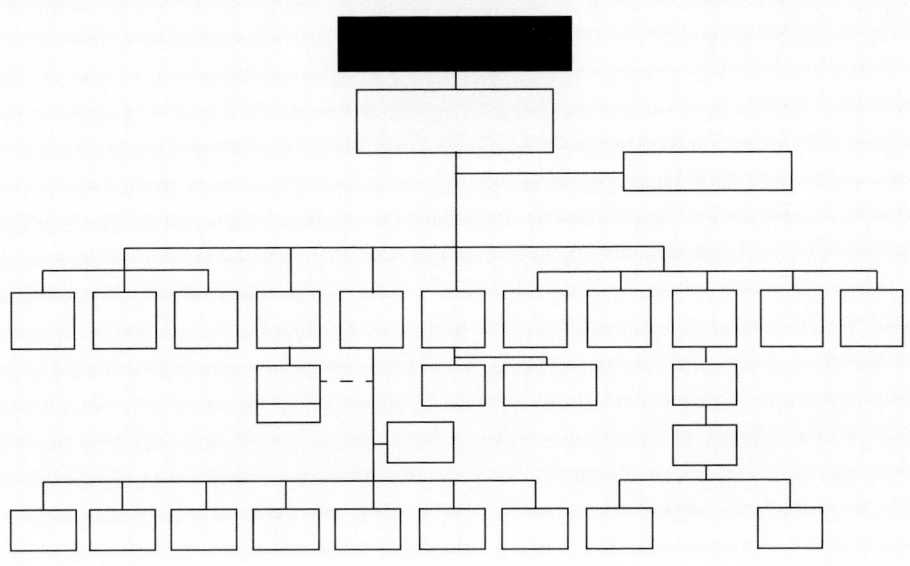

1971
Abbott, Merkt & Company

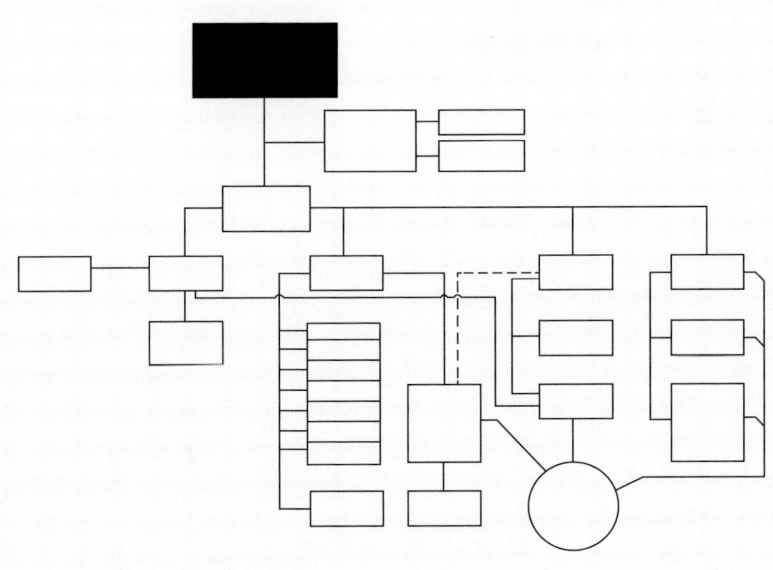

1983
Smithey & Boyton Architects

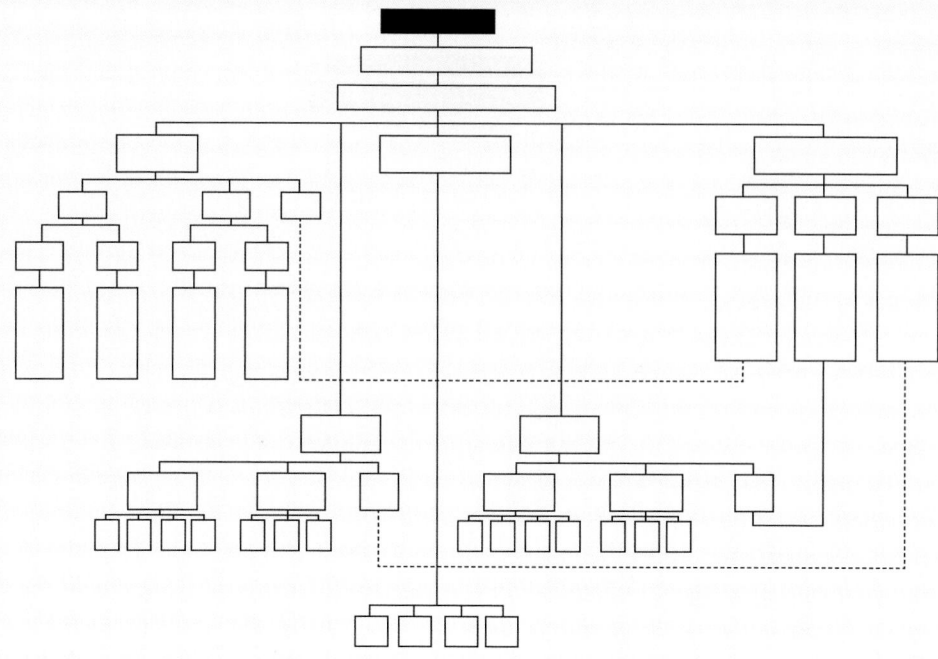

1986
The Business of Architectural Practice
Derek Sharp

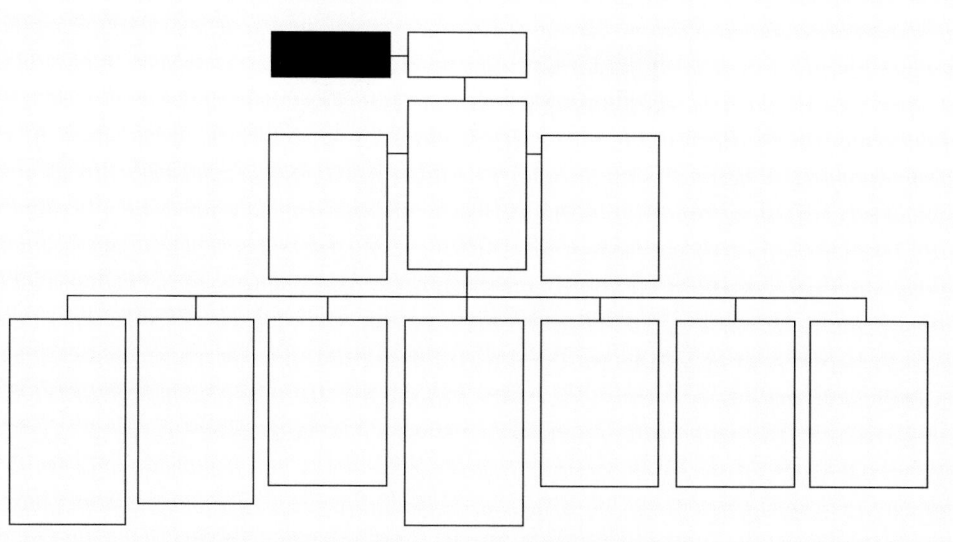

2013
Epstein

2014
AECOM

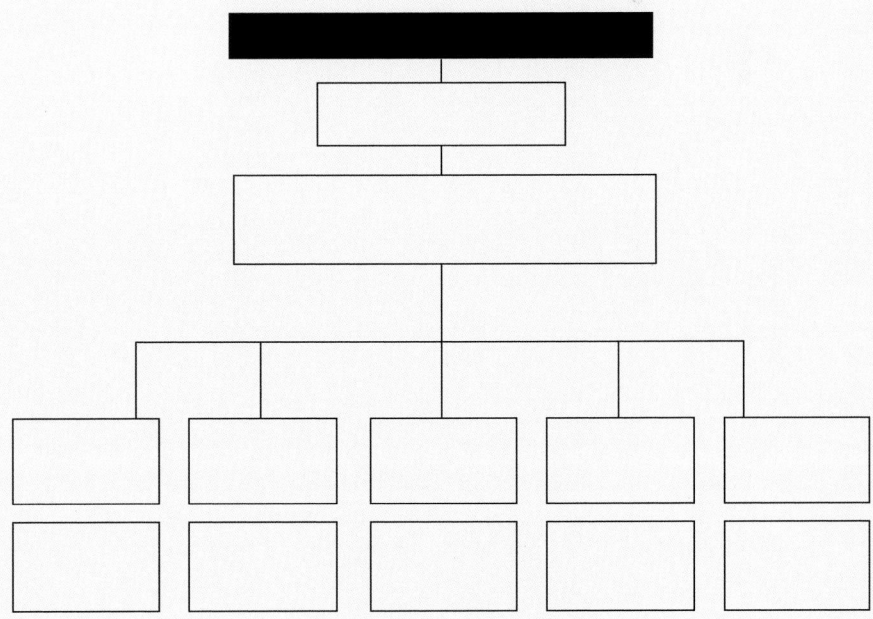

2014
Integrus

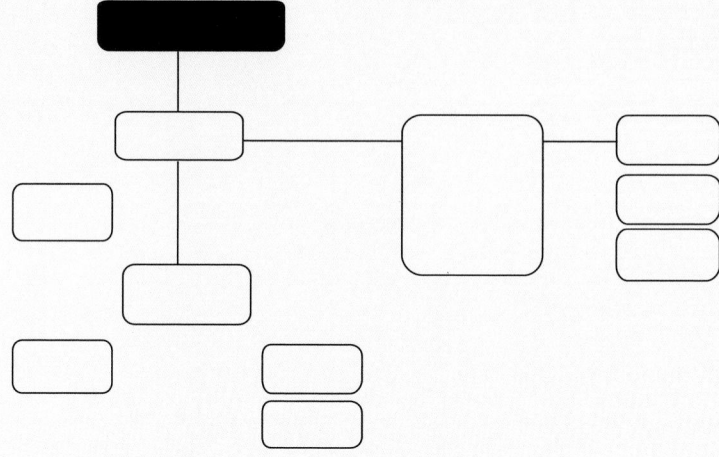

2014
MACK Architects

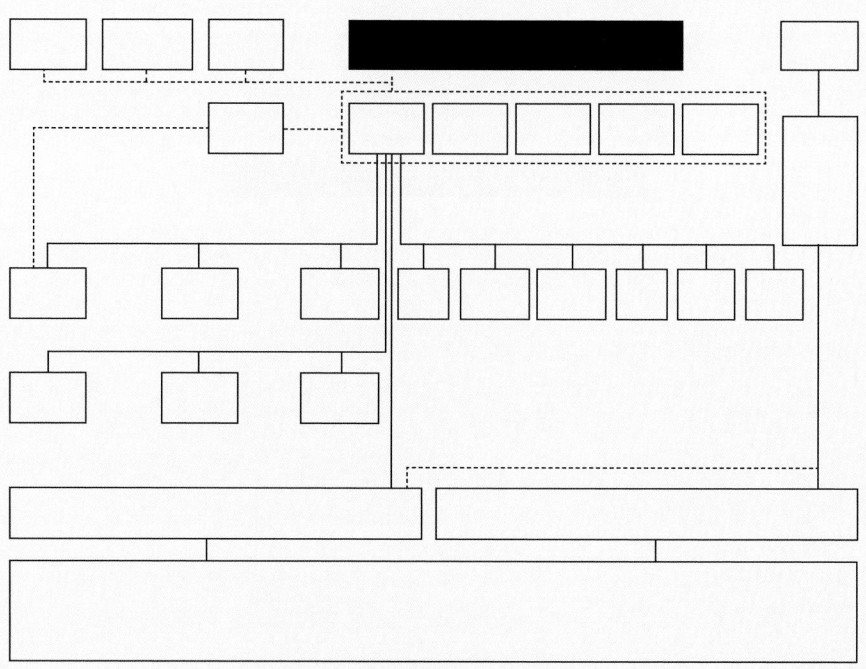

2014
Davis, Brody & Associates

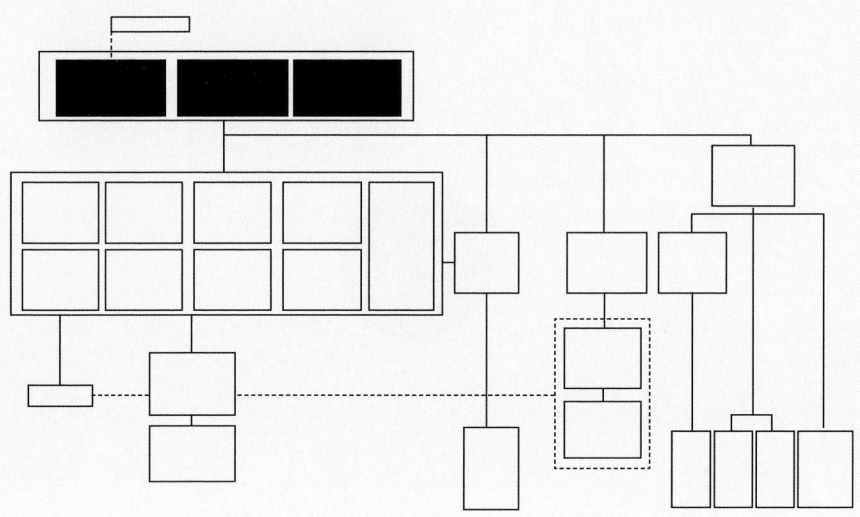

2014
Adrian Smith + Gordon Gill Architecture

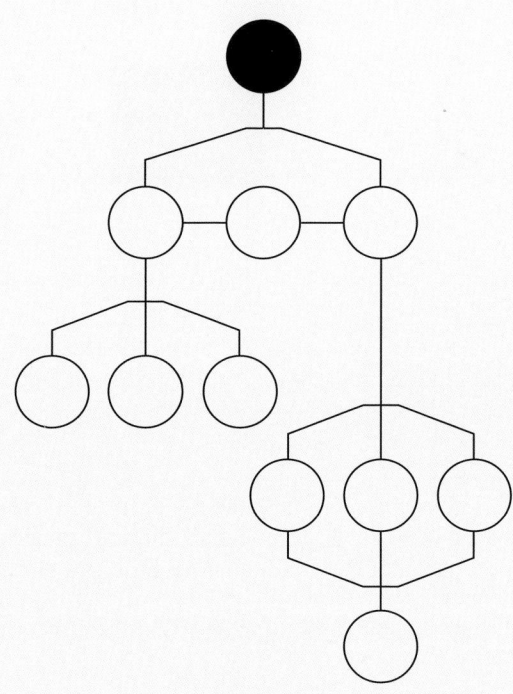

2014
Sorg Architects

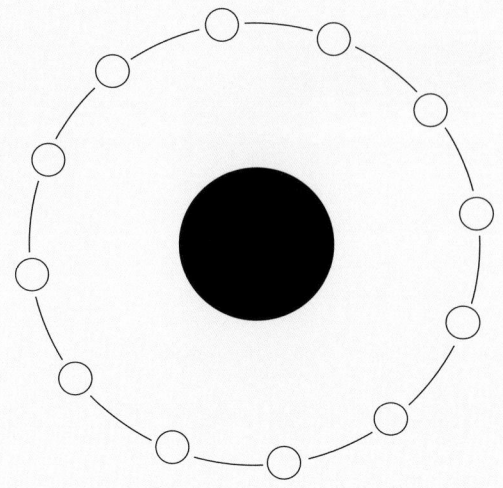

2014
Höweler + Yoon Architecture

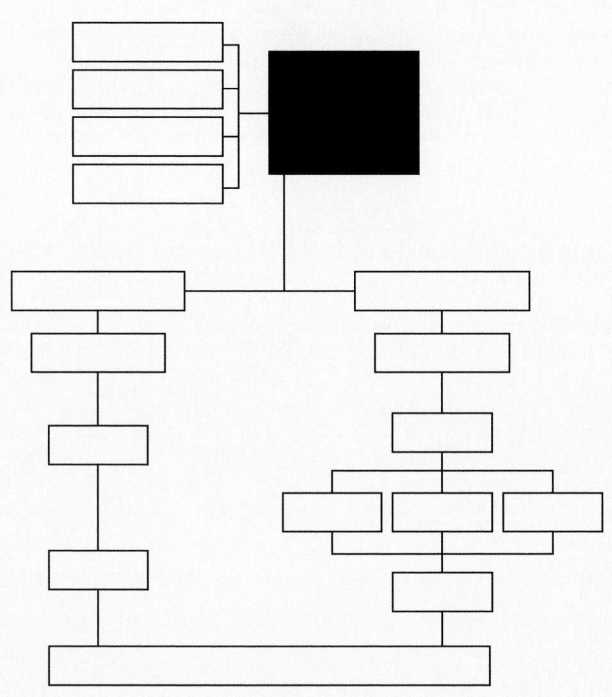

2014
WORKac

On all work except the simplest, it is to the interest of the owner to employ a superintendent or clerk of the works. In many engineering problems and in certain specialized esthetic problems, it is to his interest to have the services of special experts and the architect should so inform him.

Working drawings and detailing will be the first concern of those without the aptitude for design, and later, superintending, specification writing, or office management. Size is the usual criterion which one may deduce an office's tendency to make specialists of its workers, and it is patent that the more rounded experience of a small establishment fits better the needs of a budding architect because the one-man office is the first step of a normal evolution and its utter simplicity throws a great variety of responsibilities on its one man.

For years, CRS has had a simple rule for selecting team members. We say that a person "first must know his stuff and then be a good guy." It is the "good guy" part that qualifies him for team play. How to make a person into a good guy is quite a problem.

The procedures necessary to employ the best quality staff often change according to market conditions. During boom periods, when there is a shortage of available staff, you may have to offer high salaries or endeavor to meet people who can be enticed from other practices to yours.

Before you hire someone, first design the job.

3 — 1 HIRING POLICY

To deliver technical solutions by interpreting stakeholder requirements to ensure that all solutions are technically appropriate and meet customer and company requirements.
     —Boilerplate Clause in Recruitment Ads, 2000–2015

In spite of strenuous efforts to discredit this romantic myth, the history of design is still written and taught as if noteworthy buildings spring into existence, fully formed, from the foreheads of a few gifted individuals. The complex organization of physical labor that brings these constructs into being rarely merits even a footnote, even though the line between *design* and *build* is quite carefully maintained in practice. Since the establishment of Canon VI in 2007, the architecture profession's obligations to environmental sustainability have been a central part of the AIA's Code of Ethics, while the stipulation that "members should uphold human rights" remains a mere passing reference under the General Obligations laid out in Canon I. Professional attention to the latter does not stray very far outside of the "Albert Speer question" relating to design in the directly complicit service of a totalitarian regime. Engineers and architects are routinely insulated against any fallout from the exposure of labor exploitation on the construction site or the materials supply chain. Legal accountability for these abuses generally lies with the contractor, and it is widely held that the designer carries no moral responsibility.

     A break in this longstanding pattern of neglect occurred in the wake of Zaha Hadid's infamous 2014 statement about her non-responsibility for the abuse of Qatar's migrant workers. "It's not my duty as an architect to look at [labor abuses]…I have no power to do anything about it." Her celebrity made her a target for self-righteous scorn in many quarters, and her response—a legal effort to punish detractors—only amplified the public hubbub. The truth of the matter is that for some years now, virtually every large architecture firm in the West relies on projects in countries where labor abuse, especially of migrant workers, is routine. This is a consequence of the global boom in urban building, driven by the desperate need to park surplus capital. Notably, there is a

...

campaign afoot, initiated by the WBYA? (Who Builds Your Architecture?) group, to make attention to labor standards part the profession's ethical codes.

Yet similar problems also exist within the professional office, where it is not uncommon to find patterns of worker exploitation, most explicitly in the use of both paid and unpaid internships. While most of the latter are illegal, and are proscribed by professional codes of conduct, the use of unpaid interns is still customary in the design disciplines. In some regards, the demands made on the time or resources of paid interns or junior employees are even more severe. It is not uncommon to hear former employees describe an office of a well-known architect as being "run like a sweatshop." At a time when architecture graduates are saddled with massive debt burdens and are faced with thin employment prospects in their chosen profession, it is increasingly considered unacceptable, even offensive, when highly successful practitioners take advantage of these straightened circumstances to squeeze their own staff in this manner.

Sustainable design is typically (and technically) focused on low-carbon throughput, but it cannot gloss over its social component—how to sustain and honor livelihoods based on the principles of fair labor. Andrew Ross

1974
Venturi and Rauch
Venturi and Rauch Handbook

The office staff has been assembled to enable the firm to meet its obligations to clients and to conduct itself as a professional business organization. Each application for employment will be evaluated on the basis of educational training, professional licensing (when appropriate), and apparent aptitude, ability and potential to participate in the firm's activities.

1979
Ibsen Nelsen and Associates
Office Personnel Guidelines

INA does not discriminate against any individual or applicant for employment because of race, creed, sex or national origin, and has taken care that applicants are employed, and that individuals are treated during employment without discrimination. Such action includes, but is not limited to, employment upgrading, demotion or transfer, layoff or termination, rates of pay or other forms of compensation, and selection for training including apprenticeship.

1991
SLR/Architects
Office Manual

In order to make this policy effective, we expect the employees to share the commitment to the principles of equal opportunity and will not tolerate any acts of discrimination by any employees against any other.

2016
▮▮▮▮▮▮
▮▮▮▮
Employee Handbook

It is the policy of ▮▮▮▮ to make all employment decisions on the basis of individual merit, personal qualifications, competence, and abilities to meet the requirements of the job, without regard to sex, race, color, religion, national origin, citizenship status, ancestry, age, medical condition, disability, sexual orientation, familial status, veteran status or marital status (except where certain characteristics are essential bona fide occupational requirements or where a disability is a bona fide occupational disqualification), as required by federal and state law.

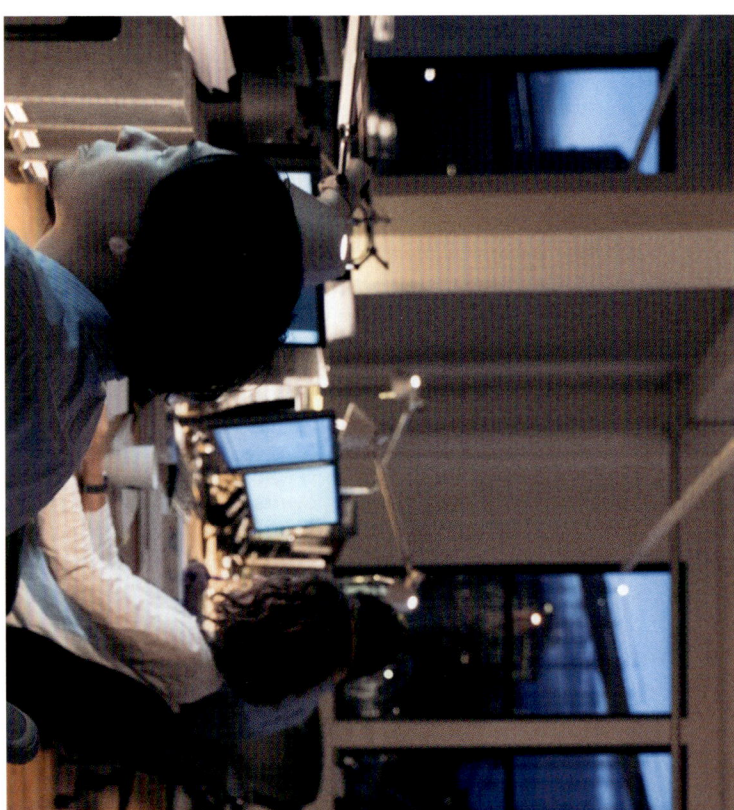

1974

1979

1991

2016

3 — 2 EQUAL EMPLOYMENT OPPORTUNITY

Equal Employment Opportunity signals our culture's desire to establish a
system in which gender, creed, color, disability, religion, and national origin are
not used as discriminating factors for employment or labor conduct. However,
the facts below, taken from the *2010 United Nations World's Women Report,*
signal that, when it comes to women, Equal Opportunity, is still an aspiration
and not yet a reality:

- *In today's world, there are fifty-seven million more men than women. This
  surplus of men is concentrated in the youngest age groups and steadily
  diminishes until it disappears at about age fifty, thereafter becoming a
  surplus of women owing to their longer life expectancy.*
- *Globally, women's participation in the labor market is about 52 percent. In
  the more developed economies, the labor force—especially the female
  labor force—is employed predominantly in services.*
- *Over the years, women have entered various traditionally male-dominated
  occupations. However, they are still rarely employed in jobs with status,
  power and authority or in traditionally male blue-collar occupations.*
- *Horizontal and vertical job segregation has resulted in a persistent
  gender pay gap everywhere. While the gender pay gap is closing slowly
  in some countries, it has remained unchanged in many others.*
- *In spite of the changes that have occurred in women's participation in the
  labor market, women continue to bear most of the responsibilities for
  the home: caring for children and other dependent household members,
  preparing meals, and doing other housework.*
- *When unpaid work is taken into account, women's total work hours are
  longer than men's in all regions.*
- *Women continue to be underrepresented in national parliaments,
  where on average only 17 percent of seats are occupied by women. The
  share of women among ministers also averages 17 percent.*
- *The highest positions are even more elusive: only 7 of 150 elected heads
  of state in the world are women, and only 11 of 192 heads of government.*
- *Of the five hundred largest corporations in the world, only thirteen have a
  female chief executive officer.*

As our world progressively moves towards equality, it will affirm that
what we can gain by achieving Equal Employment Opportunities greatly
outnumbers what we may lose. Our gender differences will be channeled in
meaningful ways allowing self-expression, creativity, wealth, and diversity
at work and throughout the spectrum of society's life style choices.

As Equality advances what makes me, me—architect, woman, mother,
South American, Jewish, brown—will become less a determining factor
regarding access to work and more a factor in the expression of what I create as
architect and give as citizen. I look forward to all the futures ahead. Galia Solomonoff

2014

Employee Handbook

It is important to understand that your employment with █████ ██████████ is "at will," meaning that either you or ████████████ may terminate the employment relationship at any time, with or without cause, and with or without notice. Nothing in this Employee Handbook or in any other document or oral statement shall limit the right to terminate employment at will. At will employment also means that ████████████████ may make decisions regarding all other terms of employment, with or without cause or advance notice. Only the President or Managing Principal of █████████████ has the authority to modify the at-will nature of the employment relationship, and any such modification must be in writing signed by the President or Managing Principal. Unless employment is covered by such a written employment agreement signed by the President or Managing Principal, this policy of at-will employment is the sole and entire agreement between an employee and ███████████████ as to the duration of employment and the circumstances under which employment may be terminated.

2014

Employee Handbook

Employment with ████████ is voluntarily entered into, and the employee is free to resign at will at any time, with or without cause. Similarly, ████████ may terminate the employment relationship at will at any time, with or without notice or cause.

2016

Employee Handbook

Employment with ██████ is entered on a voluntary basis, and employees are free to resign at any time, with or without notice. Similarly, ██████ is free to conclude any employment relationship at any time, with or without notice.

3 — 3 EMPLOYMENT AT WILL

The background legal rule throughout nearly all of the United States allows both employees and employers to terminate most employment contracts "at will"— that is, at any time, for any reason, or for no reason at all. In recent decades, however, many courts have eroded this employment-at-will rule. They often construe ambiguous employee handbook language against the employer and, as a result, may find an implied promise to terminate only for good cause. Employment attorneys routinely recommend that firms stave off these potential claims by contracting expressly for an at-will relationship, and courts readily enforce those terms.

Employers' concerns are understandable. What happens when employee misconduct or incompetence is observable but not easily verifiable? Managers may be confident that a particular employee has begun to shirk essential job responsibilities. However, this belief may be insufficient to convince a third-party decision maker such as a judge or arbitrator that the employee has transgressed and that the employer has good cause to terminate.

Conventional wisdom dictates that employers should avoid these problems by forming an at-will contract. Most employers will continue to use at-will contracts because they eliminate a modest legal risk, new hires sign them without objection, and courts readily enforce them.

But there is room in the marketplace to experiment with alternative terms governing termination. By offering greater formal job security a firm could signal to prospective employees that it is unusually committed to nurturing and investing in their professional development. The goal should be to devise terms that unequivocally send this signal without unduly increasing the firm's legal risk. Here's an effort to draft job security terms that serve both of these goals:

(1) Good Faith—[Employer] and [Employee] wish to establish a mutually productive working relationship. To that end, both parties agree that they will make a good faith effort to maintain and preserve that relationship.

(2) Termination for "Good Cause"—[Employer] may terminate this employment contract for "good cause." "Good cause" means that [Employee] has engaged in significant misconduct or that [Employee] has demonstrated an inability to perform [Employee's] duties in a workmanlike manner.

(3) Termination "Without Cause"—[Employer] also may terminate this employment contract "without cause." The term "without cause" means any termination that [Employer] initiates without "good cause" and includes any circumstances in which [Employer] has insufficient work and must reduce the size of its staff. In the event of a termination "without cause," [Employer] shall pay [Employee] sixty days' severance pay at [Employee's] then-current base salary plus ten additional days' severance pay for each full year of service up to a maximum of twelve years.

(4) Termination with Notice—[Employee] may terminate this employment contract at any time for any reason or no reason, provided that [Employee] gives [Employer] thirty days' prior notice. [Employer] will waive this notice requirement if it imposes an undue hardship on [Employee].

(5) Probationary Period—The first 180 days after [Employee] begins work for [Employer] will be a probationary period. During this period, either [Employer] or [Employee] may terminate the contract at any time and for any reason and with or without prior notice. J.H. Verkerke

1941
Royal Barry Wills
and Leon Keach
This Business of Architecture

The first year determines the general direction of a man's usefulness to an employer. A talent for design will swing him one way, or the lack of it to another more varied fate, which leads slowly towards some of the so called "practical" subdivisions of an office. Being green in such matters, the tag he will eventually wear is longer delayed in the titling.

1950
Richard J. Neutra Office
Rules for Apprentices /
Students

Training in an office is accomplished by letting you lay hands on actual current jobs which are the only projects which the architect has the time to concentrate on, and through which you can intensively learn. Your green hands burden the responsible architect with additional nerve strain. Do your best to minimize trouble to the office caused by your mistakes or negligence, which may show up at a much later date. In the smallest detail lies a possibility of damage to the architect's reputation and to the cause for which he stands. Punctuality, care and a thoroughly cooperative attitude are a prerequisite.

1988
Emery, Roth & Sons,
P.C. Architects
Office Guidelines

The first three months of employment are considered a probationary period. Thereafter, severance pay or notice is discretionary on the part of an officer of the firm.

2014

Employee Handbook

The first 3 months of employment are considered a probationary period where employment is temporary and benefits are not awarded. At the end of this period there will be a review, and depending on performance and project status, regular employment may be granted. However, completion of the 3-month period should not be considered guarantee that permanent employment is being granted.

1941

1950

1988

2014

3 — 4 INTRODUCTORY PERIOD

I'm going to make a few comments on one aspect of the introductory period concerning the employment of recent graduates in the profession of architecture. We would like to believe that this transition is a step-by-step collection of ever increasing responsibilities that introduce a new employee to the realities of practice. As naturally normative as this may sound, this is not what a new employee often does on entering many current architectural practices.

The fact is that a new employee fresh out of school knows the latest digital software. His or her first tasks are most likely rendering a finished design.

There are several problems surrounding this situation. Three main ones are as follows:

First, rendering is treated as manual labor. The production of a rendering is seen as lacking creativity, critical thought, and professional skill. This attitude can appear reminiscent of the Beaux-Arts educational system that valued a laboriously ink-washed rendering as a faithful translation of the original design parti. The difference is that today there is no argument as to how rendering ties into design pedagogy or an office ideology. The rendering is simply the last thing you do before a presentation.

Second, rendering is viewed as technical labor. It is incredibly difficult for an office to spend the necessary resources on training their current employees to keep up with the rate of change in digital technology. It is akin to an arms race, where in order to stay in the game of the escalating image war, an office needs to continually upgrade its representational output through new recruits. A new graduate's skills are valuable for their newness, *not* their disciplinary expertise.

Third, rendering is treated as devoid of aesthetic value. The assumed goal is photorealism. Digital software allows rendering to simulate with ever increasing fidelity the appearance of reality; the assumption is that the closer to the real, the better the rendering. This belief allows rendering to go un-theorized and/or neglected as part of a design process. Furthermore, it often goes unnoticed that most schools are not training students to engage rendering either conceptually or aesthetically. The students learn rendering on their own for the most part by using the most current software and following the latest visual trends.

It is more than a minor irony that one of the prime roles for a new employee in an architectural office is to practice a skill that they were not specifically trained for, is typically not understood by the employer, and is generally perceived as busy work by the profession of architecture. It may be a very valuable kind of busy work in terms of monetary expenditure, but still it is not treated with disciplinary respect. This introductory period will end for the employee when a newer graduate with more current digital skills can replace them in the task of producing images. It is only after they are obsolete that they move onto other aspects of practicing architecture. ^{Michael Young}

1909
The American
Institute of Architects
*A Circular of Advice
Related to Principles of
Professional Practice and
the Canons of Ethics*

The profession of architecture calls for men of the highest integrity, business capacity and artistic ability. The architect is entrusted with financial undertakings in which his honesty of purpose must be above suspicion; he acts as professional adviser to his client and his advice must be absolutely disinterested.

1916
Daniel Paul Higgins
"The 'Business'
of Architecture.
Part I: Introduction"
The Architectural Review

Any organization that is not efficient and harmoniously working is diseased. It is just this lack of harmony and sympathy which has wrecked many a firm's chances for success.

1940
Atlee B. and Robert M. Ayres
Office Rules

Please do not get too noisy or talkative in the drafting room.

1999
The American
Institute of Architects
*Handbook of Design
Office Administration*

All employees represent their firm. This mandates professional behavior at all times in dress, language, manners, and action. Take pride in the work of the firm and your specific contribution to the end product. Promote and exhibit a positive attitude. […] Show respect to fellow workers by practicing the virtues of punctuality, listening without interrupting when people are speaking, returning borrowed materials, being considerate of other's time, and giving credit to the accomplishments, ideas, and creations of others.

2004
Davis Brody Bond, LLP
Employee Policy Manual

DBB is committed to proving and maintaining a drug-free environment. The unlawful possession, dispensing, distribution, manufacture or use of a controlled substance is prohibited in the office.

2008
Howeler + Yoon
Office Manual

We believe in a mutually respectful environment with open communication between all members of the studio. We want to encourage a comfortable social environment, however, please mind that others are trying to work and that conversations may be distracting to others. Please use your best judgment and be respectful to others.

2014
Employee Handbook

Ethical and professional integrity both inside and outside the office is critical. We have built a high level of trust with repeat clients and this trust is reflected internally in the day to day operations of the office. All employees must think sustainably in fostering the highest standards of conduct between vendors, clients, and team members.

2016
Snøhetta
Snøhetta Guide

We respect the need for engagement of many disciplines in the development of each project. This includes in-house expertise consisting of designers, architects, landscape and interior architects, artists, economists and administration as well as any external expertise to the benefit of the project. The working method is named "transpositioning" which indicates free flow of knowledge between all project participants independent of age or experience. We strive for a continuous state of reinvention.

1909
1916
1940
1999
2004
2008
2014
2016

3 — 5 STANDARDS OF CONDUCT AND STANDARDS OF CARE

Take the *Quality* pledge.

I _____ pledge to abide by Quality Management principles and TQM (Total Quality Management) teachings as reflected in the ISO 9000 family of standards, the ISO 14000 standard for consideration of the environment, and the ISO 37120 standard for the consideration of cities. And I pledge to become a member of the International Union of Architects.

I pledge to undergo a SWOT analysis (Strengths, Weaknesses, Opportunities and Threats) and an audit by a third party expert to expose my management defects. Lesson: Climb the Quality pyramid!

I pledge to prepare a PSRRA (Purpose, Scope, Responsibility, Related Documents, Actions) report reflecting Triple3 GBB (Good Better Best) Values. Lesson: Rationalize your system to QM theory!

I pledge to adapt the PDCA (Plan, Do, Check, Act) cycle to the Ten Quality Keys matrix for Architecture and Design practices. Lesson: Respot the leopard!

I pledge to be MODERN:
- Practice like it's 1949! The global Middle class is "US"
- Offer US investment strategies to make "them" more like "US"
- "US" Don't do politics; "US" Do Do consensus
- "US" Experts say it with Econometrics
- Avoid Risk with "US"
- Time to change the structure of the USOffice: Never!

I pledge to improve my "Are you a total quality person" rating.
Lesson: There are many mirrors!

I pledge to lead a client-centered life as per the 73-point "customer profile" pro forma.

I pledge to answer the phone with the question "USOffice! How can I respond to your needs with excellence?" and end each phone conversation with the question "Has USOffice responded to all your needs with excellence today?" And I pledge to tabulate and analyze responses to these questions with a checklist for continual improvement. Lesson: There are many grains of sand in a mountain!

I pledge to request all office employees, suppliers, marketers and clients to "JOIN US" and take the Quality Pledge. Keller Easterling

An architect should be mindful of the public welfare and should participate in those movements for public betterment in which his special training and experience qualify him to act. He should not, even under his client's instructions, engage in or encourage any practices contrary to law or hostile to the public interest.

The Architect is not only obligated to certain things by his contract with his client, but has another obligation through his relation to the contract between the client and contractor. A client has the right to the best possible handling of the interests he entrusts to his Architect.

There are still other responsibilities that are inherent in the practice of architecture. The architects should be consulting experts in regard to building laws and restrictions and real estate values, and in regard to the obsolescence and depreciation of buildings and their equipment; and in regard to the cost of operating buildings devoted to commercial and industrial uses and the income that may be derived therefrom.

The true professional attitude is one that involves responsibilities which are self assumed. The architect professes to have more than ordinary knowledge of architecture in all its phases and complex subdivisions, and in so profession he assumes a grave responsibility to all with whom he deals, to protect them by the free and unfettered use of that knowledge. A code of ethical conduct which embraces every phase of this responsibility should be the controlling principle of professional life.

The ultimate responsibility for the firm's projects is vested in its principals. Much of this responsibility is delegated to a project manager for each project.

3 — 6 PROFESSIONAL RESPONSIBILITY

There are three kinds of professional responsibility.

LEGAL

We should not get sued, but if we do we should be prepared to face it. Thus we should maintain a clear scope of responsibility, or, in this case, liability.

To ensure that the above happens, we engage with all kinds of specialists. We seek consultation on the ever-expanding volume of codes and regulations binding the design and construction of buildings, such as accessibility, water-proofing, wind and weather, acoustics and zoning.

We must take all of the necessary precautions to cover ourselves against legal action. The architect's professional language is strengthened with a variety of clauses and keywords that act as barriers of responsibility, while a number of inventions such as email disclaimers, backup software, and insurance policies are called forth to protect us.

SUSTAINABLE

It is our responsibility to perform and execute work of high quality in order to maintain our business. Our clients' investments have to see successful results, and for that we are expected to perform at the highest level: meeting goals and schedules, delivering inclusive drawings, being responsive, and providing feasible and budget-conscious solutions.

To maintain quality standards we have developed an extensive control system stemming from experience, office hierarchy, and training. We have also developed methods of synergy with the client and ego management mecha-nisms that allow us to complete projects in smooth and efficient ways.

MORAL

We are architectural visionaries of a romantic kind. The soul of our work lies in our responsibility towards the community, our desire to serve it, and our fantasy to improve it.

Our projects are manifestations of ideals respecting the context, the environment, and the future users.

We seek to contribute to the city in any way possible (public spaces, enlarged sidewalks, interactive facades) and raise issues of contemporary living. We have our design agenda and we feel the duty to apply it, evolve it, and communicate it. [ODA]

1920
Howard Dwight Smith
"The 'Business' of
Architecture, The Position
of the Supervising Architect
in the Organization"
The Architectural Review

It is the architect's province to assume the position of artistic mentor to his client, to lead him and educate him as he may require.

1939
American Institute
of Architects
"Standards of Practice of
the American Institute
of Architects"
*The Octagon, A Journal
of The American
Institute of Architects*

Architects […] should seek opportunities to be of constructive service in civic affairs, and, to the best of their abilities, advance the safety health, and well being of the community in which they reside, by promoting therein the appreciation of good design, the value of good construction, and the proper placement of structures, and the adequate development and adornment of the areas around them.

1974
Venturi and Rauch
Venturi and Rauch Handbook

Active participation in the affairs of the community is a responsibility of every citizen. Participation by architects benefits both the public and the profession since this brings increased professional attention to the activities of the community and results in greater public awareness of the capabilities of architects.

2008
The American
Institute of Architects
*The Architect's Handbook
of Professional Practice,*
14th Edition

The very nature of our work offers architects leadership opportunities at the center of public life. Many successful architects have gone one step further and taken their professional expertise into roles as civic volunteers, community and cultural leaders, public service appointees, and elected government officials.

1920

1939

1974

2008

3 — 7 PUBLIC SERVICE

Who is the public and why are architects enlisted into public service? The professionalization of the architectural practice is tied to the advent of nation-states and urbanization in the nineteenth century. Earlier, architects served the bastions of religious and political power. Patronage, first the church, then the aristocracy, and eventually the mercantile class, had been the avenue through which the gentleman architect pursued his craft in Europe and the Americas. With the rise of liberalism and new state and social formations with the emergence of the nation-state and modern society, the need to house new institutions such as the courthouse, the museum, the university, and the library prompted the professionalization of the field of architecture.

Entities like the American Institute of Architects, created in 1857 to formalize the practice of architecture, established that, beyond the contractual relationship with a client—who could be a government, a civic body, or a private individual—the architect, by nature of the fact that building engaged a myriad of social relations, also had a responsibility to the public, characterized in a 1909 Ethics Code as "public betterment" and "public welfare." What public meant at that moment was defined by a set of local and national political allegiances. Social progress defined the ethos of public service, which charged the professional white male architect to improve the welfare of the lesser sex, the other races, and the lower classes.

The boosterism of Progress has thankfully waned, but today when architects are enlisted into public service whom do they serve? As global finance, media, and culture erode the boundaries of communities and nation-states, who the public might be has become more elusive and less political. As large scale agglomerations of social relations become established by tech platforms like Facebook and Twitter, where people can have millions of followers, the "friend" and "follower" becomes a new moniker of the public.

Transnational architectural practices are becoming more typical in the United States. Architects based in New York, Chicago, and Indianapolis now build regularly in the Middle East and Asia, with increasingly more commissions accepted in South America and Africa. These projects may be for states whose authoritarianism is disguised in the principled rhetoric of education, sustainability, and cultural enhancement. The architect's relationship with the society in these contexts is mediated by differences in language and cultural practices, but also by the large apparatus of transnational building networks where architects are one of thousands of actors working on large-scale construction projects. However, there are nonetheless social relations established through these projects, and there are still constituencies to be addressed in these contexts. The ethics of practice has always informed the imperative of public service. With the recent global protests and rising resource scarcity, perhaps the "people "or "commons" become the new public for architects to serve. Mabel O. Wilson

3 — 8 OFFICE HOURS

Office hours are from 9 A.M. to 5 P.M. During the summer months a half-holiday is given on Saturdays, which is made up by an extra-hour during the other days of the week.

During the months of September to May, inclusive, the office hours will be from 9 a.m. to 12:15 p.m. and from 1:15 p.m. to 5:15 p.m., except Saturdays, which shall be from 9 a.m. to 12:15 p.m. During the months of June to August, inclusive, the office hours will be from 9 a.m. to 12:15 p.m. and from 1:15 p.m. to 5:35 p.m., except on Saturday, when the office will be closed.

REGULAR HOURS OF WORK
Total number of working hours per week: 44
8:30 AM to 12; 1:00 PM to 5:40 PM Monday to Friday
8:30 AM to 12:30 PM on Saturdays

WORKING TIME
Total numbers of working hours per week: 41½
Working hours are from 8:00 am to 5:30 pm, Monday thru Thursday, and from 8:30 to 5:00, Friday

The hours of work from this office are from 8 AM to 5 PM, Monday thru Friday, a 40 hour week, 1 hour for lunch.

Office Hours are from 8:30 a.m. to 5:30 p.m. with one hour off for lunch. The lunch hour is to be taken between 12:00 noon and 2:00 p.m.

The workweek is 40 hours; 8 hours Monday through Friday; 8:30 am – 5:30 pm for technical staff. Secretarial hours range from 8:00 am – 5:30 pm.

The normal workweek is 37.5 hours, Monday through Friday. For technical personnel and plan desk, the hours are from 8:30 A.M to 5:00 P.M. or 9:00 A.M to 5:30 P.M., at the discretion of the Department Head. Once an employee establishes his/her hours, they are to be adhered to. For administrative and clerical personnel the hours are from 9:00 A.M. to 5:00 P.M.

The normal workday is eight hours from 8 a.m. to 5 p.m. and the normal week is 40 hours, beginning on Monday and ending on the following Friday.

The studio hours are 9AM – 6PM.

3 — 8 OFFICE HOURS

Office hours may be published, but they are rarely adhered to.

It is generally acknowledged that smaller, design-oriented firms make inhumane demands of their employee's time. Young employees are expected to give up their lives. Relationships die, hobbies are abandoned, even houseplants suffer. The amount of time employees are expected to be in the office is inversely proportional to the size of the office and, oftentimes, the renown of the office. The smaller and more well-regarded you are, the more you will work. Or so the theory goes.

My experience is that long hours are more a self-fulfilling prophecy rather than a demand made by Partners. Working long hours and sacrificing one's life convinces employees that they are doing meaningful work and that the Partners might notice their work ethic. In my opinion, good work is more valuable than time. So the question is: is time the thing that catapults ambitious offices into the realm of influential offices? Is work made better with more (sleep deprived) time? Or does work get better after a pleasant weekend spent with your lover in a place far, far away? Charles Renfro

1901
W. Kaye Perry
Office Management:
A Handbook for Architects
and Civil Engineers

Every member of the staff should enter his name in an attendance book when he arrives, with the exact hour of arrival. It should be the duty of the junior clerk, or office boy, to remind the member of the staff that the name must be signed, and the principal should from time to time glance through the book to see how time is kept.

There is a great laxity in many offices as regards office hours, and even the best assistants are inclined to lapse into unpunctual attendance if the book be neglected.

1971
Abbott, Merkt & Company
Procedural Manual

In the event you are unable to report for work, you should inform your superior or the supervisor at 9:00 A.M.

1980
Archonics
Personnel Information

All time and payroll reporting is on an honor system. All employees are expected to be available for work during these periods. Certain individual responsibilities require that the employee be out of the office at varying intervals. It is expected that the receptionist and the immediate superior be notified as to the whereabouts of the individual.

1990
Cannon Design
Office Protocol

Your absence from the job on a scheduled workday causes a hardship on your fellow workers and on the company as a whole.

2016
Diller Scofidio + Renfro
Office Manual

An attendance calendar is kept in Google Calendars and is visible to all employees.

1901

1971

1980

1990

2016

3 — 9 ATTENDANCE

Attendance Stack

STAYING IN-STREAM

All employees are required to remain in-stream at all attendance stack levels at all times. Maximum acceptable response latency will be adjusted to account for weekends, holidays, transport, and sleep.

BASE STACK

New employees will be issued accounts in all layers of the base attendance stack. Email will form the foundation layer for inter-firm operability and correspondence with the board. A proprietary Slack layer with Trello and Github integrations will follow for project team communications, agile production scheduling, and product versioning and feature requests. Note that some departments may still use Asana in place of Trello, but we are working to phase out all one-dimensional list interfaces. Holacracy sits on top of the Slack-Trello-Github cocktail for self-organized project-based group formation. Liquid Democracy is used for firm-wide decision-making, such as retreat topics and the softball batting order. The wiki is used as an information store and intranet to share confidential events and updates not suitable for social. Google Calendar sits on top of the entire stack for inter- and intra-firm meeting schedules and space allocation. WhatsApp is required for employees who expect to travel, except for those traveling to the Middle East, China, or Russia, or interfacing with journ-alists, in which case Wickr should be substituted.

SOCIAL STACK

In addition to the base stack, all employees are required to maintain an insightful and inspiring personal social stack and follow all firm channels. The exact composition is left mostly to the employee's discretion, but a minimum of five layers is expected. Facebook, Twitter, Tumblr, and Instagram are required. Employees should post regularly, particularly early in the morning, after lunch, and in the evening, about contemporary events related and unrelated to firm activities as well as firm-specific content. Inter-layer automation with IFTTT is frowned upon but may be acceptable in some instances where well-crafted custom recipes have been created.

...

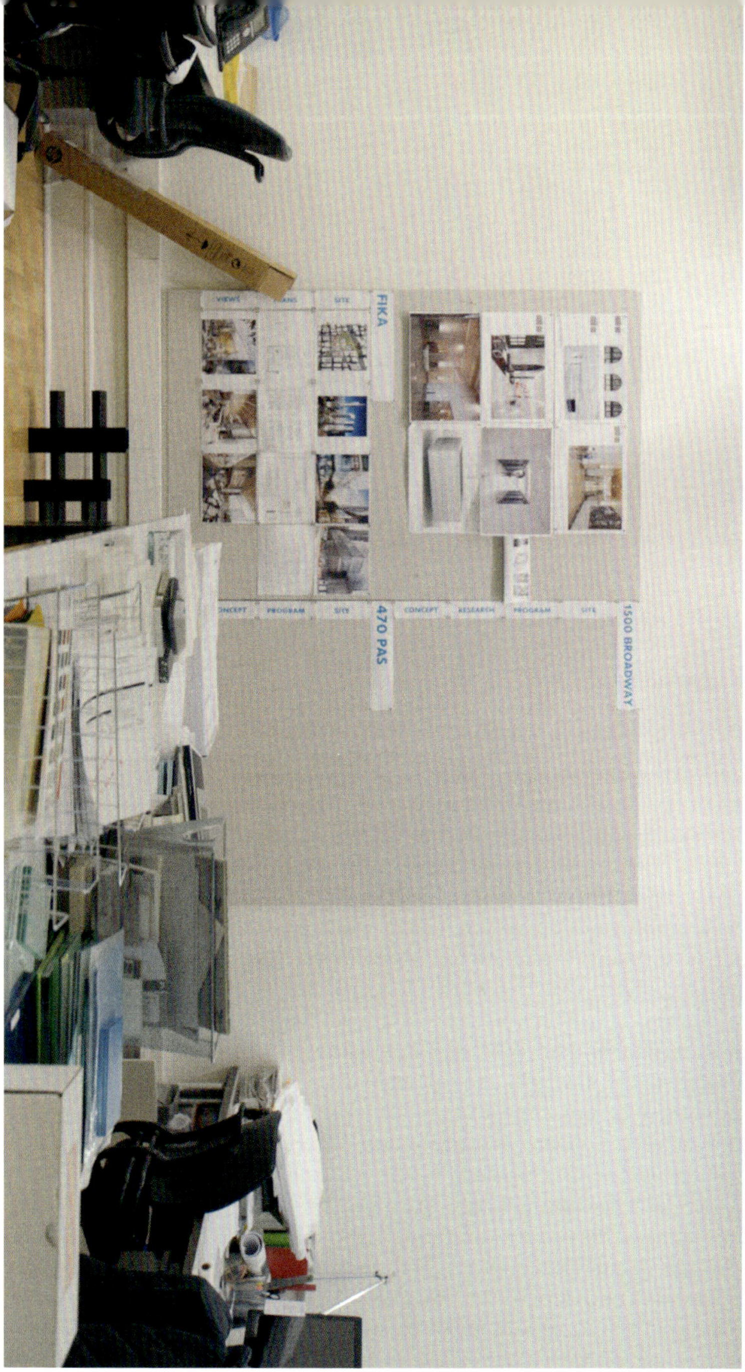
FIKA
470 PAS
1500 BROADWAY

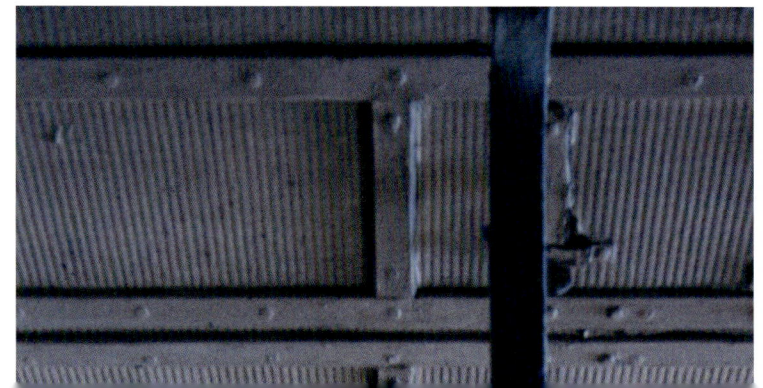

ICING

Individual teams may ice the attendance stack with other non-proprietary layers to increase morale, make decisions, or integrate extra-firm supplements into the innovation process. Examples include Predict.It for crowd-sourced prognostication through prediction markets and Amazon Mechanical Turks for high throughput menial tasks.

LATENCY AND THROUGHPUT

In-stack communication frequency is tracked automatically and weighted inversely to employee age. Median firm-wide response times and message output are reported in daily Slack posts by Latebot with special alerts for employees who drop more than two standard deviations below. Maximum acceptable latencies are adjusted for weekends, Thanksgiving, and Rosh Hashanah, during underground or in-air vehicular transport, and while sleeping.

ARTIFICIAL INTELLIGENCE ASSISTANCE

AI-assistant micro-layers like X.AI for scheduling, Largebot for procurement, or M for general mental wellness are encouraged. Please see the firm Github bot repo for a list of approved AIs. If you would like to suggest others, please submit a pull request for the attendance stack admins to vet.

GROUNDS FOR PROMOTION AND TERMINATION

Any employee more than two standard deviations above or below both the median latency and throughput for two consecutive quarters in multiple layers will be either promoted or terminated immediately on grounds of stack leadership or truancy, respectively. Troy Conrad Therrien

1928
Atlee B. and Robert M. Ayres
Office Rules

Let everyone be on time so we can quit on time.

1964
Richard J. Neutra Office
*Rules for Apprentices
– Students*

**Punctuality, care and a thoroughly cooperative attitude are
a prerequisite.**

1980
Archonics
Personnel Information

**Any tardiness is to be made up during the day of its insurance. Any
habitual tardiness by an employee is subject to disciplinary action by a
supervisor.**

2008
Höweler + Yoon Architecture
Policy Manual

**Punctuality is important as it allows us to schedule internal meetings
and coordinate daily critiques. If an employee is unable to work
as scheduled, the employee is to call one of the principals as soon as
possible or in advance.**

2014
Diller Scoffidio + Renfro
Office Manual

You are considered late if you arrive after 9:30.

1928

1964

1980

2008

2014

3 — 10 PUNCTUALITY

Punctuality is not a value, it is evidence of a life well managed.

Arrival or delivery in a timely manner indicates to others that you respect your relationship enough to ensure that the inevitable chaos we all experience in life and business is not put off on them.

Modern technology should make it easier to be punctual, not easier to fail at it. Adam Hayes

Time off will be deducted.

When obligated to perform annual service in the military reserve for a period not to exceed two weeks per year, full time personnel may be paid the difference between the sums received from the military and the individual's regular wages.

Chronic or excessive absenteeism will not be tolerated, even if the Member has sufficient accrued leave to cover the absences, and will be grounds for discipline up to and including discharge.

Time off for medical or dental appointments will be applied as sick leave, or made up by working the time within the same week. Period-ically, an employee may need to take time off for religious holidays, meeting with a child's teacher, renewing a driver's license, etc. Time off for these purposes must receive approval prior to taking it, and can be made up by working the extra hours within the same pay period.

3 — 11   TIME AWAY FROM THE OFFICE

Time away from the office depends on the office. Every practice is different, but "time away" doesn't exist for us. We're a small collaborative art practice. We don't keep track of our hours. We set goals, and work towards them. Sometimes it takes a late night, or an early morning; sometimes all weekend. We don't keep track of vacation days. We don't have rules for holidays. There are no off-limit hours. When we have a thought, we text. When we're tired, we sleep. When we want a beer, we drink. When we're awake, we work. When we need to turn off, we turn off, but we're never away. Everything is everything and energy breeds energy. Time away is time off, and the sign at PlayLab, Inc. is always on.
PlayLab, Inc.

3 — 12 MOONLIGHTING

1972
Lewis Clarke Associates
Handbook of Office Policies

All work will be handled through the office and "moonlighting" is strictly banned as unprofessional to the team effort.

1991
SLR Architects
Office Manual

The firm does not attempt to dictate to employees as to how they use their own time and, therefore, the following policies will be observed: Anyone providing outside architectural services is under obligation to advise their client that the work is not by, for, or in the name of this firm, and that this firm does not assume liability or responsibility for such work. Outside work must not interfere with regular assignments.

2011
STUDIOS Architecture
Employee Handbook

Members are expected to devote their services and best efforts exclusively to further the interests of STUDIOS. Members may not engage in professional practice or any other outside activities which conflict in any way with job responsibility, client relationships, business development or other interests of STUDIOS. All outside projects, employment and service other than volunteer work for charitable or educational organizations must have prior approval of a STUDIOS' Managing Principal in order to help avoid the perception or reality of a conflict of interest.

2014
██████████
Employee Handbook

Employees engaging in any moonlighting activities must, before engaging in such activities, provide an acknowledgment on a form letter provided by the Firm that they are engaged in moonlighting services and are abiding by the ████████ policy governing such activities and in which they identify any clients for whom they are providing services. They also must provide a letter of acknowledgment from their clients that the Firm has no involvement in these services.

1972

1991

2011
2014

3 — 12 MOONLIGHTING

Engaging in outside professional work while employed full-time is usually discouraged, if not banned outright. For many employers, the notion of "full-time service" is an expansive, hard-to-define loyalty that extends well outside of office hours. Doing independent work for hire is considered a form of cheating: the employee could be working on company time, profiting indirectly from the company's resources, or even competing directly with their employer for work. Worse, the employee's extracurricular activities may expose the company to unforeseen risks. No surprise, then, that most companies view outside employment as a zero-sum game that enriches their employees at the expense of the company.

For employees, however, there is little downside to taking on side projects. The appeal of independence, a sense of ownership, and additional income is irresistible. And so it seems that everyone is engaged in something on the side: a bathroom renovation, a competition entry, their condo's roof deck, or a weekend house for their parents.

There are a few ways a company could respond. A zero tolerance policy is unrealistic and amounts to "don't get caught." On the other hand, there is little incentive for an architecture firm to embrace side projects along the lines of the tech industry. Companies like Google have historically supported employee's "passion projects" on the hunch that they will result in new, marketable products for the company. As a service profession, the business model for architecture is fundamentally different: architects don't get paid for the quality of their ideas, they get paid for billable hours. Until architecture firms can profit from a great building design in the same way software companies profit from a killer app, an investment in employee's side projects—effectively, non-mission driven R&D—is unlikely to pay off.

Short of reinventing architecture's traditional business model, then, the most prudent policy on outside work is one that manages risk by requiring employees to meet the following conditions:

- The employee's primary commitment is to the company and must not be compromised by outside activities.
- The services offered must not compete with services offered by the firm.
- The employee must not perform work during office hours, or using office equipment or stationary.
- The employee must demonstrate that they have informed their client and other interested parties that they are performing services independently and not under the auspices of the company.
- The employee must demonstrate that they have obtained their own professional liability insurance. Gabrielle Brainard

Overtime shall be paid at same rate as regular time.

Overtime work shall be done only when authorized by the Chief Draftsman and commenced and terminated each day at such hours as stated by the Chief Draftsman. Authorization must be obtained each day. Payment will be made at the unit hourly base of the weekly salary.

Overtime work shall be done only when authorized and commenced and terminated each day at such hours as agreed to. Authorization must be obtained each day. Payment will be made at the unit hourly base of the weekly salary.

Although it is in everyone's best interest to complete work during regular office hours, the nature of the profession of architecture sometimes makes this impossible. The firm expects every member of the staff to be available for overtime work during critical rush periods.

On a normal workday, no employee is to work beyond 8:00 P.M. without taking at least a half hour for supper; on a non-working day, such as Saturday, no employee shall work more than 5 hours without at least a half hour break for lunch. No employee is to work beyond 10:00 P.M. on a normal workday or beyond 5:00 P.M. on a non-working day, and no more than 8 hours on such day.

If you are a non exempt (hourly) employee and are required to work beyond your normal eight hours, or if you are asked to work on a weekend or holiday, that time will be considered as overtime if, when added to your normal hours, the total exceeds 40 in any given work-week. In all cases such overtime work must have been required by the company and have the prior approval of your department head/group manager in order to be considered overtime. Payment for such over-time work will be made in accordance with statutory regulations on the basis of your employment classification.

It is generally expected that assigned tasks will be completed within normal working hours; however, should presentation deadlines, etc. require an unusual effort, overtime hours may be required based on the following conditions:
– Professional staff and senior administration staff are paid an annual salary. There is no payment for time over the 40 hours' week.
– Overtime for clerical personnel must be approved before the work is done. Approved overtime for clerical personnel is paid at one-and-one-half times the regular hourly rate for work over 40 hours per week.

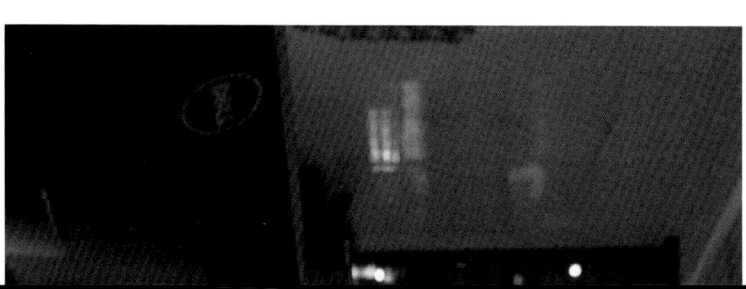

3 — 13 OVERTIME

CONTEXT

How much free labor is given away via the misguided management principle of overtime? When pricing contracts and negotiating with clients, most design firms estimate their proposals (n.b. cost is different from value) against the estimated time it takes to produce deliverables. An estimate of an estimate, there are two margins of error from the outset. Additionally, the downward pressures on fees as demanded by the marketplace, and accelerated timelines as made possible through technological innovation, have resulted in a common and unfortunate management practice of understaffing and overworking designers = overtime. This management practice is a direct response to measuring design output against time, for designers lack any other "measurable" unit for pricing their services, and have great difficulty in staying within the bounds of time that they themselves set forth.

SOLUTION

Designers Assembly proposes that design firms monetize their value against a separate unit of measurement altogether: connectivity to the electric grid. If the time-space continuum does not discourage designers from underpricing their contracts and/or overworking their staff, we know that connectivity to electricity will. No business, design included, can produce whatever they offer to the market without electricity that powers our computers. Will it be the looming global energy crisis or a societal awakening to our biology that awakens with the sun and rests with nightfall, which legally limits us to work, let's say, forty to forty-five hours per week?

In this scheme, the cost of electricity is scaled to be cheapest during 9 A.M. to 6 P.M. and becomes extraordinarily expensive at all other times. As a firm owner, your responsibility is to manage the time and output of your design staff during the most advantageous hours, and to absolutely bar them from working at all other times. Imagine the impact on the culture of design, in which working late into the evening marks your failure and a lack of commitment, not a mark of it.

...

SCENARIO 1

When a client requests a lot of work suddenly at 5:55 P.M. the manager will respond: "Do you mind that our hourly rate will increase, thereby exhausting the remaining fee in ten seconds?"

SCENARIO 2

When a design firm is able to properly execute its contracts between the legal working hours of 9 A.M. to 6 P.M. it receives tremendous accolade and well-deserved respect from the design community, design staff, and the public at large.

SCENARIO 3

Expulsion of design firm owners that try to game the system. Absolute authority and erasure of free will has not been in fashion in many aspects of society such as: politics, industrial production, education, and marital convention. So the next time Principal A exercises his or her authority over a staff person's free will to leave at 6 P.M. because "Creativity cannot be predictably scheduled"— Principal A will join the ranks of historical figures that have attempted, and failed, to maintain absolute control.

In summation, Designers Assembly is interested in creating an equitable and sustainable workplace culture by abolishing the practice of overtime from the design profession. We believe that time is finite, focus is finite, and talent is finite. There is value in actively managing our time and energy, it translates to physical and psychological health. Each of us has only one body, and one day at a time, to be the person that we most want to be. Designers Assembly (Masako Ikegami, Alda Ly, Nora Yoo)

Beyond the draughting room again is the coat and washroom, marked "gymnasium," and generally used for that purpose. It has been equipped by the firm with foils and masks, several pairs of Indian clubs, and a set of chest weights, and all the apparatus shows evidence of appreciative use, which has had a very good effect on the health and spirits of those who patronize it.

One hour for lunch.

Lunch hours are to be taken between 12 and 1 in order to keep office fully staffed during above specified office hours. Coffee break of fifteen minutes, morning and afternoon. Please telephone if any unusual delay of fifteen minutes or more is encountered.

Take the case of our national award-winning buildings—the fifty or so that were judged by the profession as being very good. With but few exceptions, each building was conceptualized during what we refer to as the CRS squatters—an on-the-spot, uninterrupted block of time (usually one week), team-effort design and programming session. No phone to bother us, no interruptions to speak of, and no disruptive breaks.

One hour from 12:00 to 1:00 P.M. for all personnel, and from 11:45 A.M to 1:00 P.M on Wednesday for check cashing. Any variation in this time shall be an exception and not the rule and shall be approved by Management.

The standard lunch hour is from 12 noon to 1 p.m. You should discuss any other working arrangement with your supervisor.

Lunch is limited to one hour, either in the office or out, preferable to be taken from 12:30 pm until 1:30 pm.

A one-hour lunch can be taken at any time convenient to your schedule.

3 — 14 BREAKS

"What makes me sad is when people have these lunches where they all go
out individually, and then have plastic containers of salads, and sit in front
of computers."
—Urs Fischer

"Owing to the pressure of work gentlemen are requested to confine the lunch
hour….between 12.30 & 1.30. The tennis lawn can only be used during the
above mentioned hour. No game or set to last over thirty minutes…."
—H. H. Richardson

Lunch is a cultural activity. The attitude toward lunch often defines the culture
of an architectural practice as well. Whereas Philip Johnson treated lunch at
the Four Seasons as an important social ritual, Mies van der Rohe advised his
employees to "skip lunch and buy art." For some, the lunch table provides an
important forum for debate and exchange of ideas. For others, lunch is nothing
but a nuisance to be dealt with as efficiently and simply as possible.
        When office and lunch are joined together to become *office lunch*, it
becomes a peculiar social activity with added significance. The level of comfort
one feels at an office lunch is indicative of the way the office is organized.
Office lunch is much more difficult to organize, for instance, in large corporate
practices. Even for a small, *atelier*-style practice, an office lunch is possible,
or enjoyable, only if its organizational structure is generally horizontal and
non-hierarchical. The duration of office lunch, the method of paying the bill
either collectively or individually, and the dominant topic of conversation during
lunch are all indicators of the office culture. Conversely, an architectural
practice can define and assert its values and cultural attitude by setting up
specific protocols for office lunch.
        When I moved my practice from New York to Seoul eight years ago, I
decided to adopt the Korean custom of eating lunch together every day.
(Whereas *hwesik*, or the office dinner in Korea, is mainly insular and private,
focusing mostly on brotherly bonding through heavy drinking, an office lunch is
much more open and public, leading to more sober and civic community
engagements.) At noon, we take daily walks through our neighborhood around
the Sewoon Arcade, searching for a new place to eat. The streets are flooded
with workers from various trades doing the same. It is at once an excursion
and lunch.
        Soon after beginning this routine, our neighbors began to recognize us
as a group. This recognition, in turn, gave us a sense of unity. Korean office
lunch, I realized, was not about efficiency or health, but a public display of your
presence as a group, or an organization, within the neighborhood. The public
display leads to trust, and the sense of trust and inclusion leads to referrals for
work, or collaboration within the community. Through this daily engagement
with our community, we, as a team, have been able to form productive partnerships for public art projects within our neighborhood. Office lunch has
expanded beyond the walls of our office both literally and figuratively. Choon Choi

A "business organization" is the machine by means of which all the other forces of architecture and building are made effective. An efficient organization, like a good machine, must work with a minimum loss of energy. […] A business organization which is to assist and direct the other forces of an architect's practice should not cause nor permit any dissipation of energy. Many a practice conducted haphazardly is, in the absence of proper business methods and specialization of function, wasting energy which should be conserved and realized in the form of direct profits.

The decisions made at the meetings would be sent to the drafting room for execution without further arguments over the draftsmen's tables. This procedure, we believe, would not only expedite the work, but would eliminate the high cost of conversation.

Time is a most important factor in all building operations. At no stage of the work should the architect procrastinate in the matter of securing decisions and expediting the progress of the drawings.

Non Productive Items: Time Lost. Here we include the non-productive time of draftsmen, such as intra-mural conversation on important international problems, oversleeping, talks with visiting friends, personal telephone calls, sickness, long luncheon hours, hot day closing, etc. A little observation on your part will reveal the surprising total of one-half to an hour a day. It is true that this is commonly charged as drafting time on the time cards but it is useful information in determining *true* drafting time.

Any architectural office in a major western city keeps a parrot in the drafting room. He walks along a mezzanine railing and screams at the employees below: "WORK! WORK! WORK!"

Procrastination is a major reason why people don't always do what they say they are going to do. It has a variety of causes, but they are less important than what you can do to avoid it.

Procrastination is a real problem which will not go away on its own, and it is a very real barrier to accomplish work. If procrastination is serious and debilitating enough, it may even require professional help for the person that is stuck. In a simplistic view, the problem may center around issues with authority, fear of failure, lack of discipline or even fear of success.

Do your best work ever, and have fun!

3 — 15 PROCRASTINATION

Many articles and books paint procrastinators as miserable and unproductive folk, inflicting stress on themselves and those around them, and driving our economy into the ditch. But this can't be right. Go through history, and remove all the novels, poems, plays, inventions, and business innovations that people came up with while they were supposed to be doing something else. You would gut civilization. The person who came up with the wheel was probably putting off building a sled; Shakespeare probably wrote his first play while he was supposed to be copying scripts for the older actors in his troupe; and so on and so forth right up to the well-known college goof-offs who have been responsible for the computer revolution. Procrastination breeds creativity.

Most procrastinators are *structured procrastinators*. Their way of not doing what they are supposed to be doing is to do something else. They often end up accomplishing a lot. Nevertheless, such people feel bad about being procrastinators and often annoy their co-workers. So here are some tips.

- Avoid the most common advice: "Keep your commitments to a minimum, so you won't be distracted." This is a way to become a couch potato. It's better to have lots of things to do, so you can work on some of them as a way of not doing the task that, for whatever reason, you seek to avoid.
- Don't feel bad because you lack willpower. Most of us lack all kinds of powers. I can't lift my car by the bumper in order to change a tire. That's what jacks are for. Tools give us the ability to make up for what we lack in native powers. The procrastinator has tools that allow her to manipulate herself to achieve results she can't get with willpower alone: alarms to get her out of bed in the morning; co-workers to nag; online pop-ups to do the same thing; and the talent for last minute, all night work sessions to meet deadlines.
- Avoid perfectionist fantasies. Often procrastination is just a way of giving ourselves permission to do a less-than-perfect job on something that doesn't require a perfect job anyway. We put it off until mere adequacy is the only possibility. Analyze the importance of the task when you accept it; give yourself permission then to do a less than perfect job, in the normal case when this is all that is needed, and avoid the turmoil.
- Most importantly, avoid annoying the non-procrastinators around you. For starters, be honest. Admit that you are a procrastinator, and it is a flaw. Maybe someday you will pursue some self-help regimen that will eliminate this flaw from your personality. But for now, don't compound the flaw with denial. If you admit to being a procrastinator, others will probably try hard to find something nice to say about you; if you are a structured procrastinator, with lots of accomplishments to your name, they may not have far to look. John Perry

3 — 16 SEVERE WEATHER CONDITIONS

In the event that the office is unable to open due to inclement weather or other emergencies, employees will receive their regular base pay for the period of time in which the office is officially closed. In such circumstances, employees should check their pre-selected communication preference for emergency closure notifications. Notices will be sent by 7am on the impacted day.

In the case of severe weather conditions operations will continue. In the event the offices are closed, the outgoing message will so state. If the office is operating and you are unable to get to work, the day will be counted as a personal or sick day.

3 — 16 SEVERE WEATHER CONDITIONS

The risks of Climate Change—as expressed by the increasing frequency and severity of weather—necessitates an explicit office policy. It probably necessitates a new approach to work: a resilient practice. To anticipate thoughtfully, prepare thoroughly, and bounce-back swiftly—for the work must go on.

   If every day is a snow day then new ways of working must be called upon:

- Foresight. Weather forecasting is notoriously fickle, but preparedness is not only knowing, but also creating options and maximizing the productivity of the "dry day."
- Prioritize workflow—what can, and cannot, wait out the storm—and shepherd resources accordingly.
- The provision of space, equipment, data, and personnel must be adaptive. The desire for uninterrupted access suggests redundancy and flexibility; whether it be through cloud services, out-sourcing, or the sharing economy.
- Lemonade. Make a virtue of severe weather impacts, like entering a competition on post-storm rebuilding; or developing expertise, defining a point-of-view, and building a new office preoccupation around resiliency.

The consequences of severe weather can, and should, be managed. Moreover, approached right, there is also the potential to catalyze a greater transformation in the way we work. ^{Daniel Pittman}

The reward of the employee may be fixed, not by an arbitrary fixed rate per hour or day, but in proportion to the results of his efforts.

An architect may not net a profit on occasion, but he has got to win a better than average architectural living to make it worth while maintaining an office. I know a very capable man who runs a small office, as long as he can pay himself a salary of one hundred dollars a week. But as soon as he falls below that average for a short time he closes up and goes to work for another architect at something like sixty five dollars a week (under present conditions), believing that the logical thing to do.

1918

As determined in the study, principals' salaries and draws range from an average of $12,886 per year in small firms (under $150,000 annual billings) to an average of $29,629 per year in very large architectural firms (over $2,000,000 annual billings).

Like it or not, everyone gives grades. Everyone gets them. School children get them. I take them home every month in the form of money; my salary is my grade. The amount is determined by people who judge the quality of my performance. There is nothing new about assigning numbers to quality of performance.

1941

In boom periods there are always difficulties with staff claiming rises, wanting to cash in on the expansionist phase. In slumps, salary increases are less of a problem, but there is always an atmosphere of insecurity which has to be allayed so that productivity can be maintained.

Firms want to be confident they are paying their employees a competitive wage compared to other firms that draw on the same pool of prospective employees. Firms also want assurance that their internal pay relationships are consistent and equitable based on employees' responsibilities.

1968
1971

1986

2008

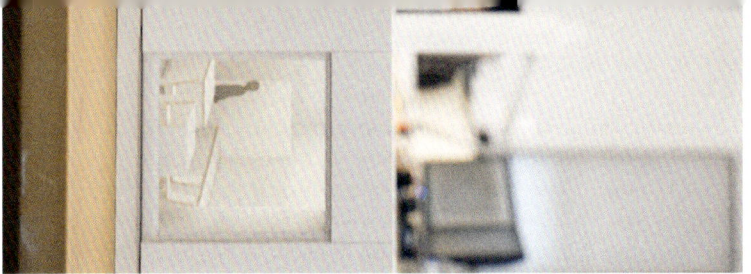

3 — 17 SALARY

There are three options for determining your office's salary structure. All are flawed, and some doomed.

The first is to offer salaries in accordance with seniority, as is the custom in many companies. Needless to say, talented, hardworking junior staff members will, rightfully, feel resentful that mediocre senior staff members automatically receive better compensation. Given the litany of familiar complaints that results from such an arrangement, it is understandable why one might turn to other options, even if one's concern for office morale is really a concern for the negative effect it has on productivity.

The second option, which is in truth only a variation on the first, is to announce in advance an absolute range within which salaries are to be kept. For example, you might announce that the highest salary cannot be more than ten times the lowest. Despite its appeal to a semblance of transparency and fairness, this arrangement will not prevent some from complaining. Why ten and not nine, they will ask? And in fact, any number greater than one will be deemed in need of justification.

This leads us to the third option, which is in fact to offer everyone an identical salary, regardless of experience, responsibility, and performance. This arrangement might have many disadvantages but one merit of this option—only ever implemented in smaller offices run by self-proclaimed socialists—would seem to be that it leaves no room for complaints. But of course this is not the case, and in surprising ways too. It is understandable that senior staff asked to forego what they think is a deservedly higher salary will be dissatisfied, but surveys show that junior staff benefiting from such an arrangement are often also deeply unhappy. This might be attributed to the difficulty that present-day human beings have in inhabiting social arrangements based on desires that the human beings of a fantasized better future are meant to embody. The impasse between the subjectivities produced by capitalism today and the subjectivities we hope to reach one bright day after the gross inequalities of capitalism have been dismantled in fact makes reaching that bright future an especially daunting task. This means that dismantling today's inegalitarian salary systems in your office can in fact come across to your employees most benefiting from it as a sort of carnivalesque reversal—enjoyable for an evening but unbearable if the carnival were to go on and on. At some point, the usual hierarchy needs to be reinstalled, for everyone's sake.

Given all these difficulties, it is clear that option one—the status quo—is best; it is the most recognizable option and the one that will be most comforting to most of your employees—which will no doubt be of great comfort to you as well. But a touch of the carnivalesque is always welcome, especially given its role in reinforcing the status quo. So here's a concrete recommendation for you to consider: at the end-of-year office party, arrange for the entire staff to be photographed in a line in order of salary. Do not forget to include yourself. Give a framed, signed copy of the photograph to each employee when the office reopens after the holidays. ^{Sina Najafi}

The reader will probably recall many men of his acquaintance who seek to create an impression by adopting a pose and manner either fashioned after some social celebrity or a creation of their own imagination. Such poser is nothing short of egotism. The egotist is next door to a fanatic. Occupied with himself, he has no ability to realize the bad impression he is creating […] Go hunt the architects in any community who are successful, and who have done most for their own and the general good, and you will find that they are almost uniformly the serious, overworked class.

Dress appropriately. This will provide self-confidence and send a message to others that they are dealing with a professional.

Each member of the studio will be issued Office Slippers. Office Slippers are to be worn in the office (this is to limit the amount of dirt in the office as well as to limit the transmission of sound to the residential floor below).

Examples of inappropriate clothing items that should not be worn during work hours include: Sweatpants, Warm-up or jogging suits and pants, Shorts, Spandex or other form fitting pants, T-shirts, T-shirts or sweat shirts with offensive messages or images, Visible undergarments, Open-toe sandals, Visible Tattoos, Revealing Clothing, Faded or torn denim.

We have a relaxed dress code and the best we can say is: Dress appropriately. You are the best judge of that.

3 — 18   OFFICE ATTIRE AND DECORUM

When meeting a client, corporate architecture firms largely stick to the protocol that governs other professions: always out-dress the client, but not so much as to make him or her feel inadequate. If the client is wearing jeans, wear slacks. If the client is in business casual, wear a suit. If the client is formally dressed, wear a three-piece suit. If the client is adorned with military medals, it's time to take out your AIA lapel pins. The goal is to project professionalism and gravitas without outshining the audience.

But the contemporary client's wardrobe has diversified beyond the typical range of accountant-chic. Across industries, the spectrum of acceptable attire has widened so far as to disrupt such a strategy of one-upping. What do you wear to meet a foreign dictator? Or a tech Svengali? Or a community board?

Along with the need to diversify the architectural workforce itself, this widening sartorial landscape further cements my conviction that architects need a uniform exclusively appropriate to the profession's idiosyncrasies, one that can transcend the diverse landscape of clients and contexts. Like a doctor's coat or a butcher's apron, a uniform can equalize the relationship of a professional to a client regardless of rank and status.

Perhaps an architect's license should come with such exclusive, codified regalia. Don't think I'm about to further promote the oppressive black-on-black garb of architecture lore—far from it. In order to preserve the sartorial personality of each architect while adding a veneer of professional codification, I imagine what is needed would have to be a cross between a caftan and a kimono. It should be performative, easily transitioning from the workshop to the desktop, from the airport lounge to the boardroom. Rami Abou-Khalil

1928
Atlee B. and Robert M. Ayres
Office Rules

Please keep drafting tables in a presentable condition at all times. […] Draftsmen will be responsible for any damage that they may incur to architectural books, plates, etc. No books will be taken from the office unless permission is given.

1942
W. J. Bonn, J. J. Sullivan
*Manual of Instructions for
Junior Architects*

Provide yourself with a metal or celluloid protractor, a triangle and a small French curve, as these are indispensable in making a neat set of notes.

1977
Robert Koehler,
The American Institute
of Architects
*Personnel Practices
Handbook*

The firm will furnish each employee with basic equipment and expendable materials such as parallel edges, pencil leads, erasers, drafting tape, paper, etc. Employees are expected to furnish their own drafting equipment, including pencil lead holders, drafting triangles, scales, lead sharpeners and other common instruments of a permanent nature.

1990
Cannon Design
Office Protocol

The company will provide you with appropriate basic equipment (Such as drafting boards, parallel edges, typewriters, etc.) and expendable materials (such as pencil leads, drafting tape, paper, etc.) You are expected to furnish your own drafting equipment such as lead holders, triangles, scales, and other common instruments of a permanent nature.

2011
STUDIOS Architecture
Employee Handbook

Every Member has a responsibility to maintain and enhance STUDIOS' public image and to use company equipment in a productive manner. The Firm reserves the right to inspect anything on company property, including equipment, computers, files, voice mail, desks and lockers.

1928

1942

1977

1990

2011

3 — 19 USE OF OFFICE EQUIPMENT

Memorandum
To: XXXX XXXXXXX
From: Andrew Atwood
Date: September 10, 2015
Subject: *Last Office Memo*

This is my last office memo. From now on I think we should keep all our communications to iMessenger or maybe Snapchat. I also think we should start calling our *office* a *studio* again. I understand why we did it back in 2011. We wanted an architecture office, not a design studio and *office* sounded more official. An office sounded like it was a *practice*. It also had that whole OMA thing going for it. And *Office* definitely sounded better than *Group*. Maybe these concerns are the only important ones? But it strikes me now. Now that it's over and I am writing something on the *Use of Office Equipment* that an architect's space is largely made up of the stuff that goes in it. *Our Equipment*. The obviousness of this *observation* is a little embarrassing, but a quick survey of the things we might call our office equipment reveals that we never really operated like an office. Mostly books and laptops, really. We do have that one binder from LegalZoom. The one with the LLC papers. And a few tax forms lying around. And all the parking tickets...But other than those things, our stuff is not very office-like. We made a list one time, before one of our trips to Office Depot.

...

I recently found it. It includes many of the things you would expect to see in an office.

- – Stapler
- – Staples
- – Copy Paper
- – Pencils
- – Scotch Tape
- – Erasers
- – X-Acto Knife
- – and Blades
- – Post-it Notes
- – Folders
- – 3 Binders
- – Scanner/Copier/Printer Combo
- – 2 Folding Chairs
- – Extension Cord
- – Power Strip
- – The thing that goes over the extension cord so we don't trip

… it goes on forever but I wish it were more boring. More like Beckett. Instead it's just a list. A fake list of equipment for a fake office. If we were PhD-types, we might use the word *instruments* instead of equipment. Making the whole thing seem very scientific. We could say we have a *lab* or a *laboratory*. Frankly, that sounds worse. Like we are super experimental or something. And everyone knows we are far from that! So if offices have equipment and laboratories have instruments, what does a studio have? Tools? Does it even matter? Maybe we should just call it *stuff*. And we can make a policy called *Use of Studio Stuff*. The USS for short. Seems to fit us, right? We could make a movie about it! It would be like a Tom Sachs video or something. ^{Andrew Atwood}

Housekeeping: Please clean sinks after each use, wash dishes, take out the trash, change light bulbs, etc. We are all expected to pitch in and do what needs doing. Please do not use the entrance hall for sorting packages and bicycles.

There is only 1 Bathroom for the Office and Live space. Please be respectful of other people as they use this shared facility. Toilet seat is to be placed DOWN after use. There is a "plunger" located in the closet in the bathroom if the toilet gets stopped up. Please inform principal if there is a problem with the toilet or sink.

Clients expect their projects designed by an efficient, organized and well managed architect. A cluttered and chaotic workplace is a sign of the opposite. PM's ensure their project work spaces are maintained and tidy. Drawings, documents, samples and materials are returned to the project reference shelf, the library or their appropriate storage space at the end of each day.

You can use available space in the fridge to store your food. Label it if you find that helpful. Please do not leave your leftovers to rot and stink up the fridge, and don't assume that they will be dealt with for you! Your nice Tupperware containers are special only to you […] Clean up after yourself!

3 — 20 CLEANING

*Please respect the general cleanliness of the bathrooms and wash after yourself,
with the idea that you are sharing these premises with many others—individuals
of varying sex, orientation, and standards. Please be mindful that we all clean the
bathrooms weekly, and thus your actions impact us all democratically.*

*Bathroom #1 is an older bathroom, and thus, has a weaker flush system. Please
do not overload it, as it is predisposed to getting clogged.*

2006
Office dA
Office Manual

---------- Forwarded message ----------
From: David Richmond
Date: Fri, Nov 10, 2006 at 12:39 PM
Subject: the oda flush.
To: da@officeda.com

Those of you present both Friday evening and this afternoon will have noticed
that we have something of a problem at Office dA. We have a finicky toilet.
As this finicky toilet is, unfortunately, our only toilet, it would not be going too
far to say that it represents the weakest link in the Office dA infrastructure.
Without a working toilet, Office dA employees are forced to spend their valuable
time searching out alternate venues for relief. Furthermore, if abuse of our
plumbing system continues on the same level that we have witnessed over
the past several days, it will also become a direct fiscal liability. Repairs are
expensive. As Nader wisely pointed out, "Your shit is cutting into our profits."

Thus, a cautionary and instructive email: Please be mindful of the unimpressive
flushing power of our toilet. Be sure that the only thing that makes its way into
the bowl—outside of your own productions—is toilet paper (NO paper towels or
sanitary products of any other variety). Should the magnitude of your situation
demand the flushing of an inordinate quantity of any of these bowl-acceptable
materials, please try to stagger the process. A careful parceling of your sewer-
destined matter should go a long way toward preventing future backups. Please
also remember that toilet-paper comes from trees and, given its destiny, cannot
be recycled in any conventional manner. Become more adept and efficient
in using it. Even behind closed doors, your actions have an impact on Office dA
and the world as a whole.

Cheers,
David

...

---------- Forwarded message ----------
From: Nader Tehrani
Date: Fri, Nov 10, 2006 at 1:05 PM
Subject: the oda flush.
To: da@officeda.com

yes, please.

if you feel it is going to be a big number two, take a break in the middle of your
efforts, and find the generosity of pushing down the flush lever. this way,
the toilet will get half the amount and swallow it all down with less problems.

and yes, please do not get too aggressive with toilet paper either. many things
clog, paper included. using less paper preserves forests, but if you are so
prone, that is to burn the forests, then flush them down in smaller increments.

also, if you need to brush up on this whole matter at a more intellectual level,
please refer to rodolphe el-khoury's translation of the infamous 'histoire de la
merde', published but a few years ago.

nt Nader Tehrani

1909
American Institute
of Architects
*A Circular of Advice
Related to Principles of
Professional Practice and
The Canons of Ethics*

An architect should urge his draughtsmen to avail themselves of educational opportunities. He should, as far as practicable, give encouragement to all worthy agencies and institutions for architectural education. While a thorough technical preparation is essential for the practice of architecture, architects cannot too strongly insist that it should rest upon a broad foundation of general culture.

1969
Richard J. Neutra
*Excerpts of Ideas for Possible
Use in The Neutra Office*

Boosters of office morale and production:
– **Professional advancement seminars**
– **Office newsletter**
– **Reference data blown up for wall display**

1983
Smithey & Boynton
Architects and Engineers
Operating Manual

Each employee, by study and by attendance at seminars and other educational programs, is expected to continually improve his own professional and technical capabilities.

1990
Cannon Design
Office Protocol

The company supports the pursuit of specialized formal training and assists in furthering the work-related educational aspirations of its regular full-time employees through a tuition reimbursement program.

2014
███████████
Employee Handbook

████████████████ is an AIA/CES registered provider. The Firm's continuing education program consists of in-house courses, many of which qualify for AIA continuing education credit. These courses are taught by employees, guest presenters, and product vendors. All architecture and interiors staff are expected to attend 12 hours of in-house courses each year.

1909

1969

1983

1990

2014

3 — 21 CONTINUING EDUCATION

An Architectural Education does not stop with the granting of a degree:
Licensure requires office experience. Poised between the open horizons of
university culture and the focused aims of professional culture, the Intern
fosters the Office's perpetual renewal. Ensuring such progress requires culti-
vating the Intern. Inciting ambition combined with altruism yields innovation.
Successful Principals are clear, patient, and compassionate, but also exacting,
challenging, and hard-boiled. Collaboration is key, but a whiff of competition
trumps a wave of compromise. Teach street smarts not organizational behavior.
Do not infantilize through managerial role-playing, reward incentives, or
passive retreats. Foster intelligent exchange with regular seminars, communal
lunches, and frequent happy hours. Encourage cultural and civic engagement.
Lead through example. Always include excellent food and drink. Recognize
when an Intern is ready to move on. Successful teaching can be measured by
that jump, even if it is to another Office.

  Principals who don't teach invariably exploit. But never forget:
Exploitation Backfires. Sarah Whiting

1909
The American
Institute of Architects
*A Circular of Advice
Related to Principles of
Professional Practice and
the Canons of Ethics*

The architect should advise and assist those who intend making architecture their career.

1939
American Institute
of Architects
"Standards of Practice
of the American
Institute of Architects"
*The Octagon, A Journal
of the American Institute
of Architects*

Architects […] should accept mentorship of the young men who are entering the profession, leading them to a full understanding of the functions, duties, and responsibilities of architects.

1972
Lewis Clarke Associates
Handbook of Office Policies

The office respects the rights of an individual especially to grow professionally and encourages this growth through writing, lecturing, and teaching for mutual advantage.

2014
Diller Scoffidio + Renfro
Office Manual

Part time teaching is permissible as negotiated with Partners and Project Leaders. It is with the understanding that time away from the studio will be made up on evenings or weekends.

1909

1939

1972

2014

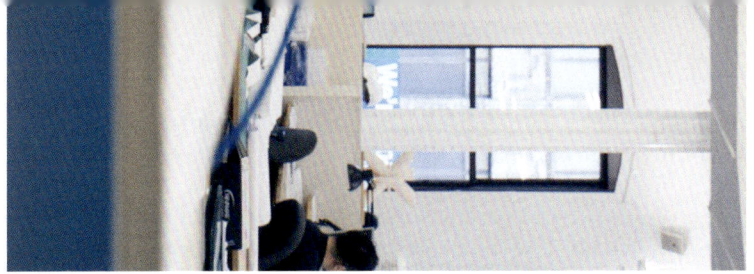

3 — 22 TEACHING, WRITING, LECTURING

Whereas in most disciplines teaching is considered antithetical to a vigorous professional practice ("those who can, do; those who can't, teach"), in architecture it is virtually axiomatic that the most inventive and vital offices are those with a parallel commitment to teaching. Contrary to the conventional perception of academic research as impractical conjecture divorced from the realities of praxis or of professional work as the repetition of rote standards incapable of fostering innovation, the coupling of teaching and practice in architecture provides the ideal grounds for creative evolution within a rapidly shifting disciplinary environment. For architects, periods of intense productivity are often coincident with a deep engagement in academia, the radically speculative nature of the design studio both feeding into and benefiting from corresponding work in the "real world." Moreover, as a discipline driven by a multiplicity of constraints and pragmatic demands—from environmental performance to material behaviors, from economic scarcity to logistical considerations— innovative solutions in architecture arrive as frequently from the front lines of practice as from scholarly speculation. In this way, teaching and practice can be seen as complimentary modes of working and thinking, providing a means to ward off a narrow professionalism on the one hand or a detached academicism on the other.

Teaching can provide a laboratory in which programs, issues, or conditions encountered in a professional context can be examined with increased scrutiny and subjected to protracted experimentation rarely feasible within the confines of client-driven work. In its most debased form, this tendency leads to design studios that replicate the active projects in a given instructor's office—a custom that can lead to misuse and resentment. However, it can also generate the possibility of teaching as an extended field of inquiry in which the consequences of ideas arising in practice can be more thoroughly evaluated and explored, creating a collective resource of imaginative research with unpredictable applications. In return, students benefit from exposure to the material conditions of the profession and a greater understanding of restrictions and parameters as generative opportunities and as catalysts for design invention. To the same extent, protocols that characterize the academic environment can be deployed to reinvigorate the habits of the professional studio, with collective pinups, iterative design exercises and open discussion as a means of fostering a less hierarchical, more agile office. This feedback loop between teaching and practice is invaluable to both the efficacy of architectural education and the advancement of the profession, and is evidenced in their ongoing exchange of instrumental technologies, formal methodologies, critical attitudes, and even descriptive language.

Finally, perhaps the single most important benefit of teaching resides in the need to precisely articulate ideas in order to clearly communicate and transmit them: to teach means to commit to (if only temporarily) what it is that is worth teaching. To teach is to define what is most important to us as architects and by extension what might constitute a meaningful practice. Marc Tsurumaki

1972
Lewis Clarke Associates
Handbook of Office Policies

Much of the work in the office is private and confidential and should not be discussed or details disclosed outside of the office.

1974
Venturi and Rauch
Venturi and Rauch Handbook

The professional relationship between each client and the firm demands that there be no disclosures of any information about projects without proper authorizations. This includes responses to inquiries about projects or potential projects from the press, contractors, other professionals or the public.

1991
SLR/Architects
Office Manual

The professional relationship between each client and firm demands that there be no disclosure of any information about projects without proper authorization. This includes responses to inquiries about projects or potential projects from press, contractors, other professionals, or the public.

2004
Davis Brody Bond, LLP
Employee Policy Manual

As a professional organization, the work performed involves matters of a highly confidential nature. In recent years, every commission executed by the firm has had contract conditions stipulating that information concerning the project can be publicly released only upon written approval from the client. It is the policy of DBB that individuals do not make available to outside organizations any information regarding the firm's work. An individual should not give any presentations or talks, speak with the press or write any articles for publication, without the prior approval of the director of business development, or a Partner.

2014
██
██ *Employee Handbook*

The firm respects the right of any employee to maintain a blog or website or to use other social media tools. Nonetheless, the line between work and personal life often blurs. Juggling personal matters during and outside of work are your responsibility; yet, activities that might affect your job performance, the performance of colleagues, or ████'s business interests are why we need to adopt a policy. As technology enables instant exchange of information with other professionals, clients, and the public, we encourage you to share your insights and expertise in a manner that does not compromise your position and ████'s business interests.

1972
1974

1991

2004

2014

3 — 23 CONFIDENTIALITY

In offices both large and small, substantial resources are devoted to finding ways to be seen and heard. It's inconceivable today for an office not to have a website and, increasingly, Twitter and Instagram accounts. And as the collective demand for immediate and infinite access only grows, the line where confidentiality goes from beneficial to detrimental fluctuates and bends. Because as communication about every facet of everything becomes increasingly public, protecting the ability to study, try, fail, and invent without exposure becomes infinitely more crucial.

A certain level of confidentiality exists on all the projects we undertake. Sometimes confidentiality is only an issue at the beginning of a project and loosens up once the concept is approved and the first images are ok'd for the public. Many times confidentiality is self-imposed, allowing us to protect IP and to revisit old ideas for future projects. It's funny in these instances that confidentiality, inherently about not talking about something, is so closely tied to public identity—confidentiality used as a marketing tool to construct a public face that seems deliberate, clear, and confident.

At other times there's an assumption that the work, or at least our involvement in the work, will remain confidential long after construction is completed and the doors are open. At that point, confidentiality has to be counterbalanced by something else: experience gained, higher fees, lasting personal connections. Because as communication about every facet of everything becomes more and more public, not being able to talk about something means that it virtually doesn't exist, it can't help us gain more work, and it can't help to grow the office. Just as confidentiality allows us to do our work in peace, it can also be the reason we don't get to do more work.

Basically, confidentiality can be awesome. It can also suck. Family (Dong-Ping Wong and Oana Stanescu)

circa 1963
Richard J. Neutra Office
*A Tentative Outline, Summed
up from various suggestions*

Retention of all rights in (I) Writings; (II) Lectures; (III) Photographs to Date; (IV) Kodachrome slides, exhibitions, clippings, etc.

All these instruments of public relations represent a very substantial monetary value, require beyond the original expense and effort, cost and labor of reproduction, ordering, indexing, filing, together with related correspondence and travel. They and resulting benefits in Prospective trust and confidence, substitute for what other architectural firms expend in representation, paid publicity, hospitality, etc.

1984
Bob Greenstreet,
Karen Greenstreet
*The Architect's Guide
to Law and Practice*

A notice of copyright should appear on each item of the work in the following form:
    a. The word "Copyright," abbreviation "Copr" or symbol ©, followed by
    b. The year when the work was first published.
    c. The name of the copyright owner. Example: © 1982 John Green

2008
The American
Institute of Architects
*The Architect's Handbook
of Professional Practice,*
14th Edition

According to statistics from the CNA/Schinnerer design professional liability program, 95.2 percent of intellectual property claims against architects and engineers from 1994 to 2003 involved allegations of copyright infringement. Of those claims, 79 percent involved architects and 42 percent involved residential projects.

2016

Employee Handbook

All work related documents and materials developed or produced in connection with ▉ business by an individual while employed at ▉ are the property of ▉ and shall remain the property of ▉ upon departure from the Firm under any circumstances.

1963

1984

2008

2016

116

3 — 24 INTELLECTUAL PROPERTY

How is architectural creativity measured and traded? Most often in bulk: weekly, in ten or eleven hour chunks. The industry of marking and defending intellectual property—fastidiously appending the c-in-a-circle, filing registration forms, prosecuting infringers—suggests a finitude of ideas and a systemic inability to sort through the few we have. If you knew what the good ideas were, you wouldn't have to waste time on the rest, but that's exactly the point. Just in case one of those ideas turns out to be a gem, just in case one of your employees is a secret genius, just in case something you can't even imagine is about to happen, own everything, copyright it all, batten down the hatches.

If intellectual property is the output, education, the consumption of culture and information, is the input. But did your firm pay for all that? Were the principals sitting there with you in the middle of the night as you frantically prepared a model, in the process planting a seed for the idea they're now market-ing? The reward for having a really really good idea is that it's definitely not yours. So how can you protect your investment?

The only real resistance here is to have bad ideas, to come up with un-original (but unspecific) concepts and to traffic in clichés. If the company's battery of lawyers can't defend an idea in court, it loses its value. The cloak of an easily recognizable architectural style is a good start for a truly radical defense, and the hallmarks of a style are nowhere so clearly defined (and easily referenced) as in records of litigation on architectural copyright.

For a clear roadmap to unprotectable design elements, seek out the strange legal narratives of protection denied. We learn from *Charles W. Ross Builder, Inc. v. Olsen Fine Home Bldg., LLC* (2012) that hallmarks of Colonial Georgian architecture include "symmetry; aligned windows; gambrel, gabled, or hipped roofs; paneled doors accentuated by classical pilasters and a proportioned, pedimented entablature." Those elements, especially in that grouping, are unprotectable and would be worthless to an employer bent on defending company property. *Trek Leasing v. The United States* (2005) estab-lishes that the elements of the Pueblo Revival style are "defined by a flat roof with parapet, stepped-back roof lines, wood canales, apparent wood lintels, outside walls made of stone, heavy massing, and muntins used to divide the glazing on doors and windows." What more invitation to operate in a litigation-free, shared vocabulary could one need? Sarah M. Hirschman

1909
The American
Institute of Architects
*A Circular of Advice
Related to Principles of
Professional Practice and the
Canons of Ethics*

The display of the architect's name upon a building under construction is condemned, but the unobtrusive signature of buildings after completion has the approval of the Institute (AIA). The use of initials designating membership in the Institute is proper in connection with any professional service and is to be encouraged as helping to make known the nature of the honor they imply.

1922
McKim, Mead & White
Manual of Office Practice

No changes should be made without the owner's knowledge and consent, or without consultation with a member of the firm, and the specification writer, and the financial result of such change clearly understood and properly authorized.

1950
Richard J. Neutra Office
Interoffice Memorandum

The following line will be used:

.... of the office of Richard J. Neutra

2006
The American
Institute of Architects
*The Handbook of
Professional Practice*

U.S. copyright law protects the creativity captured in the architect's instruments of service such as design and construction drawings, models, and other design representations. To protect themselves from copyright infringement, architects should be familiar with their rights under the law.

2016

*Confidential Inform-
ation and Invention
Assignment Agreement,
Employee Handbook*

All inventions, developments or innovations ("inventions"), whether or not patentable and whether or not reduced to practice, made or conceived by me (whether made solely by me or jointly with others) during the period of my employment with ■■■■ which relate in any manner to the actual or demonstrably anticipated business of ■■■■, or result from or are suggested by any task assigned to me or any work performed by me or on behalf of ■■■■ shall be held for the benefit and become the sole and exclusive property of ■■■■ or its nominee or successors, I will disclose any invention promptly and fully in writing to ■■■■.

1909

1922

1950

2006

2016

118

3 — 25 AUTHORSHIP

Architects design themselves first, collect references, pick an aesthetic, express values, curate their Instagram feeds, project an attitude and tone. Their work is a byproduct. Clients buy architects before they buy a design. Today, we've moved beyond Authorship towards a paradigm of Identity. Authorship, like Originality, feels naively simplistic, entangled with romantic notions about the solitary act of design, the ingenious designer, the inspired sketch. Whereas Identity is a cultural product, it's a social effort, constructed over time, through a body of work, in relation to others. Michael Meredith

1999
The Society of Design
Administration
*Handbook of Design
Office Administration*

Harassment on the basis of sex is a violation of Title VII, Section 703 of the Civil Rights Act. Unwelcome sexual advances, requests for sexual favors, and other verbal or physical conduct of a sexual nature constitute sexual harassment when 1) submission to such conduct is made either explicitly or implicitly a term or condition of an individual's employment, 2) submission to or rejection of such conduct by an individual is used as the basis for employment decisions affecting such individual, or 3) such conduct has the purpose or effect of unreasonably interfering with an individual's work performance or creating an intimidating, hostile, or offensive working environment.

2014

Employee Handbook

Sexual Harassment is unlawful and will not be tolerated. Any retaliation against an individual who has complained about sexual harassment or retaliation against individuals for cooperating with an investigation of a sexual harassment complaint is similarly unlawful. Officers will respond promptly and confidentially to complaints and where it is determined that such conduct has occurred, will act promptly to impose corrective action as is necessary, including termination.

2016
Employee Handbook

▮▮▮▮ condemns and prohibits harassment of any individual because of the individual's sex, race, color, religion, national origin, citizenship status, ancestry, age, medical condition, disability, sexual orientation, veteran status, familial status, marital status, or any other characteristic protected by law.

Harassment includes, but is not limited to:
- Verbal harassment, such as epithets, derogatory comments, or slurs;
- Physical harassment, such as assault, impeding or blocking movement, or any physical interference with normal work or movement directed at an individual;
- Visual forms of harassment, such as derogatory posters, cartoons, or drawings, and
- Sexual harassment, such as unwelcome sexual advances, requests for sexual favors, and other verbal or physical conduct of a sexual nature, such as name calling, suggestive comments, or lewd talk and jokes.

1999

2014
2016

3 — 26 SEXUAL HARASSMENT

11 things not to be said with a wink:

1. "That's a pretty big file you got there."
2. "How may I service you?"
3. "I'm sure we can find a solution that will make both of us very happy."
4. "I have a big load for you today."
5. "I wouldn't mind going through your hard drive sometime."
6. "So, I heard you like to work extra loooong hours?"
7. "Are you going to bring your delicious cakes to the company picnic?"
8. "You're really working overtime on these clients."
9. "You have a really big...personality."
10. "Here's a package for you."
11. "You really nailed that one." Felix Burrichter

1909
The American
Institute of Architects
*A Circular of Advice
Related to Principles of
Professional Practice and
the Canons of Ethics*

An architect should not falsely or maliciously injure, directly or indirectly, the professional reputation, prospects or business of a fellow architect.

1909

1973
Hugh Stubbins Associates
Office Manual

A guard will be on duty between the hours of 5:00 P.M. and 11:00 P.M. Monday through Friday to admit and register employees not holding keys. All personnel should be out of the building by 10:00 P.M.

2014

Employee Handbook

▮▮▮▮ reserves the right to search any employee's office, desk, files, locker, or any other area or article on our premises. It should be noted that all offices, desks, files, lockers, and so forth, are the property of ▮▮▮▮ and are issued for the use of employees only during their employment with ▮▮▮▮. Inspections may be conducted at any time at the discretion of ▮▮▮▮.

2014

▮▮*Employee Handbook*

As a security measure, a card-based or FOB-based security system has been installed at most locations. Your assigned access card allows entry to the building during specified hours.

1973

2014

122

3 — 27 A SAFE WORKPLACE

In response to the Hugh Stubbins Office Manual, 1973

A developer walks into the office.

"I thought I was walking into a dive bar or something…" he says.

There is:
no revolving door,
no lobby,
no marble floor,
no escalators,
no elevators,
no receptionist in uniform and hat,
no suitable ID-screening system
(no planters, no plants, no waterfalls, no recessed lights)

Is it unsafe? Is it menacing?

What kind of safety does a guard—with his or her glossy paraphernalia—really
guarantee?

What kind of safety does the lack of a guard—with his or her glossy paraphernalia—really challenge?

Is it safe to trust someone to work unsupervised—a large work load, from 5 P.M.
to 10 P.M.—and to not trust them to freely enter and exit with keys?

What happens between 10–11 P.M.? Ada Tolla

1993
Francis Baden-Powell
Building Overseas;
Butterworth Architecture
Management Guide

This is a fundamental aspect of working overseas, which needs to be recognized. In many countries local officials are poorly paid and expect to make up their salaries to a living level by the granting of favors (at a price). This is endemic from the issue of customs clearance certificates at one end of the scale to political contributions and awarding contracts at the other.

2014

Employee Handbook

In order to maintain the highest ethical standards in the conduct of our business, employees may not accept gifts or favors from clients, vendors, suppliers, or others, which could be construed to influence favorable action. This prohibition does not apply to entertainment at a luncheon or business meeting, advertising or promotional materials of nominal value, and awards by charitable or civic organizations or gifts of nominal value on special occasions.

1993

2014

124

3 — 28 GIFTS

You're probably expecting this entry to tell you that you shouldn't accept gifts so let's get that part out the way right from the start. In your professional capacity don't accept gifts. Pretty simple. Don't do it, not even a coffee or a cocktail, because then you'll be on the hook, in debt, obligated.

Let's face it; architecture is part of an exchange economy. People want what you have. You're gifted and others—clients, bosses, curators, editors, maybe even friends—want that gift. And they may not want to pay for it. They may want you to give it to them. And that's when they'll provide you with a gift: the gift of telling you that you're gifted. And that since you're gifted then shouldn't you share that gift? Their gift of admiration for your talent may be accompanied by an actual gift, a token that says "I understand you, and oh, by the way, I've got an opportunity for you…"

And that's where it gets tricky. You need opportunities, right? Keith Krumwiede

1920
Howard Dwight Smith
"The 'Business' of
Architecture, The Position
of the Supervising Architect
in the Organization"
The Architectural Review

The functions of the position are largely executive. That is to say, by way of management and direction he determines the line in which the energies of the organization should be discharged. He should also, therefore, be in a position to determine whether or not the objectives sought have been attained—a director, a general, to pass upon the acceptability of the others' work.

1974
Venturi and Rauch
Venturi and Rauch Handbook

Each staff member's performance is reviewed semi-annually to determine those individuals meriting salary increases.

1991
Norman Kaderlan
Designing Your Practice

There are four steps in assessing employee performance:
1. Observe what the person does.
2. Develop standards or criteria that define different levels of performance.
3. Compare the observed behavior with your standards.
4. If there is a difference between the performance and the standard, make a judgment of how important the gap is and what it means.

2014
■■■■
Employee Handbook

Evaluations are an important way to sharpen objectives and analyze past efforts for strengths and weaknesses. ■■■ conducts evaluations with the goal to provide frank feedback, gauge professional goals, measure responsibility, and improve office atmosphere.

- 1920

- 1974

- 1991

- 2014

3 — 29 ASSESSING PERFORMANCE

A SHORT SONG
For the door that is welded shut, Hallelujah!
For the shed that can't be entered, Hallelujah!
For the delegates who are struggling, Hallelujah!
For the CT and CGT, Hallelujah!
For the struggle that has been engaged, Hallelujah!
And the rights that will be won, Hallelujah!
To the many who have been abandoned, Hallelujah!

A FARMYARD IN FRANCE NOT FAR FROM SOCHAUX
Come close, come close. This is the chance of your life. Come. Come. I am here,
I am here. I have arrived! You are in stagnation. In misery. It's finished. I am here.
Not only will I bring you opportunities. But glory too. You search for work? I will
bring it to you. What work! The most beautiful, the most noble. For the greatest
glory. For your patriotism. For your nation. You are going to build automobiles!
The bad luck that has afflicted your region, I am here to repair this injustice. And
you, the young, it is you who I address. Beautiful, strong, like young Turks. (We
have some of those already!) I can't let you vegetate here. And what to I demand
for all this? A tiny signature.

> "Are there unions here?"
> Unions?
> "Are you well paid here?"
> A fortune!
> You can become a shareholder and participate in the benefits
> of this enterprise.
> "Where do I find this car factory?"
> In the most beautiful region of France.
> Sochaux, in Franche-Compte.
> "And the accommodation?"
> For single people there is a castle!
> "And leisure?"
> Leisure?
> We have everything.

...

Parties, pinball. There are women. Dances. Football. Fishing. Boating.
Victory my darling!
Victory my children!
Oh my God!
Drink! Victory! Drink! Victory! DRINK!

Initially they had noticed that the doors of the administration block had been left open. No one had secured the building and no one had wrecked it either. They started to spend their time in their old work place, looking out at the countryside through the large windows that were installed in order to give them a more beautiful working environment when the factory was originally built. In the past they had to work with their backs to the windows, now they have time to sit and stare at the countryside surrounding the factory while discussing what to do next. Their feelings about the place are ambiguous: they would never damage the building, but they like to reorganize the signage, spending part of each day reconfiguring the former signs and information boards throughout the plant so that they now provide a complex reflection of their schizophrenic relationship to their former work place. The nuanced work and practices that they grew up with de-emphasized the idea of absolute quantification of speed over technique, and promoted the idea of flexibility and interactive teamwork.

These concepts, which have become general, are increasingly thought of as repressive or symbolic of corrupted behavior of our group. They were part of an experimental process that de-emphasized the idea of absolute equality. In the past if you were the person who had to cast the wheels, you were the person who had to cast the wheels. In the hierarchy you had a clear place as a wheel caster. If you were the person who trimmed seats, you were a seat trimmer. The introduction of experimental models meant that you lost this absolute equality between identified specializations.

Instead the idea had been to create a complex sequence of relation- ships that depended upon ability and focus, towards the alleviation of boredom and alienation and towards increased control by the workers over the amount of hours spent on hard work during any given shift. They discuss the idea that this suppression of specializations led to the ultimate failure of their working environment.

Those who accepted flexibility now admit that they were the architects of their own collapse.

But there is no way that they can re-adjust or rediscover new models of work without acknowledging difference and desire so they decide that instead of making people specialists again, or treating them as if they can work and think separately but out of sync, that there should be an attempt at developing an equality of production instead. Their working environment was nuanced and complex and now they develop a theoretical model where what goes in will come out but with no addition, deletion, waste, or surplus. One element of energy, stuff, thinking, or desire will produce one unit of energy, stuff, thinking, or desire. They will account for everything. Liam Gillick

Should an employee wish to quit, it is expected that he gives two weeks notice. Should the company release an employee, two weeks' notice will be given.

Give one month's notice in case you have by true necessity to leave the office.

Personnel who are terminated from the Firm due to business conditions will be compensated on the following basis:

Months of Service from Date of Hire to Termination	Compensation
Under 12 months	None
Over 12 months	10 normal work days

Employment at DBB is for no specified time. Just as you have the right to leave employment at DBB for any reason, we also reserve that same right to end our relationship with you at any time, with or without notice, for any reason not prohibited by law.

Termination can result from: Poor job performance; Negative client feedback; Excessive tardiness or unexcused absenteeism; Insubordination or lack of cooperation; Theft, dishonesty, falsification of records or any illegal acts; Unprofessional or inappropriate behavior; Excessive personal phone, email, or chat communications, which affect work performance.

3 — 30 SEPARATIONS

If you act gross, you're gone. It's really that simple.

We aren't as mean as that sounds. We're talking about really gross. Like, I'm throwing up on my shoes next to the photocopier kind of thing.

We get that you might have to quit. Who hasn't? Quitting is part of life. Just do it with some class. We'd prefer that you give us advance notice. We have to find someone to replace you. We have to figure out what to do with whatever work it is that you do. So give us a heads-up.

We realize we've reserved the right to kick you out without notice, but that's only if you're acting gross. So you're wondering what constitutes gross? Well, it's more a question of degree. Like, not only are you not being efficient at work, but you're sitting in your cubicle playing Tetris, or playing telephone pranks on people. Or maybe you're sexually harassing people. Don't grab people or invite them out (well, if they say yes, then invite them out.) Just don't be gross about sex stuff. Oh, and you can't not do your job or tell your boss that they aren't in charge. It's like the military. We have a chain of command. Don't be a weak link.

And also, don't make us look bad. Like, if you go on Facebook and start talking about racist stuff, that's crazy. But also, come to think of it, don't be too liberal either. I mean, you can be gay-friendly, but not, like, super gay-friendly. Unless maybe we have a gay-friendly product…then, acting gay-friendly on Facebook would be awesome. But in general, just keep it chill on social networking. Keep it to vacation photos. You know that picture with everyone tan drinking Coronas? Who doesn't like that pic? You will thank me for this.

Oh, and we also might go broke or shift direction. It might not be anything you did. That's business. As Tupac said, don't hate the player, hate the game.

Also, if you suck at your job, you're gone. What kind of business would we be if we let everyone that sucked stay? That's communism! We'd be like the place where you get your driver's license. No way.

Finally, what if you were like this psycho we hired? Like, you weren't just sucky, but you were almost the opposite: the genius sucky worker. You didn't lose money; you stole our money! Or you had some hacker skills and you would get into our Excel sheets and put some code in and then all this money would be going into your bank account, but no one knew 'cause you were smarter than everyone. And then during the day you acted all normal, and on Facebook you were just a world of beach photos, but you were actually not even who you said you were and you were stealing all our money! Oh man, that would be awesome. We would fire you of course, but who cares? You'd be rich! Nato Thompson

TOOLS

1

MEASURING

Wooden Ruler

Wooden Triangle

Wooden Scale Ruler

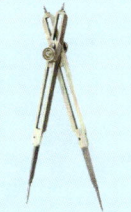

Proportional Divider

Wooden Folding Ruler

Measuring Tape

Flexible Ruller

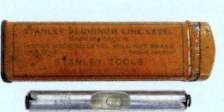

Aluminum Leveling Tool

Spring Retractable
Measuring Tape

Aluminum Set Triangle

Wood Architect's Scale

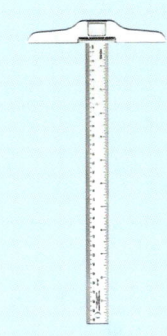

Aluminum T-Square Ruler

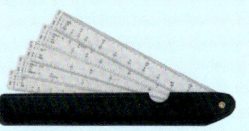

Plastic Fan Scale Ruler

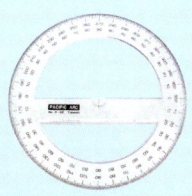

Plastic Protractor

Clear Adjustable Triangle

Angle Rolling Ruler

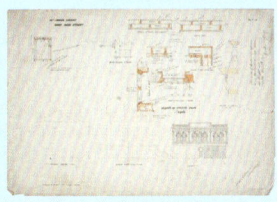

Parchment Paper

Mimeoscope

Drafting Vellum

Plastic Architect's Scale

Tracing Paper

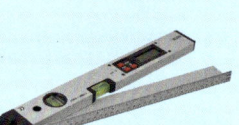

Laser Measuring Device

Wooden Drafting Table

Adjustable Drafting Stool

Digital Angle and
Level Ruler

Adjustable
Drafting Stool

Light Box

Laser Level Tool

Drawing Paper

Office Chair

3D Laser Scanner

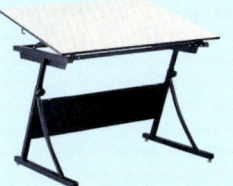

Composite Laminate
Drafting Table

3

DRAWING TOOLS

Section Liner

Adjustable
Drafting Stool

Ruling Pen

Equal Spacing Divider

Personal Computer (PC)

Polygraph Drafting
Template

Graphos Technical Pen

Brass Drawing Compass

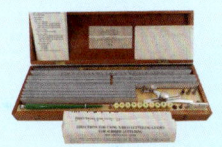

Lettering Set

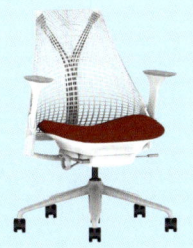

Office Task Chair

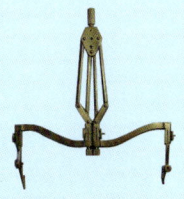

Metal Drawing Compass

Dusting Brush

Laptop

Artgum Eraser

Draft-Clean Powder

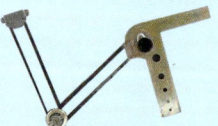
Drafting Machine

Mechanical Pencil

Eraser Shield

Drafting Dots

Drafting Machine

Technical Pen

Lead Pointer

Mayline Straightedge
Parallel Bar

Clear French Curves

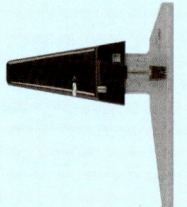
Hatching Tool

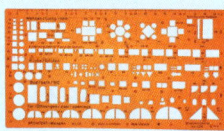
Drafting Template

Computer Mouse

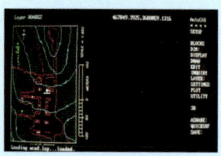
AutoCAD
Version 1.0

GRASS GIS
Version 1.0

Adobe Illustrator
Version 1.0

Adobe Photoshop
Version 1.0

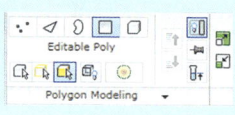
3D Studio Prototype
Version 1.0

Rhinoceros
Version Beta 1.0

Adobe InDesign
Version 1.0

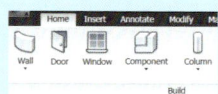
Autodesk Revit
Version 1.0

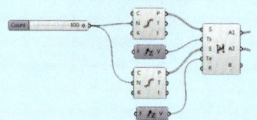
Grasshopper
Version 1.0

4

REPRODUCTION

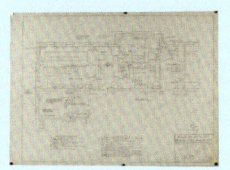

Diazo Print

Automated Copier Machine

Blueprint

Copier Machine

Flatbed Pen Plotter

Carbon Paper

Fax Machine

Still Camera

Brownie Camera

Slide Film

Drum Pen Plotter

Van Dyke Print

Slide Projector

Circular Slide Projector

Document Scanner

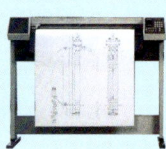

Large Scale
Drum Pen Plotter

Flatbed Document Scanner

Digital Camera

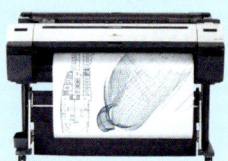

Large Scale Inkjet Plotter

Virtual Reality Headset

5

MODEL MAKING

Hand Saw

Animal Glue

Steel Ruler

Utility Knife

Powdered Glue

X-Acto Knife

White Glue

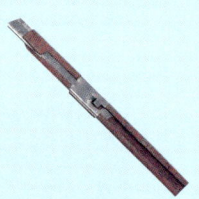

Retractable Blade Cutter

Tweezers

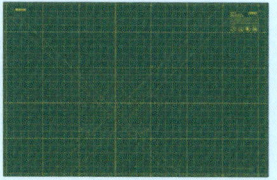

Cutting Mat

Glue Gun

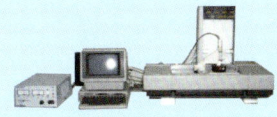

3D Printer

Portable Laser Cutter

Scale Figures

3D Printer Plaster Powder

Portable 3D Printer

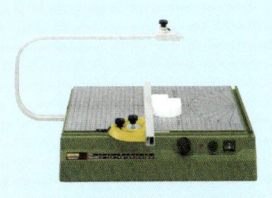

Hot-Wire Foam Cutter

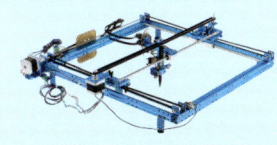

Axis Robot Cutting Plotter

Metal 3D Powder

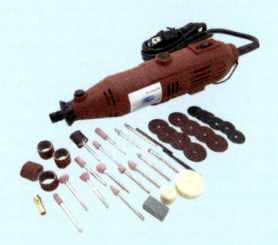

Rotary Tool Kit

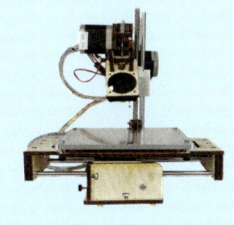

3D Printer Bot

3D Printer Filaments

Laser Cutter

CNC Machine

5 Axis Robotic Arm CNC

PROCEDURES
04

1901
Kaye W. Perry
*Office Management;
A Handbook for Architects
and Civil Engineers*

The writer believes that it is a golden rule never to do personally routine work which can be equally well done by a paid clerk, and to content himself with making sure that the clerks discharge their duties methodically. The more this habit is cultivated, the more time the principal will have to grapple with the really important duties which should receive his personal attention.

1918
Daniel Paul Higgins
"The 'Business' of
Architecture"
The Architectural Review

To make a success in architecture nowadays requires about equal parts of skill in organization, talent in promotion, art, construction and financing.

2001
The American Institute of
Architects
*The Architect's Handbook of
Professional Practice, 13th
Edition*

Although architecture services usually lead to the construction and operation of buildings, an architecture firm's "product" is not the building. Rather, it is the design process and the production of technical ideas and information necessary to construct buildings. Architects are purveyors of knowledge. People, then, are an architecture firm's most valued resource. People, not capital investments, equipment, or computers, are the essence of an architecture firm.

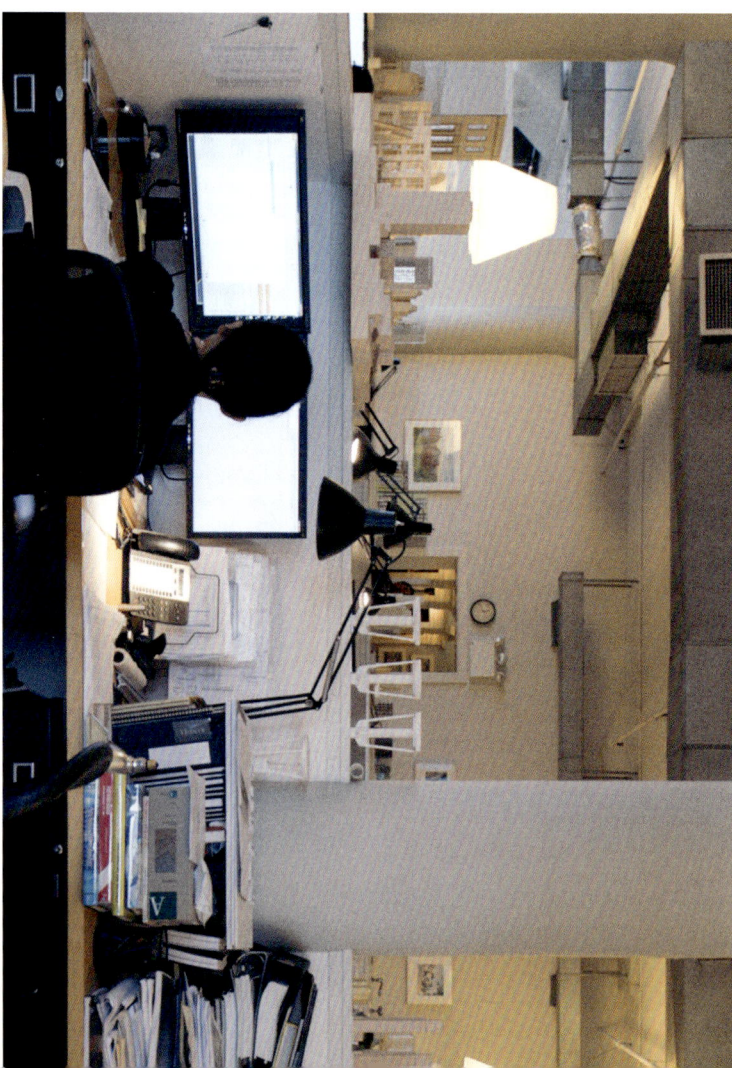

4 — 1 GENERAL PROCEDURES

General office procedures (operations, administration, conduct) imply a static means to an end—one set of processes or steps to achieve a singular result. This catchall category, fundamentally generic, contradicts the nature of contemporary practice. As practitioners we are challenged with an evolving set of tools, rules, and parameters. Buildings must perform better, teams must design more efficiently, and designers must have fluency with a growing set of skills. For general office administration, software is in constant development to answer this need to manage ever-increasing information, to streamline access to and dissemination of data. Our protocols and techniques for office process are informed by those of our design process.

Everyone does everything. Despite an increasing demand for specialization in architectural practice, we are committed generalists. This extends from our appetite for diverse project types to our expectation that designers be well-rounded and versatile: analog and digital, Office and Creative Suite, back and front of house, concept and construction, intra and extra.

We are flat; flatness belies hierarchy. Office hierarchy exists to facilitate project delivery and access to information. Collaboration is fundamental to our approach—two principals on every project, studio director oversight, project director engagement, project manager leadership, project team design. Design is developed iteratively, shared regularly, and critiqued publicly. Avoid ownership of projects.

Show and tell. The pin-up occurs at all scales—two-person meetings at a desk, team meetings by a wall, office-wide critiques in a conference room. Keep project areas pinned up and refresh regularly; show process, techniques, and current design. Extend this model to other areas of office management. Weekly meetings focus on overall office updates, operations, staffing, marketing, and finances. Monthly meetings focus on systems, research areas, marketing, and finances. Promote transparency of information.

Office administration is project-based. Human resources are assigned to office resources (library, shop, archives, website). Special projects are assigned flexibly based on availability, interest, and skill set, promoting a shared work load for office projects (differentiated from design projects). Avoid long-term, dedicated responsibilities by area. Manage resources flexibly to take best advantage of the individual for the collective office.

As in design, generate, iterate, and refine to evolve the office model. Kim Yao

1901
Kaye W. Perry
Office Management;
A Handbook for Architects
and Civil Engineers

Every member of the staff should enter his name in an attendance book when he arrives, with the exact hour of arrival. It should be the duty of the junior clerk, or office boy, to remind the member of the staff that the name must be signed, and the principal should from time to time glance through the book to see how time is kept.

1986
Bertrand Goldberg
Associates
Interoffice Memo

When leaving the office for any reason (excluding lunch) the office must know where you can be contacted. A check out log is provided at the receptionist desk for this purpose. Record the time of departure, where you will be, anticipated time of return, and actual time returned.
If you are attending an early meeting, you are expected to "sign out" the night before.

1986
Society of Architectural
Administrators
Handbook for Architectural
Administrators

Sign in/sign out sheets, which undoubtedly make life easier for the receptionist, are a difficult item to enforce. Again, the secret is: IF THE PRINCIPAL OFFICERS OF THE FIRM ARE WILLING TO COOPERATE, the rest of the employees will follow suit. This form will tell the receptionist where the architect is (meeting, lunch, punch list checkout, etc.) and what time the architect is expected to return to the office.

2016
Snøhetta
Snøhetta Guide

First one in.
– Turn on lights.
– Have a look around to check if all is well.

Last one out.
– Check that any machines that should be off are off.
– Turn off lights.
– Make sure that both doors are locked.

144

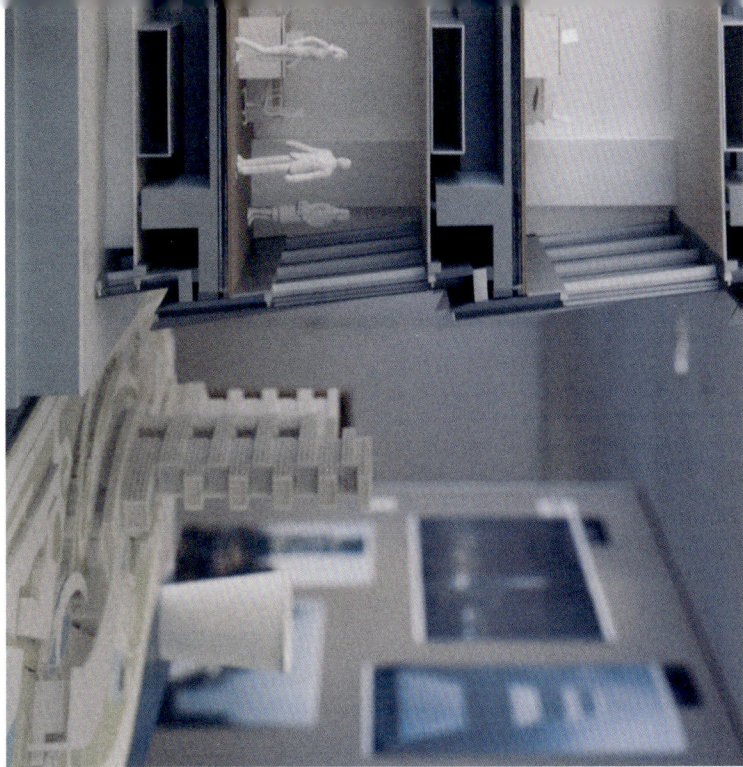

1
http://www.gallup.com/
poll/175286/hour-
workweek- actually-longer-
seven-hours.aspx

2
http://20somethingfinance.
com/american-hours-
worked-productivity-vacation/

4 — 2 SIGN IN / SIGN OUT

"Work to-day is more intense, and is carried on at a quicker rate. Actually the whole question becomes one of daily intercommunication with a view to settling the state of the market and the conditions of labor. The more rapid this inter-communication can be made, the more will business be expedited. It is likely, therefore, that the working day in the sky-scraper will be a shorter one, thanks to the sky-scraper. Then, perhaps, the working day may finish soon after midday. The city will empty as though by a deep breath."
      —Le Corbusier, *The City of Tomorrow and Its Planning*

In his 1929 *The City of Tomorrow and Its Planning*, Le Corbusier's work day was divided into equal parts: eight hours of sleeping, eight hours of working, and eight hours of repose. Le Corbusier suggests that in the future, this balance might shift so that the work day takes only six hours, and leisure time increases accordingly to ten. While a proponent of technology, capitalism, and speed, Corb's proposal is also part of trajectory that recognizes the detrimental effects of the new modern way of working on the body and the mind.

      Today, Le Corbusier's notion of ordered sign-in and sign-out times is be-coming less and less clear, and work hours have certainly not changed for the better. Contemporary hours worked in America have, for one, shown an exorbitant imbalance in favor of work over life relative to other countries. With a work week that exceeds the commonly held standard of forty hours by seven on average,[1] it is not surprising that annual totals for work hours exceeds other countries by weeks or even months: Americans work thirty-seven more hours per year than Japanese workers, 260 more hours per year than British workers, and 499 more hours per year than French workers."[2] And while many other countries require a significant amount of time off per week, the US represents a small group of countries that have no such provision.[3] Furthermore, amongst

...

3
http://www.motherjones.
com/politics/2011/06/
speedup-americans-
working-harder-charts

4
http://resources.
alljobopenings.com/
architect-jobs

5
Ibid.

6
http://www.archdaily.
com/234633/
worklifework-balance

American workers, some of the longest hours are worked by architects, whose work-week often exceeds fifty hours.[4,5]

Le Corbusier's optimistic aspiration that technology would shorten the workday, of course, presumes that work and repose are separate (in both time and space) and that the former should be carried out efficiently to maximize the latter. It is possible, therefore, that the increase in hours worked is due to the resulting conflation of previously divided work and repose, a line that sign-in/sign-out books once defined rigorously. Today, however, the sign-in/sign-out book seems to have largely disappeared from architecture (and most other) offices. Employees, once strictly categorized as either on or off-the-clock, now frequently straddle the line between work and repose; for instance, by routinely checking personal e-mails while physically being present in the office. Furthermore, the obscured boundary between work and life is articulated in what Slavoj Žižek describes as the exploitative work-place tactics of the contemporary office. Here, employees are simultaneously presented free food, free coffee, kitchens, and break-out spaces that are designed to manipulate staff into working more hours. Through this informal nature of the office and its pleasant surroundings, an image of the employer as friend is fostered, thus, generating a contemporary instrument of control that is psychological in nature as opposed to the sign-in/sign-out book's straightforward ordering.[6]

With the obsolescence of sign-in/sign-out books, employers instead rely on digital technologies to monitor hours worked regardless of location: e-mails arrive time-stamped on weekends while late-night cab ride receipts denote time of payment and, therefore, the point in time and space at which one has clocked out. Perhaps the much-maligned book that once operated as a control mechanism was, in the end, more liberating to the worker than the blurred line of the contemporary office in which workers can never truly sign-out. Caroline O'Donnell & Michael Jefferson

The next step in the preparation of an exact and detailed cost analysis would require reference being made to the costs records, one of which is shown in the draughting-room card record. On this card each drawing, its kind, the draughtsman's name, its beginning and completion date, is recorded, and from information available thereon it is possible to give accurately the cost of producing each drawing—thereby enabling the architect to distinguish between the inefficient and the efficient employee, and so immediately to place his finger on and correct any unnecessary leakage of his profits.

Time records shall be filled out each night before leaving, giving to within one half hour the time spent on different jobs.

Some offices issue a separate [time] card for each job a man is concerned with, though more often the draftsman has a single card for all jobs and information on it is unified later when the bookkeeper transfers its details to the job-cost book.

Provide hour chart on each sheet (rubber stamp or printed) for comparison with hours allotted.

Each Friday, at the end of the working day, the total hours worked are recorded on a timecard; the timecard is signed by the employee and submitted to the Accounting Department.

All technical employees are required to submit by 9:00 A.M. Monday morning a weekly time sheet listing the hours spent on each job that week.

You are required to keep accurate time records as they serve as the basic documentation for client billing, project cost control, payroll records, and your pay. You should complete your time sheet each day as directed by your supervisor. Time increment of 30 minutes or longer are to be recorded.

Employees must log in their hours specific to each project on the shared document and should only enter data from their own hours. As this is crucial to billing, project tracking, and IDP reports, accuracy and timeliness in supplying this information is required. Senior members will track and verify hours at the end of the week and from time to time ask for clarifications.

4 — 3 TIMESHEETS

9:30 – 10:00
Arrive at the office
Get coffee
Check emails
Prepare for meeting

10:00 – 12:30
Project team meeting
Serving good coffee and cookies at meetings is essential to create a cooper-
ative atmosphere. Over-eager meeting-cookie-types can be divided in two: those
who obsess over cookie quality to manage their own boredom; and those who
purposefully ignore them for fear they are another strategic pawn in a tactical
game of adversarial professionalism. Strangely, coffee rarely takes on this cons-
piratorial role: coffee is our universal lingua franca, it just is.

12:30 – 13:30
Write meeting minutes & send
Measuring architectural labor is notoriously difficult. The timesheet is a brutal
device of simplification and, therefore, subjugation. It individualizes labor in
terms of person-bound time according to strict demarcations of predefined
activities, over something (architecture) that can only be produced by a multi-
plicity of professionals and modes of collaboration.

13:30 – 14:30
Lunch
Of course, "lunch" is one of those categories of activity that is often qualified
as non-labor time. This is a lie, as demonstrated by a few productive activities
that typically occur during "lunch" including drawing with a sandwich dangling
from the mouth, lunch-meetings with other design team members, and—
crucially—meetings with co-workers that lubricate and enrich the cosmically
complex lifeworld of collaboration. Simply stated: No lunch = No work.
Of course, the most advanced organizations have long understood that "lunch,"
and other space-times of "non-labor," are the very motors of productive
innovation. Unfortunately, these organizations have simply replaced the time-
sheet with a 24/7 culture of narcissistic hyper-expression. Self-actualizing
for the sake of capital, the boundary between capital and self becomes ever
more fluid and problematic.

...

14:30 – 17:00
Site Visit
I was once asked by the Director of a leading architecture firm who was prepar-ing a fee proposal how many A0 drawings I could do in a week. I hesitated to respond "what scale, what kind, what project?" I really wanted to know: at what labor rate was he (mis-)listing me?

17:00 – 18:00
Return to the office
Issue drawings for tomorrow

18:00 – 19:00
Dinner
See "13:30 – 14:30," but with the factoring magnitude of, sometimes, beer.

19:00 – 23:00
This is an awkward time at the office. Lamps are left on at empty desks. The lonely murmuring printers and the occasional laughter can be heard nearby. Some call their mothers, husbands, or lovers, arguing in hushed tones. Avoidable mistakes are perpetrated. Things begin to take twice as long as they should. Working regularly at this time betrays the unprofessionalism of our profession, while also unwittingly making it less diverse and more unprofitable. For who can endure the social strain of a lifeworld without others (children, partners, aging mothers) but the very young, the privileged, or the sociopathic?

23:00 – 2:00
The best and the worse things happen at this time in architecture offices. Apparent strikes of genius. Love affairs. Efficiency innovations. Collective consciousness-raising. Proto-revolutionary organizing. Salary discussions. Spite and Solidarity. Model-making first-aid situations.

2:00 – 9:30
It is an open secret that some architecture offices expect their employees to sleep under their desks "after hours." This may appear reasonable in exceptional situations for the sake of a brilliant project, but as a recurring event, it will flatten life experience to one-dimensionality. I am unaware if this kind of activity is ever acknowledged on a timesheet—and if so, how it could be justified. Its occurring, and subsequent narrating by recent M.Arch graduates, is the very lifeblood of our highly self-mythologizing and ideological profession. Thus, in almost circular fashion, the "end" of the timesheet has become the bedsheet; or, rather, their obscene indiscernibility. Manuel Shvartzberg

1922
McKim, Mead & White
Manual of Office Practice

Time is usually the most important single factor in all building operations. It is therefore of the utmost importance that the architects' part of the work be handled expeditiously, as well as carefully, so that the responsibility for proper progress will remain at all times with the contractor.

1931
John Russell Pope
"Office Manual, Architect Routine and Procedure"
The Architectural Record

Time is a most important factor in all building operations. At no stage of the work should the architect procrastinate in the matter of securing decisions and expediting the progress of the drawings.

1969
Richard J. Neutra
Excerpts of Ideas for Possible Use in The Neutra Office

Reduce scale of drawings to save time.
Simplify sections and elevations—i.e. doors, windows, etc. indicated by single outline with schedule symbol and detail key.
Draw only interior elevations needed for clarification.
Use abbreviations.

1986
Derek Sharp
The Business of Architectural Practice

We frequently hear building contractors say optimistically: "We'll make up time lost and finish on programme." This is impossible. Time lost is never regained and therefore we should always carefully value time. There is a difference between timing and the control of time.

1999
The Society of Design Administration
Handbook of Design Office Administration

Make appointments on the calendar for phone calls, exercise, and other things that never happen because of a lack of time, as well as of predetermined meetings, tasks and events. If things are not given an honest time slot, they will never happen in a busy schedule.

4 — 4 TIME MANAGEMENT

1. **Time = Money**
   A. Literally. Because client fees are no longer based on piece-work [percentage of construction (or hourly with a cap, which amounts to the same thing); fixed fees] but, rather, time-work, employees are instructed to log every five-minute increment of work according to a) project title; b) task performed; and c) administrative type (see 2B below). No work can be unbillable; that is there will be no billing to "overhead" when learning new skills.
   B. Any work extending beyond an eight-hour day will be billed as overtime at one and a half; employees must indicate whether task performed is overtime. Overtime is discouraged.
   C. Working remotely is allowed when approved in advance by Project Team Liaison.

2. **Time = Knowledge**
   A. The Project Team Liaison manages the team members' time. Her role is twofold: 1. to ensure that team members do not waste time or duplicate tasks; 2. to ensure that team members coordinate with their equivalent (according to task performed) in other teams so that knowledge is shared across projects.
   B. Team members must identify tasks as a) perfunctory; b) iterative; or c) innovative. All tasks identified as "innovative" will be shared with the entire office on a Google Doc. Peggy Deamer

A dated memorandum record must be made of matters discussed at all conferences with clients and general or sub-contractors. In all cases it is advisable that a copy of such memorandum be sent to the interested parties, so that any error or misunderstanding can be corrected.

Beginning with the Chief's office, we feel that the Monday morning meetings we now have are most beneficial and that a specified hour each Monday morning is paramount for the Chief to call his meeting with the *etat-major*. A certain amount of time should be allowed without interruption.

Meeting notes are typed on ditto and follow the standard format shown on the sample, remembering to leave a 1 1/2" margin on the left side.

"Meetings, bloody meetings—why don't they make their own decision and not rope everyone in to make them collectively when they are avoiding responsibility of making decisions themselves." We have all heard people say this. Meetings are the most costly form of communication there is.

Schedule meeting at optimum times.

Monday mornings and Friday afternoons are the worst. Mornings are best. Try for an hour and a half before lunch, so you will have a natural ending. Don't get off on tangents that are not on the agenda, and don't participate when someone else does it.

Each meeting is important. If it is not, do not schedule it. When it is scheduled, careful planning and preparation are necessary for the successful use of the time spent.

4 — 5 MEETINGS

In *Star Wars*, some Jedi Masters attend High Council meetings via holographic telepresence, participating even when they are somewhere else far, far away in the galaxy. They understand the value of meetings: instant information/opinion sharing and feedback. As the Jedi Masters know, it is much easier to reach agreements and make decisions with a focused and interactive discussion compared to, for example, communicating via messages carried back and forth by R2-D2.

Today, our reach is not (or at least not yet) as expansive, and the Force is not that strong with us. But we now can supposedly overcome distance and "show up" at meetings remotely on a screen thanks to the technology of videoconferencing. This form of meeting quickly became ubiquitous in the last decade. It has tremendously enhanced the quality of long distance communication, yet we all know there is room for improvement.

Long distance meetings used to be organized only through telephone conference calls. Soon we realized that hearing words alone was insufficient for good communication. Ray Birdwhistell, founder of the field of kinesics, estimated years ago that only thirty to thirty-five percent of the social meaning of human communication was carried by words, with the remaining two-thirds of communication consisting of non-verbal behaviors such as body language and facial expressions. The invention of videoconferencing enabled these visual cues to be exchanged. Seeing people's silent reactions and gestures helps better understand what's really going on and what's implied between the lines. Document cameras and screen-sharing technologies now allow us to interact more directly and instantaneously through sketches and diagrams— another type of visual communication that cannot be achieved on a verbal conference call.

Clearly, videoconferencing is powerful, but it has limitations. We may all have experienced bad connections resulting in broken conversations and poor video quality. Some people may act strangely due to appearance consciousness when on camera. And cognitively, virtual presence remains inferior to in-person meeting because people still tend to engage more deeply with their immediate environments and the people right around them.

Let's assume however that technology will improve and people will grow more accustomed to being on camera. The fundamental problem of videoconferencing is that it still does not cover the full spectrum of non-verbal communications as outlined by Birdwhistell. A simple eye contact or a friendly handshake can establish mutual connection and trust. Basic emotional connections between people rely heavily on physical presence, which videoconferences cannot deliver. A face on a flat screen does not have the human touch—you are still not there. This is a bit like seeing a 3D virtual model on the computer screen. It lacks the intimate tactile and spatial quality of real physical presence.

So what could be next? Beam me up, Scotty! Human Wu

4 — 6 ESTIMATES

1922
McKim, Mead & White
Manual of Office Practice

Where estimates are desired the information given the bidders should be clear, concise and complete. Matters of detail should not be left to the estimator's imagination. Experience has shown it is practically impossible to hold a bidder responsible for omission from his estimate, of work not clearly shown or described, even where apparently covered by a broad or general requirement of a specification.

1931
John Russell Pope
"Office Manual, Architect
Routine and Procedure"
The Architectural Record

Preliminary estimates should be secured and submitted to the owner before proceeding with final working drawings. On securing this information the office is then ready, after a consultation with the chief draftsman, to set a definite date for the completion of working drawings.

1944
Gordon Lorimer
"The Bureau in Architecture"
*The Octagon, A Journal
of the American
Institute of Architects*

It has not generally been the practice of architects to prepare detailed estimates showing breakdown of materials and equipment, but rather to rely on an empirical general experience factor, such as cost per cubic foot of similar types of structures. While this approach is considered adequate as a means of arriving at a budget figure, if has been proven not conclusive enough to act as a basis for actual monetary appropriation for the execution of the work.

1962
Roland Green
*The Architect's Guide to
Running a Job*

Information concerning the lowest [bid] on each subcontract should be abstracted and itemized for future reference in the office for estimating purposes on other contracts.

1971
Abbott, Merkt & Company
Operating Guidelines

1. Cost Estimation shall be responsible to the Vice President for Project Managers for all matters relating to duties and assignment.

2. On specific projects, work under the direction of the Officer-in-Charge to produce cost estimates of various schemes as required for the preliminary package. Prepare statement of probable construction cost of preliminary package for presentation to the client.

4 — 6 ESTIMATES

Money is not a quantitative material. Its movement is managed by the unpredictable psychological frame that accompanies it. A budget is typically formulated before a design has been made, so it is theoretical, yet it is treated as a fully-objective figure. However, pre-design budget estimates are often made intuitively, politically, or based on typologies that don't match the conditions of the project at hand. Most of us know the outcome: evisceration of the design very late in the process. Unless everyone takes an honest look at the project goals, you can only be successful by accident. Budgets and expectations require some degree of alignment before design begins.

As everyone is well aware, projects are defined primarily by three factors. *Cost*, meaning the amount of money available to spend; *quantity*, meaning how much and how fast will it be made; and *quality*, meaning the performance of the materials and components. It is possible to manipulate any two of these three conditions, but the third must be the natural sum of the two components being directed. So $5+2=7$ or $6+1=7$, but $4+3 \neq 9$.

It is wrong to think that "Architecture" is the primary component that dictates cost. Design-y things only comprise about 20 percent of the cost outcome of a project. Program and performance standards, on the other hand, comprise about 80 percent of the cost outcome of a project. So get the program sorted out first. This means that cost control should occur during a pre-design phase, before spaces are designed but when the desired quality is understood. Unfortunately these issues are often ignored, and they only resurface deep into the detailed planning or construction periods at which point you are lucky if you can refine the cost by about 5 percent.

Architects need to be more responsible in understanding these issues and ensuring that their work is achievable within the context of the client's material framework or, when necessary, should say "no" to projects. Clients need to be more aware that a simple cost and design alignment is important prior to beginning design. Unfortunately, all of this rarely happens because the design and construction process is often approached by everyone involved as a zero-sum game rather than a conversation, which in turn deemphasizes collective success. Both architects and clients would do well to heed this advice from Angry Zodd's novel *Danny the Last Earth Man*: "You can be as morally righteous as you want—in a vacuum—but throw in a second entity and you gotta start acting in response to the other." Craig Dykers

When an estimate has been accepted, the next business of the architect or engineer is to see that this acceptance is put into legal form, by means of a suitable legal instrument, which is usually styled a contract, but which is really a form of agreement.

Nine times out of ten, a contract is just an arrangement of words on paper, but when the emergency arises it becomes your strongest bulwark of defense. How many varied and unexpected ways this may be proven!

AGREEMENT BETWEEN OWNER AND ARCHITECT
THIS AGREEMENT, made the .... Day of .... in the Year Nineteen Hundred and .... , by and between .... , Esq., ... , hereinafter called the Owner, and Royal Barry Wills, 3 Joy Street, Boston, Massachusetts, hereinafter called the Architect, WITNESSETH that, whereas the Owner intends to erect a .... at .... , now therefore the Owner and the Architect, for the consideration named hereinafter, agree as follows: THE ARCHITECT agrees to perform for the above named work professional services in accordance with his schedule of professional practice attached hereto.

THE OWNER agrees to pay the Architect at the rate of eight per cent (8%) hereinafter called the basic rate, computed and payable as stated in said schedule of professional practice, and to make any other payments and reimbursements arising out of said schedule.

....

Owner   Architect

For the usual type of project involving full professional services for design, production of construction documents, award of construction contract and construction administration, the firm will normally propose to the client the latest Standard Form of Agreement as recommended by the AIA, modified as necessary to suit our standard practice and the specific project requirements.

4 — 7 CONTRACTS

Contracts are legal instruments that represent an exchange of consideration between parties made in order to formalize their business deal. For archtects— who provide services to clients as professional agents—such contracts typic- ally comprise an obligation to provide competently delivered services to the client in exchange for specified compensation and differ in structure and intent from their parallel counterparts in construction. Construction contracts between client and builder are intended to exchange payment for the delivery of a product, typically a building or renovation. The relationship between these two, co-dependent agreements on a project, is typically described by the following diagram:

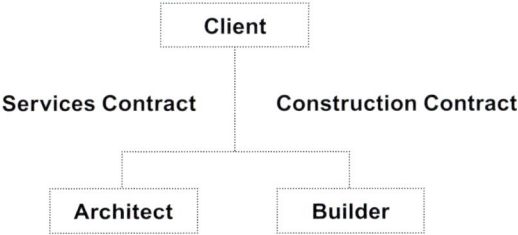

A contract is the best mechanism for systematically describing the obligations of the architect, her consultants and the client, and when properly created coordinate the obligations of the architect with the builder. Both the owner/architect and owner/contractor agreements should therefore be comple- mentary. Contract model and language should be chosen based on the type of project delivery model (hard bid, CM, design build, integrated) designated for the project.

The terms and conditions of typical architectural contracts follow a template created in the early twentieth century by what is now the American Institute of Architects and elaborated as the profession has evolved accord- ingly. Most such contracts in the United States rely heavily on this precedent, which has been successively known as Agreement B1 (originally), B141 (until

...

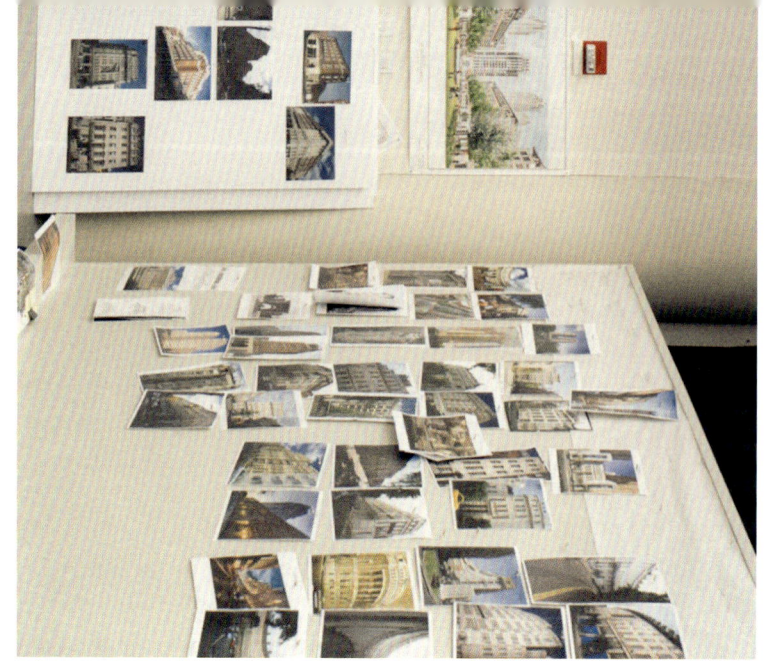

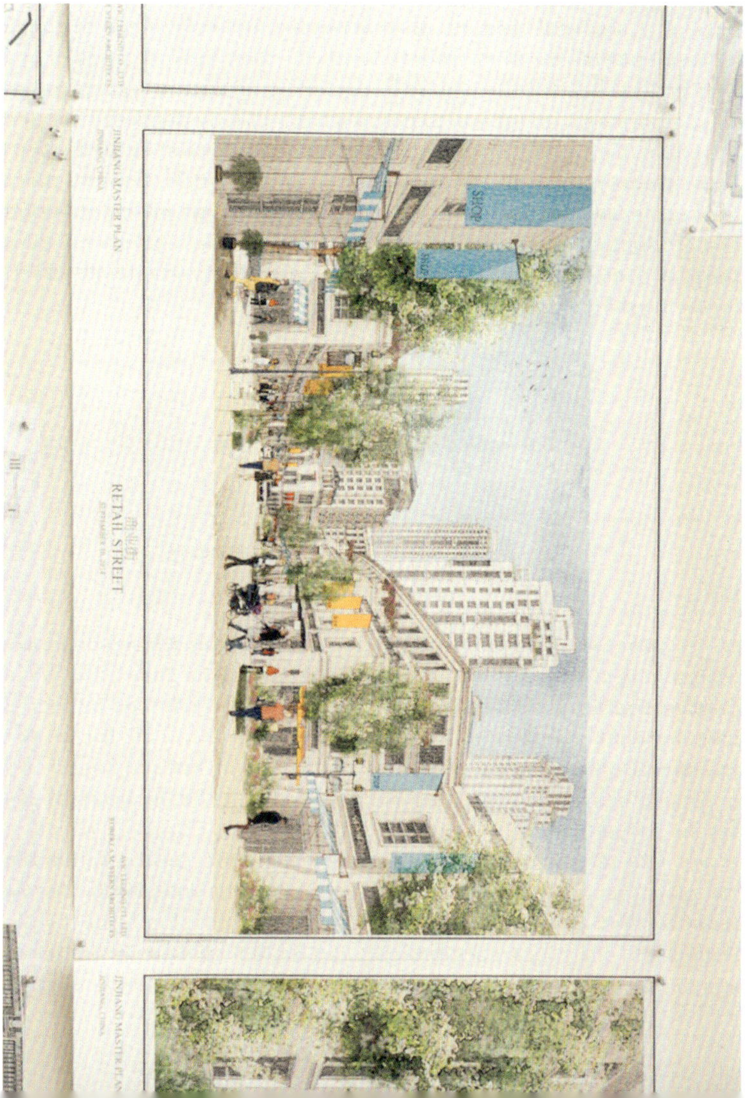
JINJIANG MASTER PLAN
RETAIL STREET

2005), and B101 (since 2005). That contract and many of its typical variants include the following components (based loosely on articles of B101):
- – Initial information: basic information such as project description, client, architect, etc.
- – Architect's responsibilities: a summary of the architect's role on the project
- – Scope of the architect's services: a phase-by-phase explanation of the services the architect is to perform for the fee and what services are considered outside that fee
- – Owner's responsibilities: defines the owner's obligation to provide certain information and support to the project.
- – Cost of the Work: explains how the project construction cost is created and managed, and the architect's responsibility therein
- – Copyrights and licenses: defines intellectual property rights to the drawings and other use of the architect's work
- – Claims and disputes: defines how disagreements between the parties are resolved
- – Termination or suspension: how either party can extinguish the contract and the implications therein
- – Compensation: defines the architect's payment for services and expenses
- – Miscellaneous provisions: where all the other terms reside.

An important component of any architect's contract for service is the professional standard of care, which is the legal principle that governs the measurement of an architect's competence (and, by implication, negligence). The standard of care—which may be explicitly stated in the architect's contract but applies anyway—states that non-negligent services are those that are provided by any competent practitioner in similar circumstances. A contract can raise the standard of care by obligating the architect to do things that fall outside this measure and care must be taken in negotiating terms not to exceed an acceptable level of resulting liability.

A new generation of contract models is emerging that embrace principles of integration and do not hew to the structure or terms of traditional agreements. Under the aegis of IPD (integrated project delivery) these agreements combine the considerations for the project under a single contract signed by the architect, builder, and owner and compensate the parties based on measurable project outcomes rather than fixed, commoditized fees. While relatively few projects today use this model, principles of integration that require strong cooperation between designers and builders are influencing traditional models in novel ways. It's expected that continued progress toward integration may eventually radically affect the obligations of architects and contract models accordingly. Phil Bernstein

1926
Frederick L. Ackerman
*Ackerman Office
Policy Manual*

No print is issued from the office without being accompanied by a receipt in duplicate, one of which is to be signed and returned to this office. Upon its return the third copy of the receipt, which had originally been retained as an office memorandum, is destroyed and the slip containing the signature is filed in its place.

1943
American Institute of
Architects
*The Handbook of
Architectural Practice*

In order that the Architect may have a competent knowledge of the results of his business, he should keep an accurate account of the costs of this work; namely, reimbursements, direct costs, and overhead.

1967
Morris Lapidus
*Architecture: A Profession
and a Business*

When I started my practice I asked an accountant friend to tell me how to keep records of incoming fees and outgoing expenses. With only one client and one draftsman at the time, I had no difficulty in my bookkeeping venture. By the time I had a few clients and two draftsmen, there was little time for me to make entries in my books. It was inevitable that my wife should assume these chores. I still treasure these archaic pages as professional memorabilia! Any architect starting a practice must keep books; but as his practice grows, a professional bookkeeper must be obtained. Sometimes a secretary can double in this capacity. The larger office will soon have a full-time bookkeeper, and as its growth continues, a comptroller, business manager or treasurer will become an integral member of the office staff. Whatever the title, he will be your "money man."

2014
Arquitectonica
*The Project
Management Manual*

Arquitectonica staff submit monthly expense reports and backup material according to the reimbursement policies and procedures of the personnel manual.

The employee prepares a separate expense report for each project; individual expenses are associated with specific project tasks. The PM signs the expense report, which is submitted with the monthly timesheets. The accounting department reviews the expense reports, adjusts them as necessary, requests reimbursement cheques and does the necessary posting. These expenses appear on the project status report issued on the 2nd day of each month.

1926

1943

1967

2014

4 — 8 EXPENSE REPORTS

"Expense" is both noun and verb, exorcising the double bind of territorial praxis within our institutions and daily lives. A living record of one's labor, the report is as much a framing of effort as it is a mapping of it only to be distributed among others whose own reports seek to quantify, schedule, and fix. The expense report establishes a litmus of both personal and professional value across multiple scenarios, rendering new ecologies of dominion within academic institutions and the workplace.

Value, when transcribed as a social construction, remains a proviso that implicates knowing as a form of becoming. Through such transfers, it may be possible to recognize one's value to a broader organization while also ascertaining what permits becoming valuable to it. If one's value is recorded and recoded in part by the expense report and aligned with that of an academic institution— yet another business—the security of our value, presupposed by continuous effort, is upended by not knowing. Value, read as expense over time, creates division. An expense report thus acts as a referendum on our present selves and the frailty of our own acts.

The expense report may also arbitrate failure at a number of scales when we "expense" something—a protocol, a gesture—which does not coincide with the act itself. This mismatch is a component of failure between ourselves and the commissioning of value(s) that may be averted or widened through or by expense. Transacting failure may first be deployed as an independent undertaking, and later revealed as that which transgresses the fragile structures that securitize and monetize the broader scope of institutional value systems.

To expense is also to establish an archive of trajectories, of visible and invisible properties across multiple intersecting economies that behave semi-independently within the institution. Managed by others, witnessed by few, these are ever-expanding enterprises within which value may be made visible at any given moment. Expenses are aggregate and in their expansion may eventually match their collapse if not vigorously regulated.

We may be implicated by our receipts, our transactions, like an errant ballistics of desire. This tension proliferates across all institutions, condemning its individuals to both a furtive repurposing of worth whilst encumbered to each other's own uneasy daily questioning. Some within the institution may not be the subject of expense—for whom reports and other methods of self-policing do not necessarily apply. It is the majority of us, however, whose value is markedly questioned from without and within, and in whose reports are the lineaments of worth, that expense reports illustrate and sustain a topology of discipline.

If value embodies both internal and external dichotomies, within the quasi-orderliness of expense reports and their editing, one is continually reminded, "You Are Here," yet lost in space. Sean Anderson

1941
Royal Barry Wills
and Leon Keach
This Business of Architecture

By adopting a cost per mile charge for automobile travel (at least six cents at the present time) it is possible to allocate the expense of longer, special trips, directly to jobs. But short radius trips, usually involving stops at several locations, are too difficult to segregate under their exact headings, and so should be grouped as Overhead.

1969
Abbott, Merkt & Company
*Accounting Department
Procedure Manual*

Travel vouchers are presented to the accounting department upon return from a trip. Vouches are to be attached, American Express, Avis, hotel and restaurant bills, and minor invoices tying into charges as presented. Voucher is added, footed, coded and charged to the proper job.

1986
Society of Architectural
Administrators
*Handbook for Architectural
Administrators*

As a rule, the administrator is responsible for the architect's travel arrangements. This includes picking up tickets and travel documents.

Required information: Once the answers are obtained, write them down and keep them beside the telephone while making the travel arrangements:
1. Where are you going?
2. When are you going?
3. What time of day do you wish to leave/arrive?
4. How long will you be gone?
5. Do you need hotel reservations? What hotel do you prefer?
6. Do you need a car rental? Which rental agency do you prefer?

1993
Francis Baden-Powell
*Building Overseas;
Butterworth Architecture
Management Guide*

Living in a different culture and climate puts great strain on people's mental and physical health and it is thus very important that they are fit and mentally well balanced and remain so during their tour overseas. They should have a medical check-up before travel and on their return.

2014
█████ *Employee Handbook*

Travel is an important part of the way we conduct business. █████'s policy is to control and limit travel expenses to reasonable and necessary amounts within consistent parameters for business travel. For specific questions not addressed in this Handbook, you may refer to the Firm-wide Travel Policy on INET.

1941

1969

1986

1993

2014

4 — 9 TRAVEL

For the architect, travel is alternately a necessity, a form of education, and a quest. To move from the office to the site, from the place where work is produced to the place which is the subject of the work, is essential and even unavoidable. Whether local or far flung, the site visit makes for critical moments of discovery. The time spent en route provides opportunities for reflection, reinterpretation, and revision. Somewhere between drawing and building, the traveling architect is allowed to let the mind wander.

No architectural education is complete without travel. Nineteenth-century Beaux Arts pedagogy involved academic tourism. Many of today's graduate school studio courses in the United States come complete with air tickets and hotel reservations, the professor serving as a guide. Intellectual discovery is related to travel experience.

Beyond the academy, and aside from the profession, there lies a form of travel with more profound implications: the quest. To visit a city or to roam the world searching for a building can constitute a goal of finding unwritten truth. Louis Kahn's voyages to the Mediterranean and Le Corbusier's *Voyage d'Orient* provide us with mythic precedents; today's frequent flier criss-crossings of the globe will yield their own sketchbook revelations. James von Klemperer

1926
Frederick L. Ackerman
*Ackerman Office
Policy Manual*

Modeler is to photograph all models and these are to be filed in the Subject File, each job in envelopes, and indexed as "Models."

1968
Harry Wesse and Associates
*Organization and
Design HWA Office*

We will standardize the procurement of photographs, both as to models and finished buildings. Photographers will be selected from an approved list by the person in charge of photography, and an estimate from the photographer will be required before he undertakes actual shooting.

The staff person assigned to this task is in charge of the dark room, its stocking, its use, and its maintenance and security, as well as all of the office photographic equipment which will be maintained therein.

Before a photographer is sent into the field, he should be briefed, given a scope, and given a set of snapshots taken by us to show the views we wish. In every case, we need one direct elevation of every facade, something quite often missing. Also crucial interiors including corridors are needed. CISDC is helpful to the photographer and can be used for instructing him.

4 — 10 PHOTOGRAPHY

Everyone has a camera. But not everyone is a photographer. And as we've said, perhaps too often, taking a picture is not the same as making a photograph. Those who make photographs of architecture have many simultaneous concerns. Some are technical, dealing with cameras and lenses, hardware and software. Other issues involve aesthetic decisions about capturing space and light at a specific moment.

The final image is that instant. Telescoping time also becomes the persistent reality of the building itself as the images are circulated and the building is identified by the photograph. Another way of considering time is to think of the viewer's subsequent visual exploration of the image. Forms and shapes represent the reality. The edges—the framed, cropped rectangular world—show the power of the photographer to determine what you see and what you don't. And the photographer has the responsibility of creating an image with layers of information for those who may not visit the building or may see it under very different circumstances, even years later, after the original structure has been vastly changed.

While the designer may imagine the project as it was visualized, from start to finish, the photographer sees the final result as it is, fully realized. This viewpoint is important as it is not filtered through design phases, renderings, aspirations, and compromises, but captures built reality by translating three-dimensional space to two-dimensional media.

For the photographer to understand the project and successfully complete an assignment, it's important to have background about the program, design decisions, and solutions, and then to spend time moving through the space, becoming familiar with the surroundings and observing changes during the day and over time. The full scenario helps the photographer determine and then make images that reflect the structure, the use, and the liveliness of the project. The most successful collaboration engages the photographer as a recent member of the design team whose images capture the layers of meaning in the final, built project.

Architects commission photography for many reasons. There are immediate needs such as marketing and promotional use, competition entries, and editorial submissions. For the long range, there are archives and historical purposes. Frequently, design colleagues, consultants, suppliers, and perhaps the building owner collaborate to commission images that will be useful to each in a different way. To ensure complete and responsible coverage the photographer should know how the images will be used. The images may be made on one trip to the site or, to describe seasonal and other changes, there may be a number of visits. Sometimes, to meet deadlines, the photographs are made before construction is fully completed. We all share the responsibility of changes made to the image to improve reality. How much fixing is enough? How much is too much? And what is reality, anyway? Erica Stoller

1941
Royal Barry Wills
and Leon Keach
This Business of Architecture

The architect is entitled to compensation for articles purchased under his direction, even though not designed by him.

1973
Hugh Stubbins Associates
Office Manual

Requests for drafting supplies should be directed to Central Services. Requests for secretarial supplies and printed forms should be directed to the Executive secretary.

1974
Venturi and Rauch
Venturi and Rauch Handbook

All purchases of routine supplies, material, equipment will be made through the administrative assistant or directly by the individual submitting receipts to the bookkeeper. Major purchases of capital items must receive the prior approval of a Principal or Associate of the firm.

1988
Emery, Roth & Sons,
P.C. Architects
Office Guidelines

No one is allowed to order any type of supplies without having filled in a requisition form. With approval of a Director, which should be processed by the head of the Plan Desk. Additionally, personal orders for supplies for one's own use are not to be ordered under any circumstance.

2014
Employee Handbook

All purchases, including commitments for printings, when related to a project, must first be approved by the Project Manager or the Principal-in-Charge. Anyone obligating the Firm for any purchase without going through this procedure will be individually liable for the cost of this purchase.

1941

1973
1974

1988

2014

4 — 11 PURCHASES

Shopping Guide:
1. Color: find light-hearted and upbeat colors that will work well in a lightbox, producing a cute and optimistic feeling. In other cases, find objects with black linework and white background.
2. Texture: look for a mixture of glossy, furry, matte, and metal. Almost behaving like a serial murderer, sort the similar textures and shapes neatly before we start composing. Make sure there's a premeditated distribution of texture percentages.
3. Architectural and Urban Qualities: look for objects with elements that may contain "columns," "ramps," "canopy," and so forth. As well, look for objects with an abundance of both soft and hard corners—the more we are able to zig-zag, the better we can compress and expand the gaps between objects in plan and in section.
4. Math of Shapes: when in doubt, select objects with clear "geometric" properties—spheres, cubes, cylinders, pyramids, etc. They can be "near-spheres" or "near-cubes," so long as we can make an argument that they belong to certain categories of geometry. Also, find objects with compositional principles such as a tripartite stack.
5. Potential for Dismemberment and Aggregation: find objects that can be taken apart and reassembled to depart from their original meanings.
6. Stories of Shapes: be funny about the objects—not only are we asking "why are you here," we will be imagining silly things we can do in them. A Laurel Broughton toaster is funny because the scales have new meanings and gaps are meant to be occupiable. An Andrew Kovacs environment is gorgeous because things look slumpy or sloppy on purpose. It is a means of defamiliarizing meanings. This demands us to imagine the implied stories when the objects can be occupied.
7. Genre of "Funny": when generating the comedic moments, consider the use of deadpan. Please avoid slapstick—it is a kind of take-away that becomes a giveaway. Also, avoid sarcasm, as it is too dark too quickly and not mysterious enough. Absurd juxtaposition is a good technique, too.
8. Size: impose a range of sizes for the objects. Preemptively chart the zones against an applied grid, and the distribution of number of objects per zone. This will help us consider the range of sizes of objects we need to acquire.
9. Defamiliarize Readability: the mix of objects should allow for most to be not clearly readable.
10. Genealogy and Relationships Between Objects: can some of them be cousins? Are there contrasting ones?
11. Orientation: can some of the pieces be re-oriented and become richer architecturally and more difficult to read as normal objects?
12. Ease of Relaying Your Shopping Stories: can the punchline be delivered in three to seven words, and would anyone from eight to eighty-eight chuckle at it? Jimenez Lai

2004
Davis Brody Bond, LLP
Employee Policy Manual

The fire and theft insurance coverage held by the firm for the office premises is the standard commercial policy in which there is no coverage for personal property. Unique or expensive items of personal equipment brought into the office or on business-related travel on behalf of the office (i.e. cameras, special tools, etc.) may be covered by a binder for a stipulated period of time that the equipment will be used for office purposes.

2004

4 — 12 VALUABLES

ARTICLE 1 FACILITIES AND GENERAL OFFICE PROCEDURES

§1.1 Valuables. It shall be the policy of Leong Leong to assist its employees in safeguarding their personal property while at work. However the office does not assume responsibility for the loss or theft of personal belongings and employees are advised not to carry unnecessary amounts of cash or other valuables with them when they come to work.

§1.1.1 Valuables or articles of personal property found on the premises should be returned to the owner (if known) or turned in to the office manager. Inquiries regarding lost property should be directed to the office manager.

§1.1.2 Employees are expected to exercise reasonable care in safeguarding personal items of value brought to the office. Such items should never be left unattended or in plain view.

§1.1.3 Equally, employees should be mindful that the office, like life, is like a river. Nothing is permanent except constant change. One should not become too attached to anything. Just let go. Leong Leong (Chris Leong and Dominic Leong)

1967
Morris Lapidus, AIA
*Architecture, a Profession
and a Business*

Attractively mounted or framed work—your work—should be what your visitors see. These can be renderings or photos of completed projects—even your best school work is acceptable until you can replace it with photos or renderings of your new work. Your state license and diploma do not belong in the reception room. The fact that you have an office is proof enough that you are a qualified architect. Your credentials belong in your office.

1986
Society of Architectural
Administrators
*Handbook for Architectural
Administrators*

All persons entering the office should be treated with courtesy and helpfulness. The receptionist should immediately greet the visitor, by name if possible. If the visitor is unknown, the receptionist should immediately perform the self-introduction, ask the person's name and determine who may best help the visitor.

2014
Office Manual

The office is willing to accommodate student and professional groups. However, in the interest of minimizing disruption during the workday, we try to limit the number of people, times of arrival and duration of their stay.

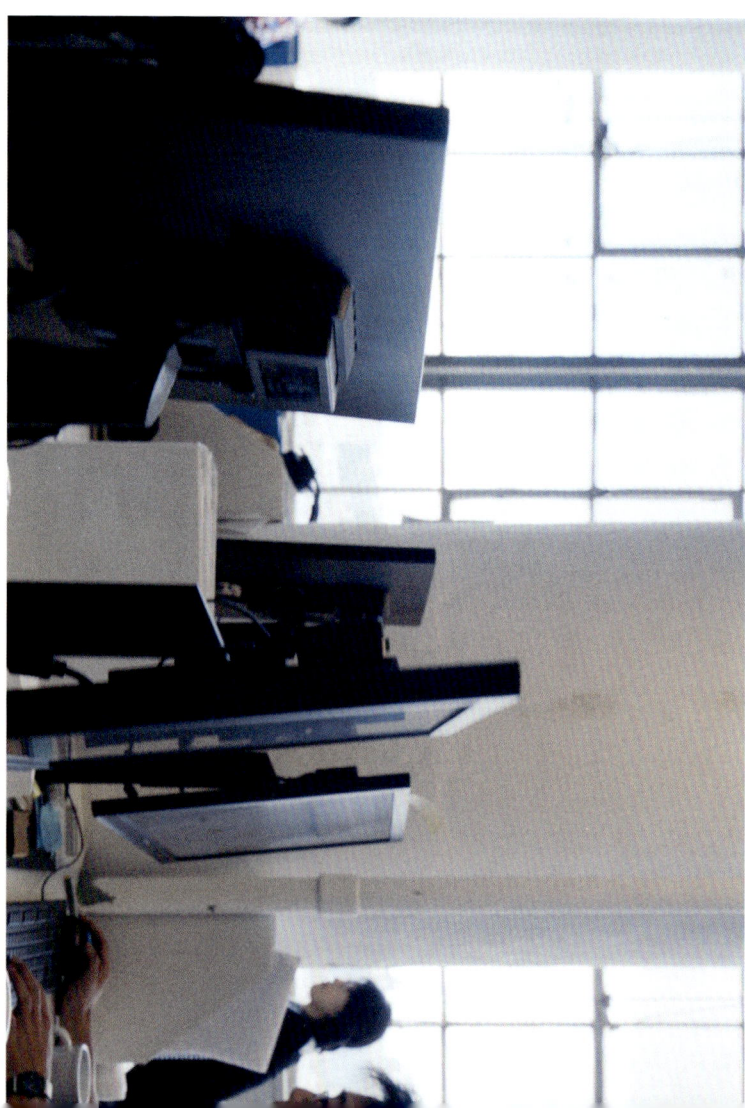

1967

1986

2014

172

4 — 13 RECEIVING VISITORS

A visit to a Very Large Corporation that builds a large number of buildings

Hello, hi, welcome! I'm so glad you could make it today. I'll put a call into the Back and someone will be right with you. Would you mind just giving me your name again?
Excellent.
And a photo ID if you have one?
That's perfect. Thanks…

Do you have a camera with you by chance? Your phone? Yes, I'm afraid that counts. Would you mind leaving that up here? We're a little cautious is all. Fantastic, thanks. That'll all be right here when you're done.

Just, ah, a couple more things: We have a little NDA, standard for all callers. Just boilerplate stuff but if you wouldn't mind just signing here… here … And also here. Great! Thank you so much. And then if you could just take a coverall. That's right, zips in the front. We like these because it helps even the playing field. Okay! All set!

Let me show you to the Visiting and Sharing Room. Right this way please! We have you in Room 11… here.

The doors *are* sound proof! How could you tell? We try to make our guests feel at ease while they are visiting with our people. Please have a seat and enjoy a snack from the Treat Bowl if you'd like. You might like the little boxes of raisins. Or maybe you're more of a single-serving Life Savers kind of person.

Oh, right, you have to kind of lift the chairs up when you scoot in. The metal legs on the concrete are kind of loud otherwise. Not that I'll be able to hear you of course, ha ha! Anyway, if you need anything, just bang on the window. I'll have a visual on you. There is some literature on the walls while you are waiting. Those are the Ten Rules for Building a Business. And those posters represent different fun ways of reminding everyone of our zero-tolerance gift acceptance policy and ethics regulations.

1. Commit to your business.
2. Share your profits with all your associates, and treat them as partners.
3. Motivate your partners.
4. Communicate everything you possibly can to your partners.
5. Appreciate everything your associates do for the business.
6. Celebrate your success.

…

7. Listen to everyone in your company.
8. Exceed your customers' expectations.
9. Control your expenses better than your competition.
10. Swim upstream.

That's pretty much what we're about. Just, like, swimming upstream? Like all swimming back to our ancestral breeding ground, you know?

Anyway, make yourself comfortable and, just a friendly reminder that "accepting gifts and entertainment can cause a conflict, or the appearance of a conflict, between personal interests and professional responsibility. Our business culture is to never accept gifts or entertainment from any supplier, potential supplier, government agent, or other third party the associate has reason to believe may be seeking to influence business decisions or transactions." So you might just keep that fruit basket for yourself.

Make yourself at home and someone will be right with you! ^{Jesse LeCavalier}

1928
Robert Maurice Trimble
Office and Drafting
Room Practice

We consider a satisfied client our best advertiser and this point is stressed throughout the entire organization—a beautiful picture means nothing if it is executed with a leaky roof or damp basement, or finished two months too late. In short, we are making an earnest effort to disprove the accusation that the architect is an impractical dreamer and a painter of pictures; still retaining, however, a practical expression of the beautiful picture.

1930
Abram Garfield
"Personal Publicity"
The Octagon, A Journal
of the American Institute
of Architects

There is another form of advertising which was somehow useful so long as it was uncommon. This is the monograph illustrating the work of an individual architect. It is convenient and may well be described as useful except that it has become so common that it has lost some of its novelty.

1928
1930

1941
Royal Barry Wills
and Leon Keach
This Business of Architecture

Competition from non-professional sources and the weakened condition of the code of ethics has made some sort of business promotion necessary.

1971
William Wayne Caudill
Architecture by Team;
A New Concept for the
Practice of Architecture

1941

In 1950 we received a call from Robert Nail, secretary of the school board, saying they were interviewing architects for a job, and that at least three of them had referred to the book. He said, "I'm curious to know about the guy who wrote the book. Would you be interested in coming to Albany to talk with the Board about it?" Would we! That night, after driving over 300 miles for the interview, we got the job.

1974
Venturi and Rauch
Venturi and Rauch Handbook

Writing articles for professional magazines and journals and participating in professional speaking programs are excellent opportunities for personal professional development. Meaning interprofessional communications benefit the staff member, the firm, and the profession.

2000
Gavin Tunstall
Managing the Building
Design Process

1971
1974

Branding the consistent use of identity art on marketing instruments, fosters recognition of your architecture and design firm within the public sector. Key to branding is your firm's identity package, which should include a logo design with the firm's name and contact information and a flexible set of business materials such as stationery, envelopes, business cards, memo forms, and business forms.

2000

176

4 — 14 PUBLICITY, PROMOTION, PRESS, AND PUBLICATIONS

Today, architecture is fractured. It lives in the physical realm that visitors experience as they walk through space; and in the media, whether in print or online, in film or photos—the ephemeral yet superficial.

The physical can't travel, the superficial travels instantaneously all over the world.

The static nature of architecture makes publicity and the image necessary evils. The reality is that an office needs to consider itself a profit-making business if it wants to survive. These days it seems to take unremitting boastfulness to be heard, but offices shouldn't get swept away in efforts to gain publicity. Never should publicity guide design; never should it be a purpose from the beginning. Architecture has too many other functions, too many responsibilities.

Do your research before blasting your news—don't bombard others without careful consideration. Just as you establish a design philosophy and process, take time to find your voice. Not every office is the same, and not everyone needs to handle publicity in the same way. Do you believe in "any press is good press," or quality over quantity? What comes first, the architect or the architecture?

Some tactics and platforms work better for one office than for another. How can we capture the spirit of a building? Magazines and blogs aren't the only outlets that can make an impact. Consider books, exhibitions, events, videos—bonus points for creativity and a fresh perspective.

Choose wisely, and avoid drowning in the waves of loud voices around you. Julia van den Hout

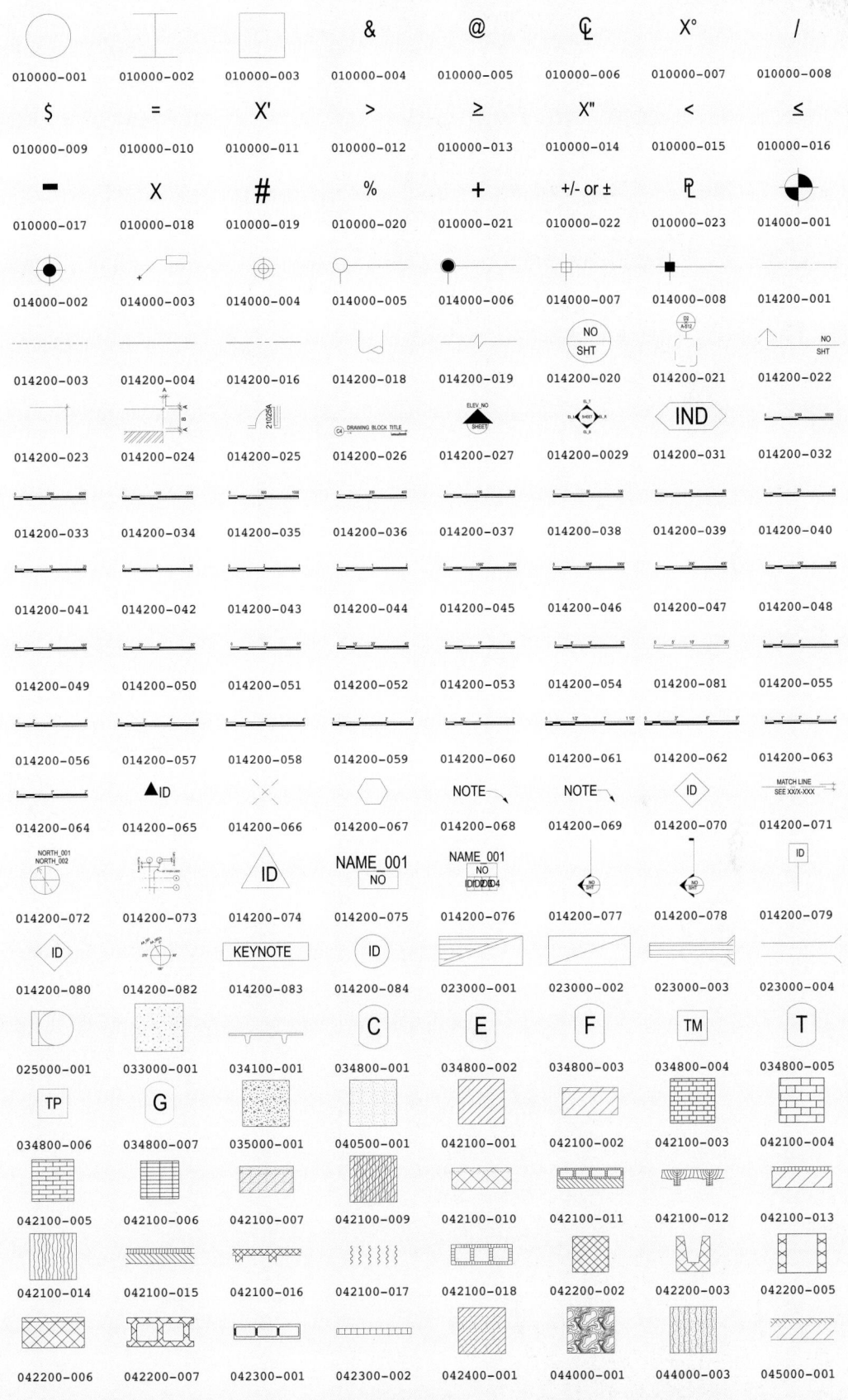

010000-001	010000-002	010000-003	010000-004	010000-005	010000-006	010000-007	010000-008
010000-009	010000-010	010000-011	010000-012	010000-013	010000-014	010000-015	010000-016
010000-017	010000-018	010000-019	010000-020	010000-021	010000-022	010000-023	014000-001
014000-002	014000-003	014000-004	014000-005	014000-006	014000-007	014000-008	014200-001
014200-003	014200-004	014200-016	014200-018	014200-019	014200-020	014200-021	014200-022
014200-023	014200-024	014200-025	014200-026	014200-027	014200-0029	014200-031	014200-032
014200-033	014200-034	014200-035	014200-036	014200-037	014200-038	014200-039	014200-040
014200-041	014200-042	014200-043	014200-044	014200-045	014200-046	014200-047	014200-048
014200-049	014200-050	014200-051	014200-052	014200-053	014200-054	014200-081	014200-055
014200-056	014200-057	014200-058	014200-059	014200-060	014200-061	014200-062	014200-063
014200-064	014200-065	014200-066	014200-067	014200-068	014200-069	014200-070	014200-071
014200-072	014200-073	014200-074	014200-075	014200-076	014200-077	014200-078	014200-079
014200-080	014200-082	014200-083	014200-084	023000-001	023000-002	023000-003	023000-004
025000-001	033000-001	034100-001	034800-001	034800-002	034800-003	034800-004	034800-005
034800-006	034800-007	035000-001	040500-001	042100-001	042100-002	042100-003	042100-004
042100-005	042100-006	042100-007	042100-009	042100-010	042100-011	042100-012	042100-013
042100-014	042100-015	042100-016	042100-017	042100-018	042200-002	042200-003	042200-005
042200-006	042200-007	042300-001	042300-002	042400-001	044000-001	044000-003	045000-001

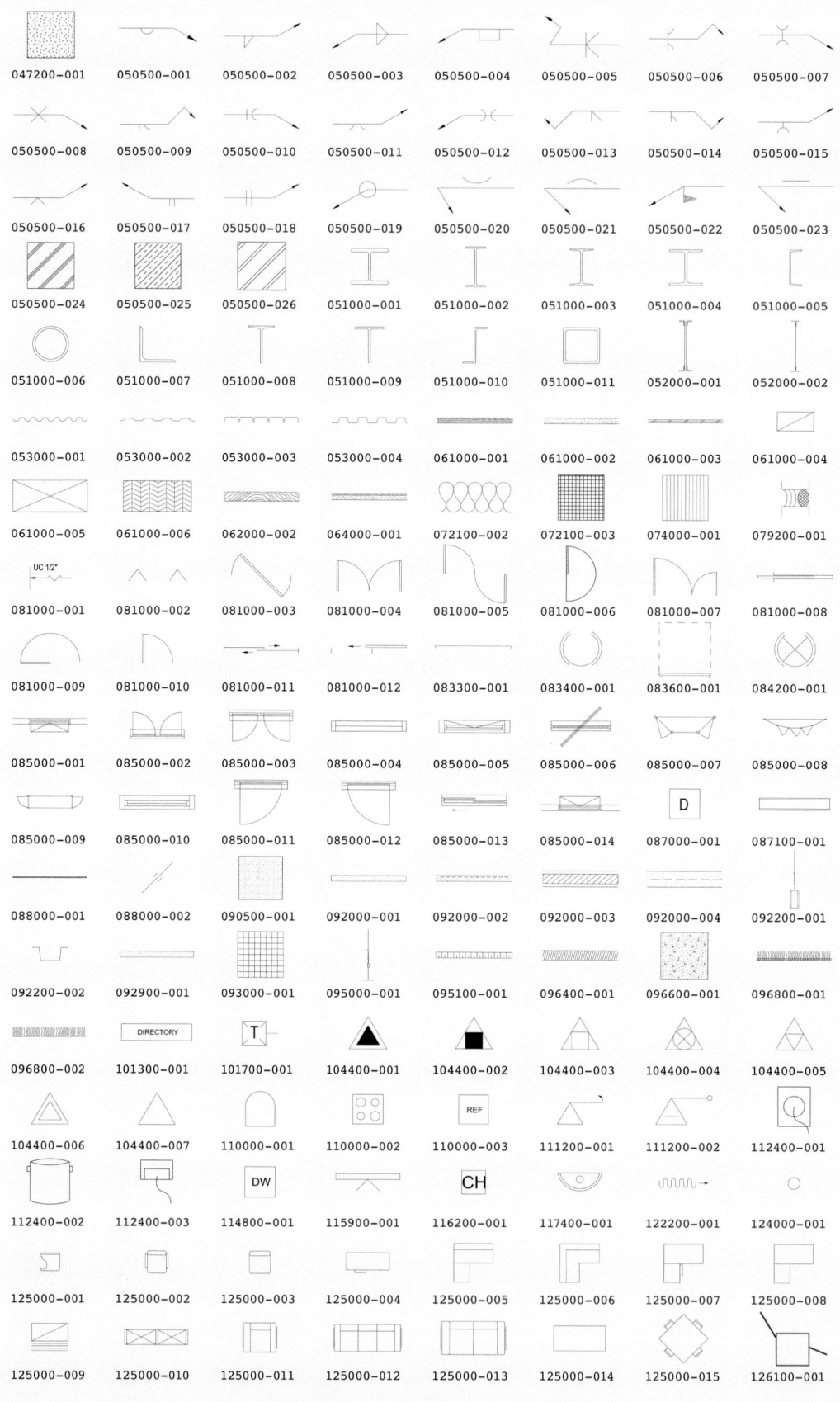

047200-001	050500-001	050500-002	050500-003	050500-004	050500-005	050500-006	050500-007
050500-008	050500-009	050500-010	050500-011	050500-012	050500-013	050500-014	050500-015
050500-016	050500-017	050500-018	050500-019	050500-020	050500-021	050500-022	050500-023
050500-024	050500-025	050500-026	051000-001	051000-002	051000-003	051000-004	051000-005
051000-006	051000-007	051000-008	051000-009	051000-010	051000-011	052000-001	052000-002
053000-001	053000-002	053000-003	053000-004	061000-001	061000-002	061000-003	061000-004
061000-005	061000-006	062000-002	064000-001	072100-002	072100-003	074000-001	079200-001
081000-001	081000-002	081000-003	081000-004	081000-005	081000-006	081000-007	081000-008
081000-009	081000-010	081000-011	081000-012	083300-001	083400-001	083600-001	084200-001
085000-001	085000-002	085000-003	085000-004	085000-005	085000-006	085000-007	085000-008
085000-009	085000-010	085000-011	085000-012	085000-013	085000-014	087000-001	087100-001
088000-001	088000-002	090500-001	092000-001	092000-002	092000-003	092000-004	092200-001
092200-002	092900-001	093000-001	095000-001	095100-001	096400-001	096600-001	096800-001
096800-002	101300-001	101700-001	104400-001	104400-002	104400-003	104400-004	104400-005
104400-006	104400-007	110000-001	110000-002	110000-003	111200-001	111200-002	112400-001
112400-002	112400-003	114800-001	115900-001	116200-001	117400-001	122200-001	124000-001
125000-001	125000-002	125000-003	125000-004	125000-005	125000-006	125000-007	125000-008
125000-009	125000-010	125000-011	125000-012	125000-013	125000-014	125000-015	126100-001

129200-001	131700-001	131700-002	131700-003	131700-004	131700-005	134800-001	211000-001
211000-002	211000-003	211100-002	211100-004	211100-005	211100-007	21100-008	211100-009
211100-011	211100-012	211100-013	211100-014	211100-015	211100-016	211100-017	211100-018
211100-019	211100-021	211200-001	211200-002	211200-003	211200-004	211200-005	211200-006
211200-007	211300-001	211300-002	211300-003	211300-006	211300-007	211300-008	211300-009
211300-010	211300-011	211300-012	211300-014	211300-015	211300-016	211300-017	212100-001
212100-002	212100-003	212100-004	212200-001	212200-002	212200-003	212200-004	212200-005
212300-001	212300-002	212400-001	212400-002	212400-003	213000-001	213000-002	213000-003
214100-001	220500-001	220500-002	220523-001	220523-002	220523-003	220523-004	220523-005
220523-006	221100-001	221100-002	221100-003	221200-001	221300-001	221300-002	221400-001
223100-001	224000-001	224000-002	224000-003	224000-004	224000-005	224000-006	224000-007
224000-008	224000-009	224000-010	224000-011	224000-012	224000-013	224000-014	224000-015
224000-016	224000-017	224000-018	224000-019	224000-020	224000-021	224000-022	224000-023
224000-024	224000-025	224000-026	224000-027	224000-028	224000-029	224000-030	224000-031
224000-032	224000-033	224000-034	224000-035	224000-036	224000-037	224000-038	224000-039
224000-040	224000-041	224000-042	224300-001	224700-001	224700-002	224700-003	230900-001
230900-002	230900-003	230900-004	230900-005	230900-006	230900-007	230900-008	230900-009
230900-010	230900-011	230900-012	230900-013	230900-014	230900-015	230900-016	230900-017

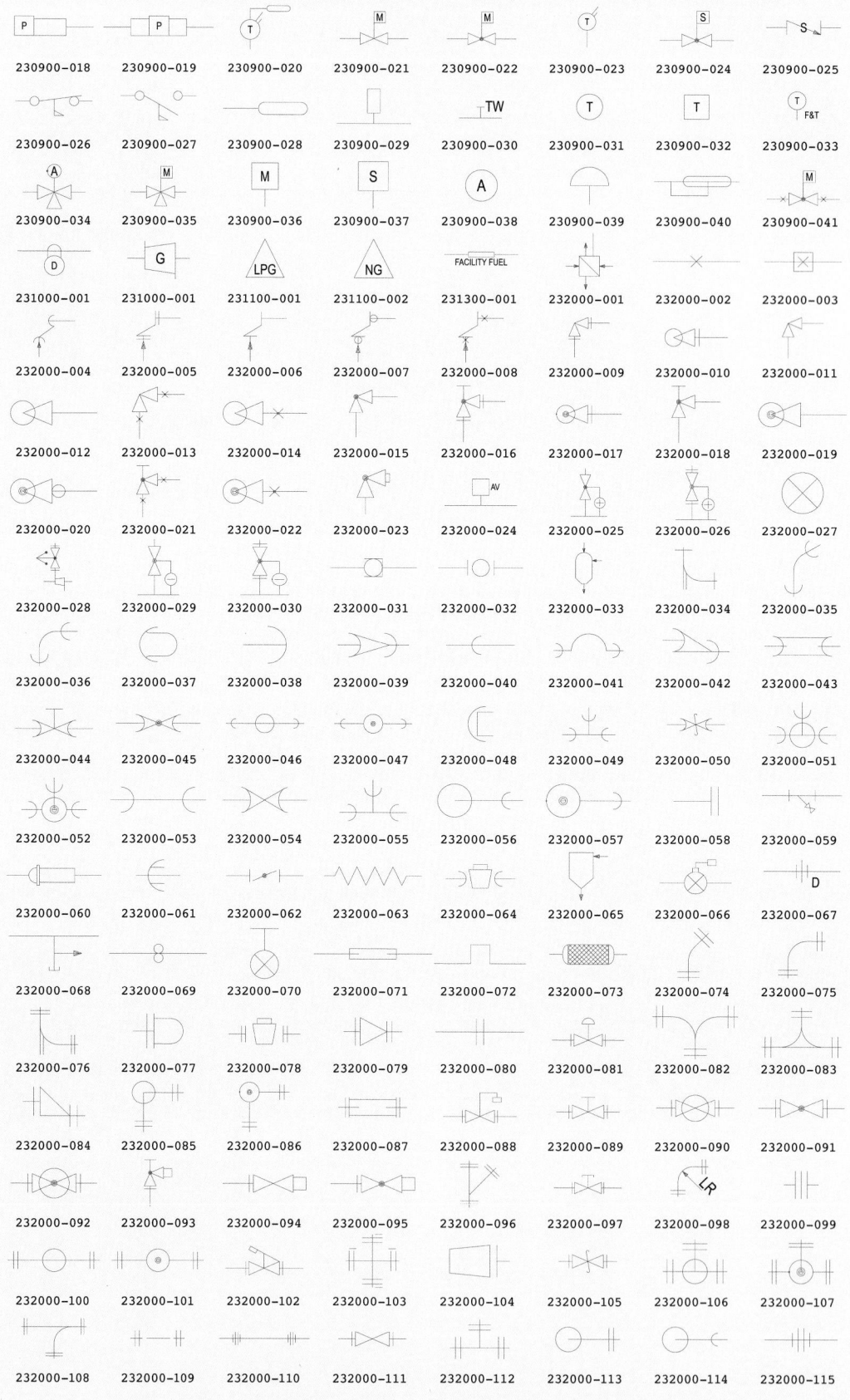

230900-018 230900-019 230900-020 230900-021 230900-022 230900-023 230900-024 230900-025

230900-026 230900-027 230900-028 230900-029 230900-030 230900-031 230900-032 230900-033

230900-034 230900-035 230900-036 230900-037 230900-038 230900-039 230900-040 230900-041

231000-001 231000-001 231100-001 231100-002 231300-001 232000-001 232000-002 232000-003

232000-004 232000-005 232000-006 232000-007 232000-008 232000-009 232000-010 232000-011

232000-012 232000-013 232000-014 232000-015 232000-016 232000-017 232000-018 232000-019

232000-020 232000-021 232000-022 232000-023 232000-024 232000-025 232000-026 232000-027

232000-028 232000-029 232000-030 232000-031 232000-032 232000-033 232000-034 232000-035

232000-036 232000-037 232000-038 232000-039 232000-040 232000-041 232000-042 232000-043

232000-044 232000-045 232000-046 232000-047 232000-048 232000-049 232000-050 232000-051

232000-052 232000-053 232000-054 232000-055 232000-056 232000-057 232000-058 232000-059

232000-060 232000-061 232000-062 232000-063 232000-064 232000-065 232000-066 232000-067

232000-068 232000-069 232000-070 232000-071 232000-072 232000-073 232000-074 232000-075

232000-076 232000-077 232000-078 232000-079 232000-080 232000-081 232000-082 232000-083

232000-084 232000-085 232000-086 232000-087 232000-088 232000-089 232000-090 232000-091

232000-092 232000-093 232000-094 232000-095 232000-096 232000-097 232000-098 232000-099

232000-100 232000-101 232000-102 232000-103 232000-104 232000-105 232000-106 232000-107

232000-108 232000-109 232000-110 232000-111 232000-112 232000-113 232000-114 232000-115

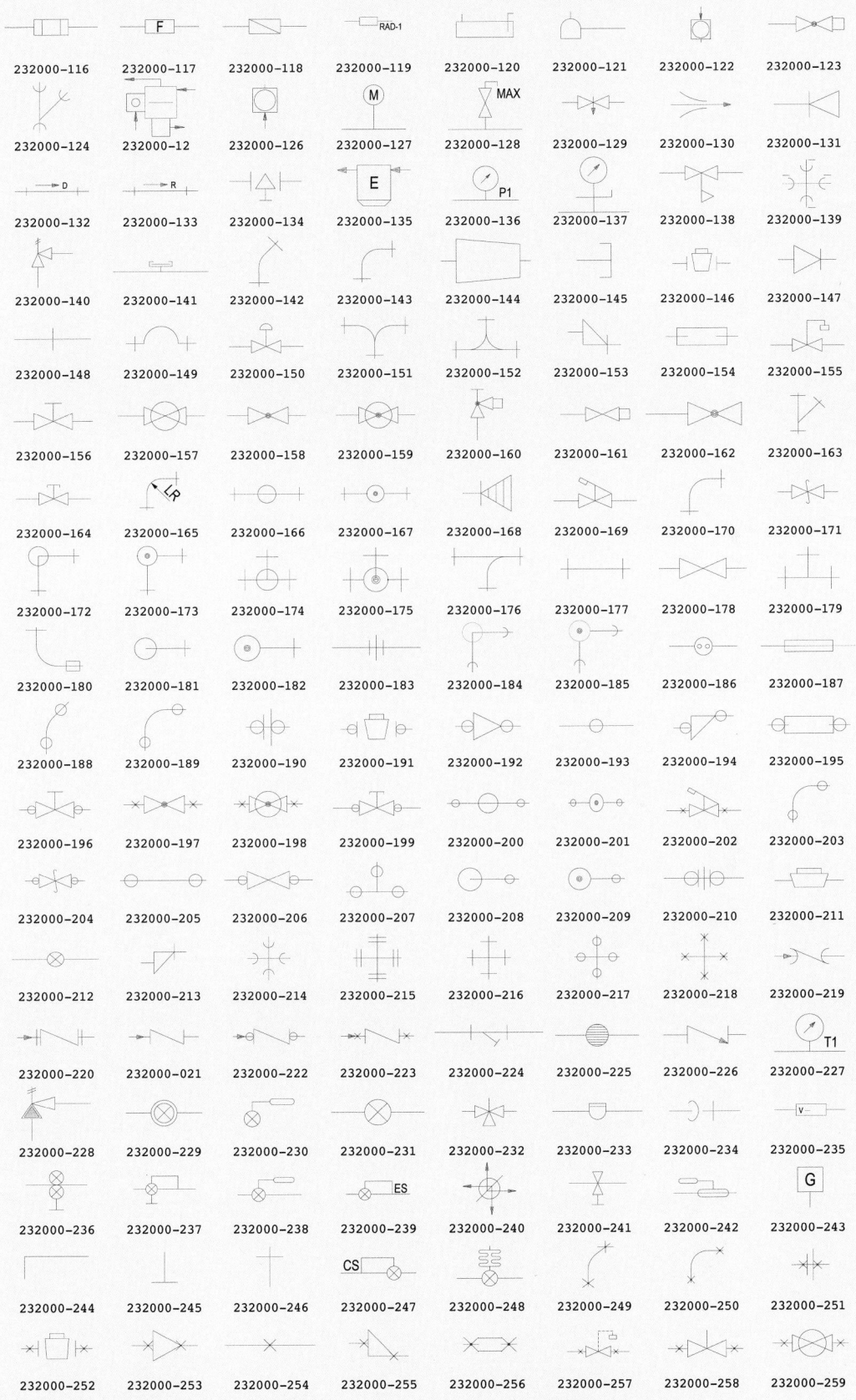

232000−116 232000−117 232000−118 232000−119 232000−120 232000−121 232000−122 232000−123

232000−124 232000−12   232000−126 232000−127 232000−128 232000−129 232000−130 232000−131

232000−132 232000−133 232000−134 232000−135 232000−136 232000−137 232000−138 232000−139

232000−140 232000−141 232000−142 232000−143 232000−144 232000−145 232000−146 232000−147

232000−148 232000−149 232000−150 232000−151 232000−152 232000−153 232000−154 232000−155

232000−156 232000−157 232000−158 232000−159 232000−160 232000−161 232000−162 232000−163

232000−164 232000−165 232000−166 232000−167 232000−168 232000−169 232000−170 232000−171

232000−172 232000−173 232000−174 232000−175 232000−176 232000−177 232000−178 232000−179

232000−180 232000−181 232000−182 232000−183 232000−184 232000−185 232000−186 232000−187

232000−188 232000−189 232000−190 232000−191 232000−192 232000−193 232000−194 232000−195

232000−196 232000−197 232000−198 232000−199 232000−200 232000−201 232000−202 232000−203

232000−204 232000−205 232000−206 232000−207 232000−208 232000−209 232000−210 232000−211

232000−212 232000−213 232000−214 232000−215 232000−216 232000−217 232000−218 232000−219

232000−220 232000−021 232000−222 232000−223 232000−224 232000−225 232000−226 232000−227

232000−228 232000−229 232000−230 232000−231 232000−232 232000−233 232000−234 232000−235

232000−236 232000−237 232000−238 232000−239 232000−240 232000−241 232000−242 232000−243

232000−244 232000−245 232000−246 232000−247 232000−248 232000−249 232000−250 232000−251

232000−252 232000−253 232000−254 232000−255 232000−256 232000−257 232000−258 232000−259

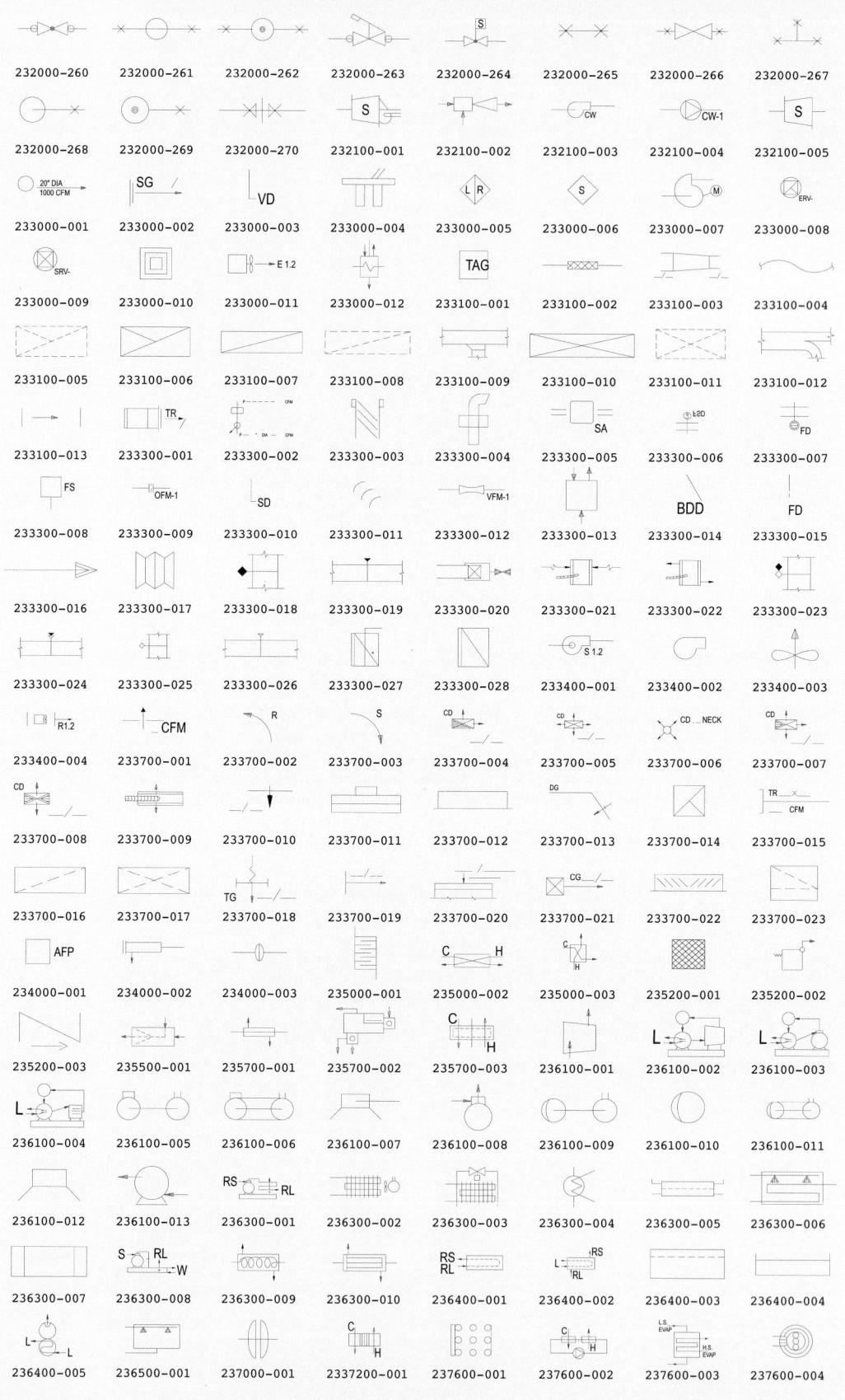

232000–260	232000–261	232000–262	232000–263	232000–264	232000–265	232000–266	232000–267
232000–268	232000–269	232000–270	232100–001	232100–002	232100–003	232100–004	232100–005
233000–001	233000–002	233000–003	233000–004	233000–005	233000–006	233000–007	233000–008
233000–009	233000–010	233000–011	233000–012	233100–001	233100–002	233100–003	233100–004
233100–005	233100–006	233100–007	233100–008	233100–009	233100–010	233100–011	233100–012
233100–013	233300–001	233300–002	233300–003	233300–004	233300–005	233300–006	233300–007
233300–008	233300–009	233300–010	233300–011	233300–012	233300–013	233300–014	233300–015
233300–016	233300–017	233300–018	233300–019	233300–020	233300–021	233300–022	233300–023
233300–024	233300–025	233300–026	233300–027	233300–028	233400–001	233400–002	233400–003
233400–004	233700–001	233700–002	233700–003	233700–004	233700–005	233700–006	233700–007
233700–008	233700–009	233700–010	233700–011	233700–012	233700–013	233700–014	233700–015
233700–016	233700–017	233700–018	233700–019	233700–020	233700–021	233700–022	233700–023
234000–001	234000–002	234000–003	235000–001	235000–002	235000–003	235200–001	235200–002
235200–003	235500–001	235700–001	235700–002	235700–003	236100–001	236100–002	236100–003
236100–004	236100–005	236100–006	236100–007	236100–008	236100–009	236100–010	236100–011
236100–012	236100–013	236300–001	236300–002	236300–003	236300–004	236300–005	236300–006
236300–007	236300–008	236300–009	236300–010	236400–001	236400–002	236400–003	236400–004
236400–005	236500–001	237000–001	2337200–001	237600–001	237600–002	237600–003	237600–004

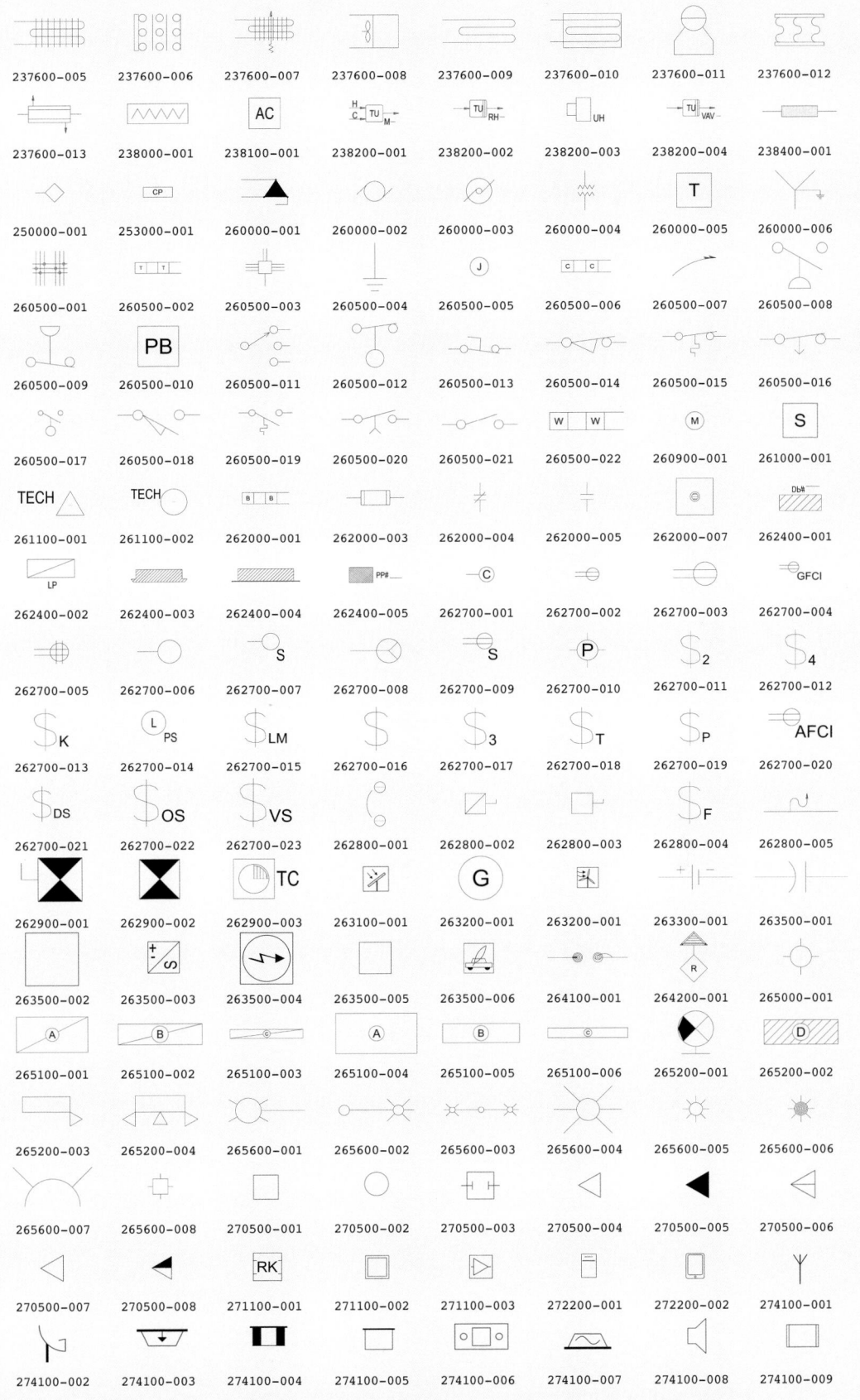

237600–005	237600–006	237600–007	237600–008	237600–009	237600–010	237600–011	237600–012
237600–013	238000–001	238100–001	238200–001	238200–002	238200–003	238200–004	238400–001
250000–001	253000–001	260000–001	260000–002	260000–003	260000–004	260000–005	260000–006
260500–001	260500–002	260500–003	260500–004	260500–005	260500–006	260500–007	260500–008
260500–009	260500–010	260500–011	260500–012	260500–013	260500–014	260500–015	260500–016
260500–017	260500–018	260500–019	260500–020	260500–021	260500–022	260900–001	261000–001
261100–001	261100–002	262000–001	262000–003	262000–004	262000–005	262000–007	262400–001
262400–002	262400–003	262400–004	262400–005	262700–001	262700–002	262700–003	262700–004
262700–005	262700–006	262700–007	262700–008	262700–009	262700–010	262700–011	262700–012
262700–013	262700–014	262700–015	262700–016	262700–017	262700–018	262700–019	262700–020
262700–021	262700–022	262700–023	262800–001	262800–002	262800–003	262800–004	262800–005
262900–001	262900–002	262900–003	263100–001	263200–001	263200–001	263300–001	263500–001
263500–002	263500–003	263500–004	263500–005	263500–006	264100–001	264200–001	265000–001
265100–001	265100–002	265100–003	265100–004	265100–005	265100–006	265200–001	265200–002
265200–003	265200–004	265600–001	265600–002	265600–003	265600–004	265600–005	265600–006
265600–007	265600–008	270500–001	270500–002	270500–003	270500–004	270500–005	270500–006
270500–007	270500–008	271100–001	271100–002	271100–003	272200–001	272200–002	274100–001
274100–002	274100–003	274100–004	274100–005	274100–006	274100–007	274100–008	274100–009

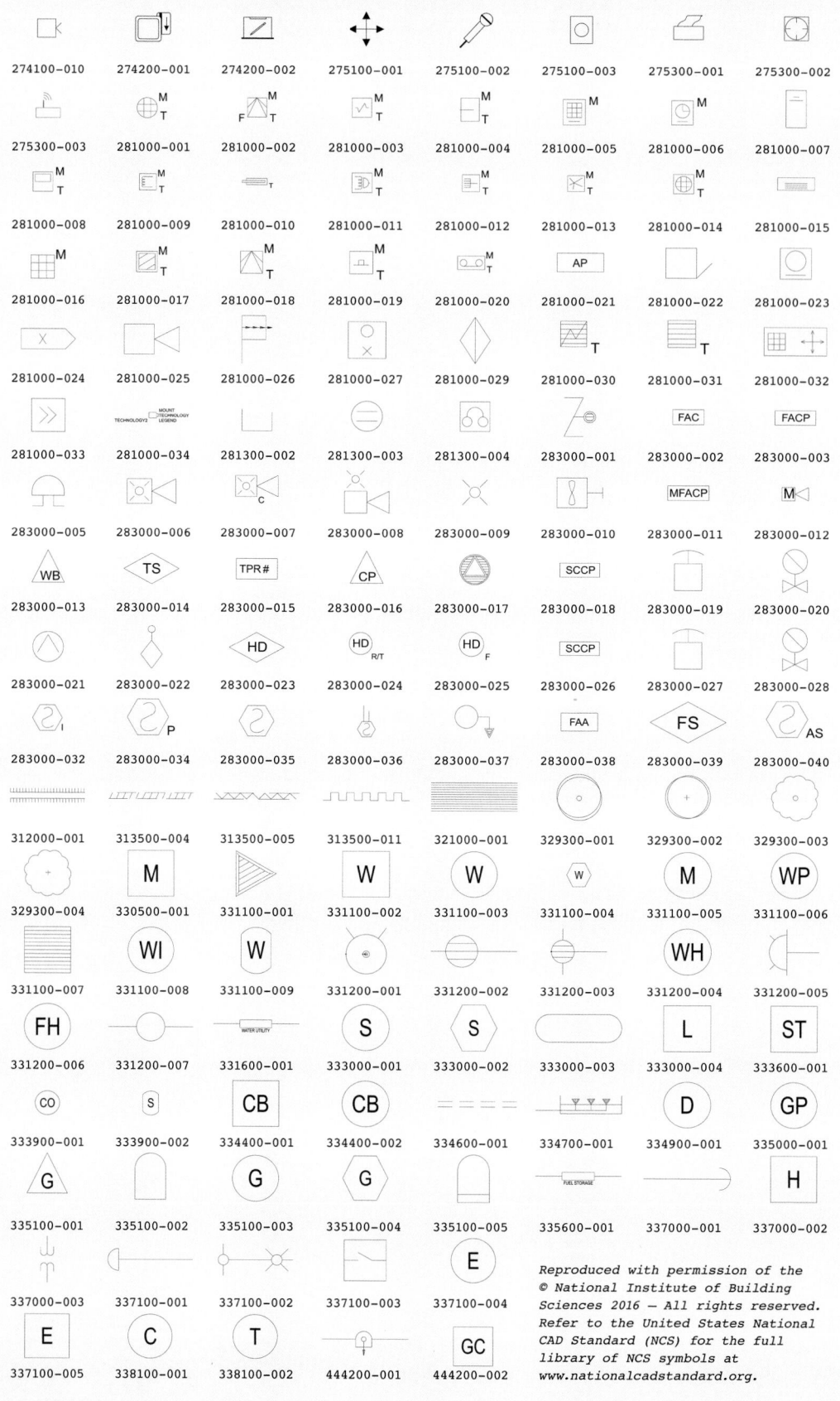

274100-010	274200-001	274200-002	275100-001	275100-002	275100-003	275300-001	275300-002
275300-003	281000-001	281000-002	281000-003	281000-004	281000-005	281000-006	281000-007
281000-008	281000-009	281000-010	281000-011	281000-012	281000-013	281000-014	281000-015
281000-016	281000-017	281000-018	281000-019	281000-020	281000-021	281000-022	281000-023
281000-024	281000-025	281000-026	281000-027	281000-029	281000-030	281000-031	281000-032
281000-033	281000-034	281300-002	281300-003	281300-004	283000-001	283000-002	283000-003
283000-005	283000-006	283000-007	283000-008	283000-009	283000-010	283000-011	283000-012
283000-013	283000-014	283000-015	283000-016	283000-017	283000-018	283000-019	283000-020
283000-021	283000-022	283000-023	283000-024	283000-025	283000-026	283000-027	283000-028
283000-032	283000-034	283000-035	283000-036	283000-037	283000-038	283000-039	283000-040
312000-001	313500-004	313500-005	313500-011	321000-001	329300-001	329300-002	329300-003
329300-004	330500-001	331100-001	331100-002	331100-003	331100-004	331100-005	331100-006
331100-007	331100-008	331100-009	331200-001	331200-002	331200-003	331200-004	331200-005
331200-006	331200-007	331600-001	333000-001	333000-002	333000-003	333000-004	333600-001
333900-001	333900-002	334400-001	334400-002	334600-001	334700-001	334900-001	335000-001
335100-001	335100-002	335100-003	335100-004	335100-005	335600-001	337000-001	337000-002
337000-003	337100-001	337100-002	337100-003	337100-004			
337100-005	338100-001	338100-002	444200-001	444200-002			

1901
Kaye W. Perry
Office Management;
A Handbook for Architects
and Civil Engineers

It should be made an invariable business rule to send by the next post a confirmation of any telegram, because telegraph messages are sometimes incorrectly transmitted, and the confirmation will correct the mistake besides reminding the receiver of the contents of the message.

1941
Royal Barry Wills
and Leon Keach
This Business of Architecture

The most important reasons for recording toll calls is because they may be legitimately charged against job cost.

1960
Office of Architect
Maynard Lyndon
Employee's Manual

Answered by Secretary when she is here. Answered by saying "Maynard Lyndon's Office." Never use expression "In Conference." Ask "who is calling" and also to wait while you check with person called. Record every message or call (date and time). Place in telephone box at Secretary's desk.

1971
Abbott, Merkt & Company
Procedural Manual

Each secretary should establish with her superior the manner in which he wishes his telephone calls handled. The general preference seems to be:
– When he is in his office, he will answer his calls;
– When he is in the office, but away from his desk, the telephone operator will page him over the loudspeaker;
– When he is out of the office, the secretary is responsible for his telephone calls and messages, unless he requests they be handled differently.

1974
Venturi and Rauch
Venturi and Rauch Handbook

Good telephone procedures and manners are important since they may be the way in which an outsider becomes acquainted with the firm. A courteous "Hello—Venturi and Rauch," and a polite "May I say who is calling?", prompt message taking and no long waits on "Hold" promote the image of the firm as an efficient business operation.

1986
Society of Architectural
Administrators
Handbook for Architectural
Administrators

Telephone courtesy demands listening carefully, answering politely, speaking clearly, and promptly handling each call. The caller on "HOLD" should receive frequent attention.

1999
The Society of
Design Administration
Handbook of Design
Office Administration

The person answering the phone leaves a big impression on the caller. This is one of the most important jobs and the least considered. Everyone in the firm should have training in telephone etiquette because insensitive telephone habits may result in a lost client.

2014
Employee Handbook

Cellular or portable phones should be off or on silent during working hours and are not to be used at your workspace unless your position requires it. While we understand they are a common communication tool, they are a disruption to our business.

2014
Employee Handbook

At the present time, the Firm will reimburse each eligible employee up to $90 for voice and data use each billing period. Additionally, the Firm will reimburse each eligible employee up to $100 every two years for the purchase of a new device.

5 — 1 TELEPHONE

The negotiation of telephony within the office space of architectural practice is especially intriguing as an interface between outside and inside, between time-based audio and the economy of inscription, between the volumetric (qua sound telephony is always a volume of vibrating air) and the two-dimensional (paper), between what was historically often male speaking and female audition.

In the fascinating archaeology of protocols governing the handling of the incoming call—greeting, registration, re-routing, etc.— one is struck, however, by the almost complete absence of the very technology whose express function was to manage that particular interface: the telephone answering machine. This is particularly curious given that the time period covered—loosely 1900–2014—is effectively synonymous with the lifespan of this now-largely-defunct apparatus. The latter date—marked by CocaCola's November 6, 2014 decision to eliminate voicemail throughout its entire organization (*Bloomberg News*, 22 December 2014)—is hardly astonishing. But the fact that telephone answering automation is not a product of the audio-cassette or even the reel-to-reel-tape era but dates back instead to the late nineteenth century is quite surprising indeed.

Barely two decades after Edison's 1877 cylinder phonograph that would go on to transform the production conditions of the office letter in the form of the Dictaphone, the Danish engineer Valdemar Poulsen (1869–1942) announced his latest invention in August 1898: the telegraphone. Presented to great acclaim at the Exposition Universelle in Paris in 1900 (where it won a gold medal and the praises of both Émile Zola and Kaiser Franz-Josef), the new device (known alternately as the recording telephone, telegraphophone, microphonograph or telephonograph) was able, according to the 1899 patent filing, to store speech electro-magnetically using a steel wire and later a steel disc. A huge improvement on the cylinder phonograph, the telegraphone enabled the capture of relatively long audio messages whose sound quality did not decay with repeated playback and whose erasure allowed for virtually endless subsequent inscriptions. Equally crucial, through its linkage to the then-still-relatively-new telephone, "a subscriber may thus receive messages which have been sent in his absence" (*Special Paris Correspondent of the Scientific American*, Poulsen Telegraphone, 22 September 1900, 181).

By 1903 the functional scenography of the office answering machine was fully in place, as confirmed by the following account of its ramifications: "The man of business who has to leave his office for a time simply places the telegraphone in its place and goes away. When he returns he finds that all the messages that have come for him have been recorded with absolute fidelity on the steel band and he has only to connect the telephone receiver to the instrument and hold the receiver to his ear to hear the words that have been spoken days or weeks before. Such records will be of great value, for at present, confusion and trouble have arisen from the fact that verbal messages or orders have to be relied upon. Besides it is often very inconvenient to leave one's work or interrupt an interview to attend to the telephone." (Herbert Fyfe, *Scientific American*, 25 April 1903, 317) Given the centrality of this device in office culture for much of the twentieth century, the minutia of its employment (or lack thereof) surely constitute another media-archaeological dimension of the history of professional architectural quotidianity. Thomas Y. Levin

5 — 2 CORRESPONDENCE

Nothing is more sure indication of the habits of a man of business than the management of his correspondence. Without ever having an interview with a person, a very complete insight can be informed into his business capabilities by correspondence. A good man of business will acknowledge the receipt of every letter the same day that it is received.

Whenever possible letters must be answered on day of receipt, otherwise they should be kept in mind and sight, and in all cases answered without unnecessary delay.

No letters should remain unanswered. If a full and complete answer cannot be given immediately, the responsible person should acknowledge receipt of the letter within at least three days, and reply in a more detailed manner as soon as possible.

All typing in this office is to be done on the computer. A rough copy is printed: corrections are made to this. It is edited on the computer and a final version is printed. The final copy is signed, copied, envelopes are addressed and it is mailed as per above section, MAIL.

Architects often do not excel at written communication. Perhaps because of their graphic and spatial reasoning skills, architects can find stringing words together into a coherent sentence a daunting task.

"Slang" should not be used in any written form of correspondence including email. While email is perceived as more casual, terms such as "Hey (name)" can be distracting to many, especially since emails are many times cc'd or forwarded.

5 — 2 CORRESPONDENCE

WEISS/MANFREDI "STATIONARY WARDROBE"

These correspondence protocols relate to the headings identified below. All information issued from the office is to be sent using standard office templates for Letters, Memorandum, Field Notes, RFI's, and other types of documents.

The purpose of these instruments of communication (including correspondence, telephone, voice and electronic mail "[e-mail]", all computer equipment, software, and the local and wide-area networks) is to facilitate transmittal of project-related information, and they are not to be used in a way that may be disruptive, offensive to others, or contrary to applicable legal requirements.

CORRESPONDENCE "HYGIENE"

All correspondence is public in nature; write accordingly. Appropriate correspondence hygiene includes following all physical and digital filing protocols.

What is in your head is not part of the filing system. What is on the top of your desk is not part of the filing system.

LETTERS AND MEMORANDUM

A letter should be used for any communication with the client and others including those not under contract to this firm, or for any correspondence of a serious or contractual nature with members of the design team. A Memorandum is to be used for intra-office communication / informational correspondence with other members of the design team (i.e. consultants).

If you need a closing and a signature, then you should be writing a letter, not a memo.

RESPONSE TO AN RFI (REQUEST FOR INFORMATION)

Be direct, succinct, and laconic. The less you can say and answer the question, the better it will be. Just answer the question. Reserve eloquence for presentations.

...

ARCHITECT'S FIELD NOTES

As with RFI responses, be direct, succinct, and laconic. Emotion and long explanations do not belong here.

EMAIL: INITIATED BY MEMBERS OF THE FIRM TO THOSE OUTSIDE THE OFFICE

Initiate emails to communicate everything that benefits from a written record and a written response. Copy only those that need to be aware of the correspondence; minimize copying everyone. All emails must maintain professional character and clarity.

As with RFI responses, be direct, succinct and, laconic. Emotion and long explanations do not belong here.

EMAIL: RESPONSE TO INCOMING EMAIL

Respond to all emails as soon as possible, ideally within twelve hours. Copy only those that need to be aware of the correspondence; excess copying to everyone generates unnecessary email traffic.

If email pin pong ensues over a challenging issue, stop sending emails and pick up the phone. Send a follow up email that restates conclusions from the call.

EMAIL: TO EVERYONE IN THE OFFICE

Communicate crucial information that must be shared with every member of the office such as conference room reservations for upcoming meetings, specifics of office wide events, new office wide protocols, excellent news, etc.

EMAIL: FROM INSIDE THE OFFICE TO AN INDIVIDUAL INSIDE THE OFFICE

Communicate crucial information that must be shared with one or two members of a team if it is not possible to convey the information in person.

Otherwise, get out of your chair, walk over to the individual, and talk to them! Marion Weiss

2001
The American
Institute of Architects
*The Architect's Handbook
of Architectural Practice,*
13th Edition

With so much hype centered on the Internet, it's little wonder some architects are confused about how this powerful information and communication tool can make their jobs easier. What is clear is that the Internet offers both quick, easy access to information and a reliable communication network.

2010

Employee Handbook

█████ may monitor usage of the Internet by employees, including reviewing a list of sites accessed by an individual. No individual should have any expectation of privacy in terms of his or her usage of the Internet. In addition, █████ may restrict access to certain sites that it deems are not necessary for business purposes.

2016

Employee Handbook

Some █████ employees are authorized to have user access to the Internet. Access to the Internet, World Wide Web, and bulletin boards systems are intended to be used primarily for business purposes.

2001

2010

194

2016

5 — 3 INTERNET

Access to the Internet began penetrating American architecture practices in the early 1990s. At the time, entree to the then-limited resources of the Web was considered a privilege, requiring special dial-up equipment. Even in those early days, before Google was a verb, concerns arose regarding the reliability of information made available mysteriously, and miraculously for free. Architects were confronted with a body of uncurated and unverified information. As technology evolved and the volume of content ballooned, some offices set up "Internet Access" stations as adjuncts to their sample and resource libraries. The stations had to be signed out and managed as a shared resource. The temptation to explore Internet content beyond the narrow boundaries of "architecture" content was overwhelming. There was simply too much out there to investigate and there is something particular to the human mind that sponsors an insatiable craving for information.

The next milestone of Internet penetration in architecture practices developed alongside the distribution of networked, desktop computers. This technology democratized and even anarchized internet access by making it available to everyone, all of the time. The policies on the facing page reflect the challenges faced by firm management (and by extension, human resources departments and risk-management attorneys) to place the burden of responsible use on the users. In the semi-public landscape of an office, it was possible for individuals to flaunt policy and explore content beyond what firm policies allowed. In this atmosphere, sophisticated firms added layers of automated protection to prevent access to problematic content, and began to track the internet activity of individual employees, and intercede when activity was inappropriate. These were generally ineffective as there was simply too much traffic to monitor and no staff with the skills to know what to monitor.

The issue of an employee's right to privacy as it relates to Internet access is also a factor in many office manuals. The approach of management is quite consistent: when an employee uses the firm's computer and communications system, the employee has no right to privacy. Her or his Internet activity can be reviewed by management, and content transmitted over a company's system can be intercepted and read. The hard line between what is an employee's private and protected information versus what is not is conceptually clear, but becomes immensely complicated by human nature and contemporary technology. An employee's personal iPhone is often their home phone, their business phone, their personal and company email handler, and their personal and company web browser. Has an employee who gambles online committed a policy violation when placing a bet transmitted over office WiFi, but not violated company policy if they step out of the office at lunch time and place the bet over a public mobile network like AT&T or Verizon? The answer is probably yes, if the phone belongs to the employee and they pay the monthly charges.

...

Distinguishing between personal and company information traffic is not something employees easily do, and the technology is intentionally designed to make the lines of demarcation invisible. This has rendered most Internet use policies ineffective as determinants of behavior, however useful they may be as a means to shift liability for inappropriate behavior from employers to employees.

Interestingly, Internet policies have a lot to say about what not to do, and very little to say about beneficial use of the Internet as part of professional practice. It is only recently that a young generation of technically adept architects has entered the field—people for whom the Internet was always there, people who cannot remember actually learning how to use it. Don Weinreich

5 — 4 ELECTRICAL OUTLETS

The circuits in the studio and in most offices are being drawn to full capacity. Please do not plug anything besides your computer and luxo lamps into the electrical outlets by your desks. Only the outlets found on the main corridors throughout the office should be used for vacuums, photography lamps, etc.

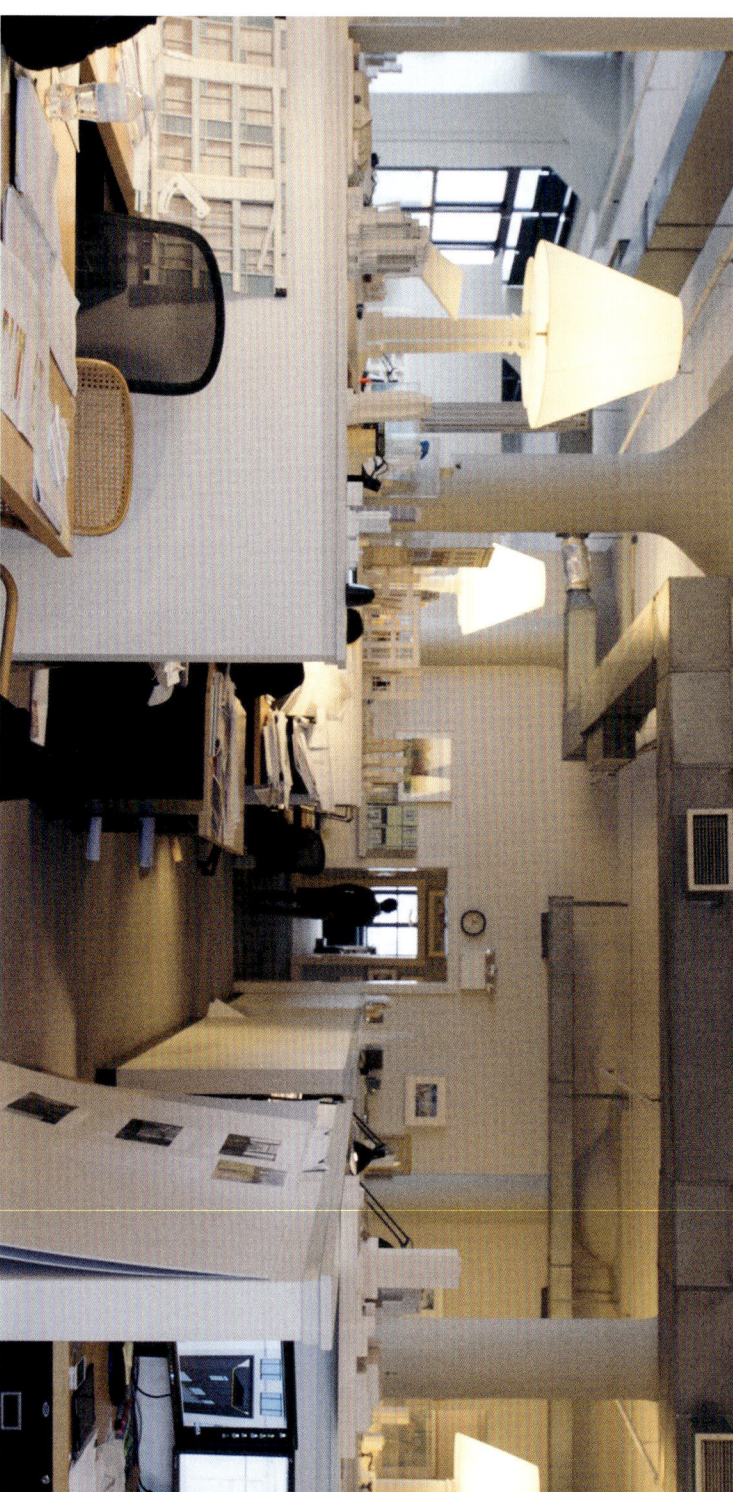

5 — 4 ELECTRICAL OUTLETS

Begin by dispensing with the overwhelming but obvious: for those with the privilege of being cared for by one or another highly developed society, to "plug in" is an action of profoundly ingrained habit. For something to be as easy as "turning on a light switch" is for that action to be evacuated of thought—for it to be an automatic, unrecounted act. Seventy-nine years ago, George Orwell described an analogous disconnect between the user and the used in *The Road to Wigan Pier*—"Down there where coal is dug it is a sort of world apart which one can quite easily go through life without ever hearing about…Yet it is the absolutely necessary counterpart of our world above. Practically everything we do, from eating an ice to crossing the Atlantic, and from baking a loaf to writing a novel, involves the use of coal, directly or indirectly."

This specter that lies beneath and throughout our world has only grown ravenously. And if electricity is a specter, its apparition is the electrical outlet. There is no clear origin of the electrical outlet as we know it today, though two-pin plug and sockets first appeared in England in the 1880s. It would take many decades for the form to be standardized, however, and before that happened homeowners looking to power an appliance often had to find a spare light socket or were even forced to displace a light bulb already in use. In his 1986 article on "Domestic Electrical Plugs and Receptacles, 1881–1931," Fred E. H. Schroeder quotes from a 1925 article from *Good Housekeeping* that asks its reader: "When you want to use your electric toaster in the morning, do you have to unscrew a lamp from some lighting fixture to secure an outlet convenient to the table? When you wish to use the vacuum cleaner in your bedroom, do you have to connect to a wall fixture and have the cord dangling across the dresser or table?" As Schroeder writes, excerpts like this one provide "pictures of a reality that is otherwise forgotten or suppressed."

Today, it is electricity, itself, that is forgotten and suppressed. The architectural office is but a small piece of the large society that floats on these ceaseless electric currents; the office's interior spatial patterns are limned by the outlets that limit the spatial arrangement of its servers and monitors, its employees' desk lamps and phone chargers. In much the same way, the city is haunted by the paths and capacities of electrical mains, lines which determine its development more than most well-intentioned urban planning precepts.

Amidst this immense system, the outlet has a minuscule, if essential, presence. Architecture, too, and architectural practice are inextricable from electricity, resting upon it with the rest of our well-tempered dailiness. Aleksandr Bierig

5 — 5 PRINTING AND COPYING

1922
McKim, Mead & White
Manual of Office Practice

Printing of descriptive notes should be carefully done, using letters standardized for the job, 1/8" high for room or space-names, smaller for notes. Place properly to give maximum legibility. Avoid duplication.

1968
Harry Weese and Associates
Design Standards

Wherever possible, 8 1/2 × 11 format for Xerox is to be followed, Xerox is the most efficient, flexible, and authoritative mediums for all uses. It is immediately available, easily altered, lends itself to filing and binding. It is one of our standard formats.

1971
Abbott, Merkt & Company
Procedural Manual

VERIFAX, THERMOFAX and RECORDAK machines are located in the mailroom for reproduction purposes. The same procedure as that for duplicating should be followed in completing the STATIONERY and DUPLICATING REQUISITION. As in the case of duplicating, all material to be reproduced must be done by the mailroom employees.

2014
*The Project
Management Manual*

Printing and copying charges are recorded electronically by project number.

1922

1968
1971

2014

5 — 5 PRINTING AND COPYING

Think before you print. Please consider our environment—ecological, political, and social—before printing. Careful and efficient contemplation of the reproduction of the digital and its conversion to the analog will save paper.

The act of physical reproduction is an act of producing, performing, and consuming waste. To reduce waste, please recycle spent ink and toner cartridges. Environmentally preferable ink and toner cartridges include reman-ufactured and high-yield cartridges. High-yield cartridges usually contain about twice as much ink and toner as an equivalent standard-yield cartridge, which translates into more printed pages per cartridge. Reusing cartridges cuts waste disposal at landfills and saves energy. Less energy is used to produce remanu-factured cartridges than to create new ones.

Please consider the value of aura before printing or copying. To what degree is the original enhanced or compromised by the 8½ × 11-inch facsimile? The 1976 Copyright Act, a by-product of modernity, presents a benchmark by which to protect authenticity and the identity (authorial and economic) of the maker. For copying to fall under the category of fair use, it must meet the tests of brevity and spontaneity. Consider our environment and saving our trees. Print double sided whenever possible.

Although imitation is the highest form of flattery, copying should not be used to create, replace, or substitute for anthologies, monographs, compi-lations, or collective works. Acts of homage, quotation, or sampling must meet criteria for fair use and/or satire or parody, see Campbell v. Acuff-Rose Music, Inc., 510 U.S. 569, 580 (1994).

You are encouraged to only print when absolutely necessary. Mimi Zeiger

Each drawing is numbered and recorded in a register kept for the purpose, in which are entered the date description and scale; and when a blueprint is issued a similar record is made of it in another book. These records are kept by a clerk who has charge of a special room called the "Record Room" in which all drawings are stored. […]
The necessity of this system will be seen when it is understood that the number of drawings on file now exceeds 18,000 accumulated during 14 years.

Originals of all working drawings except full sizes on Manilla paper, tracings of all such full sizes, copies of all sketches, and photographs of competition drawings, must be kept for office record, and so filed.

The filing department has charge of all letters and contracts, the recording of all incoming and outgoing blueprints, specifications, samples, etc. Only the file clerk shall have access to the files.

You will notice that the left side of the form is for INCOMING action, and the right side is for OUTGOING action.

We will gradually all learn how to use this form better and better, as we apply it to all the different circumstances, and suggestions are most welcome. The goal is to keep the records clear—but it's simple, rather than complicated or confusing.

The most common way to organize project information is to assign a job number for each project or commission and to use it on all documents and drawings as recommended by <u>The AIA Handbook</u>. The most common numbering systems are straight numerical sequence or a combination of the year the project began plus a numerical sequence for the individual year's work.

File Daily—preferably as you go—or at regular intervals. An established routine will make better use of time. If the paperwork stacks up, it will mean sorting, organizing into the appropriate chronological order, and then actually filing the papers.

The ▮▮▮ server has 4 main drives: Office, Proposal, Project and FTP. Every Project in the studio must have a Project Folder in the Project Drive (P:) which contains files of all project related correspondence, drawings, schedules, technical documents and written texts. The Project Folder should be labeled with the Project Number and its structure should be organized by the following subfolders: 3D Model, Drawing Set, Milestone Drawings, Photos, Presentation, Project Notebook, Research, Sketches and Transmit. The Project Folder is a dynamic record, material is added to it, but never deleted.

5 — 6 FILING SYSTEM

A filing system is a repository of an office's ideas, so how do you organize it?
The question is fundamentally historical if you ask: by what means have offices
organized their output in order to have easy access to specific pieces of
their past work? But it can also be asked more theoretically, touching on the
way that well organized ideas begin to give an identity to offices over time.
If SOM is to some extent identified with curtain walls and office buildings, then
the office building as a typology and the curtain wall as a piece of architectural
engineering, in their various iterations over time, should be accessible within
the files and understandable as comprehensible ideas from within that database.
Gaining and storing this sort of embedded identity is important for passing
office knowledge from one generation of employees to the next, and for codify-
ing an office's capabilities and disciplinary expertise in ways that produce a
clear image for potential clients. The device through which an identity is established and propagated through an ever-changing staff of designers can take
many forms but it needs to be accessible, open source, more of a public gallery
than a sealed container.

Eventually Acconci Studio will face the same question faced by every
office after a period of time: can the entity outlive the individual? While some
offices have no intention of life beyond their founders, for those that do,
establishing a viable corporate brand requires two independent attributes: a
successful operating structure and a successful identity. Like a combination
litmus test and catalyst, the humble filing system—the record of an office's
ideas and the bookkeeper of its identity—is very much the result of the former
and a necessity for the latter. Nicholas McDermott

The development of filing systems, as universal tools of organization,
is crucial to the emergence of larger and more geographically disparate offices.
Like the growth of a firm's files over time, the importance of storing and filing
increases proportionally with an office's complexity and output. As an office
grows, management becomes more necessary, hierarchies increase, and the
organization of information becomes trickier. Having more employees means
that office knowledge needs to be distributed more broadly and that there
is more potential knowledge to organize. Filing systems sit at the center of this
input-output cycle. As architects store drawings, sketches, models, project
manuals, material samples, product literature, communications, and other
paraphernalia, the artifacts add up to form a picture of the office over time.

Recently I had the chance to rifle through a portion of Vito Acconci's files.
The evolution of the artistic and architectural work was present in the chronolog-
ically arranged documents. The big shift between a first career as a solo artist
and the establishment of the design office Acconci Studio is there embedded in
the ephemera, as is the growth and development of the latter. The natural incon-
sistency of this unedited filing system (successful projects next to unsuccessful
ones, computer prints beside hand sketches, presentation material mixed
among drafts) is somewhat smoothed out by the basic consistency of the ideas.
Acconci's instinctive working maneuvers and fundamental preoccupations
are evident everywhere in this gradually accruing selection of work. Modes of
production and materials change, but over time Acconci becomes more
Acconci as the filed material gangs together to form a "professional" identity.

Eventually Acconci Studio will face the same question faced by every
office after a period of time: can the entity outlive the individual? While some
offices have no intention of life beyond their founders, for those that do,
establishing a viable corporate brand requires two independent attributes: a
successful operating structure and a successful identity. Like a combination
litmus test and catalyst, the humble filing system—the record of an office's
ideas and the bookkeeper of its identity—is very much the result of the former
and a necessity for the latter. Nicholas McDermott

1901
Kaye W. Perry
Office Management;
A Handbook for Architects
and Civil Engineers

For present purposes it is sufficient here to say that each separate work, whether large or small, is distinguished by a number. These numbers are consecutive, and as each fresh commission originates in the office, whether by verbal instruction or by letter, the work is entered and given the next consecutive number, and is thereafter known as "Work No.-"

1920
Frank Miles Day
The American
Institute of Architects
The Handbook of
Architectural Practice

1 to 99 may be plans, elevations, sections,
100 to 199 scale details,
200 to 299 structural engineering,
300 to 399 mechanical plan, heating, ventilation,
400 to 499 electrical engineering,
500 to 599 full size details,
600 to 699 shop drawings.

1967
Morris Lapidus
Architecture, a Profession
and a Business

Wherever possible, sketches are to be numbered in sequence, with job number and date. Drawing numbers shall be SKD-1, SKD-2, etc.

2008
The American Institute
of Architects
The Architect's Handbook
of Architectural Practice,
14th Edition

The National CAD Standard Sheet identification system combines a discipline designator, sheet type designator, and sheet sequence number to create a sheet identifier, as follows: AS (Discipline), 1 (Sheet type), 01 (Sheet sequence). The file-naming convention for this drawing might be expressed as T: \ 06053 \Drawings \AS-101.dwg

2014

An Architecture
Office Manual

Year-Month-Day—This date of document method (2005-02-08) ensures the correspondence will be in chronological order when scrolling within each source and using two spaces for Month and Day will keep your files aligned so that scrolling is easier to read.

1901

1920

1967

2008

2014

1
André Leroi-Gourhan, *Gesture and Speech* (Cambridge: MIT Press, 1993), 195.

2
Vilém Flusser, *Does Writing Have a Future?* (Minneapolis: University of Minnesota Press, 2011), 12.

3
Ibid., 12.

5 — 7 FILE NAMING

Both "the file" and "the name" belong to the dawn of the Orthographic Age, during the early stages of which, "the invention of writing, through the device of linearity, completely subordinated graphic to phonetic expression."[1] In that moment, a kind of prehistorical tooling—filing as *rasping*; as "filing down" stones with harder stones—found new expression in alphanumeric abstraction: filing as *inscription in stone*. To "inscribe" was to "inform" by digging forms (glyphs, proto-words) into matter; "a gesture of digging into an object with something, so making use of a tool."[2] Here, the file was a lithic instrument, both for making new digging-writing tools (sharpening, lapping, honing: perfecting the awl-become-chisel), and for ensuring the visual legibility of the labori-ously inscribed alphanumeric matter-code (abrading, chamfering, polishing: perfecting the textual-historical record). In that code, an ageless oral proclivity towards sounding out the contents of the world was transformed from mytho-graphic ambiguity into proto-conceptual phonetic precision: literacy. Was "the name," for its ability to sort the world into subjects and objects—for having allowed an animal to name itself Man—the first concept in History? We can never know.

  Filing and naming. That we should even care about the obscure anthro-potechnical origins of such mundane activities is justified by the realization that our thought is absolutely inseparable from our technics (that these are merely two different words for the same reality) and that "although *to inform* originally meant 'to dig forms into something,' it has taken on a whole series of additional meanings in the present."[3] And so we must now ask what it means to undertake filing and naming in the so-called Information Age.

  If various means of hand-mechanical writing governed the practices of filing and naming for millennia, it is certain this is no longer the case. The electronic screen belongs to the technical genealogy of image-message trans-mission—telegraphy and telemetry—in which life and its contents are reduced ("compressed") into discrete electrical charges handled by an apparatus

...

agnostic to their semiotic content. Signalization replaces signification as the primary epistemic mortar in all reasoning and imagining, and the linear time of textual inscription is replaced by the real time technics of electrical control engineering. A new, numero-alpha code is installed, anterior to the syntactical alphanumerism of orthography, arranging the preconditions for an entirely new technics of automation. "Writing" becomes a concept at war with itself, unsure if what it was (digging, inscribing) bears any sensible relation to what it has become ("word processing"). Like all other words, filing and naming are swept up in this conflict, not knowing if, as words, they still contain the capacity to describe the realities they are meant to explain.

Unlike the linear historical time of hand-mechanical informing (digging-writing), which gradually became obsessed with inscribing a record of the past as a way of perfecting the future (*progress*), the real time of electrical informing aims to eliminate completely the gap between past and future as a way of managing the present (*probabilism*). That gap was the home of all textu-al-conceptual thought, of all philosophy, all history, all politics and literature. In its place now is an uncertain terrain whose true geology is not meaning but management, where the naming of files has replaced the filing of names. John May

5 — 8 DRAWINGS

Even the unmethodical architect generally has something approaching a system for his drawings. They are the objects of his affectionate care, perhaps many of them the work of his own hands. Here, he feels himself in his element, and even if he has not elaborated a good system, he can generally put his hand on the drawing which he wants.

Drawings are primarily intended as a guide for construction. In the field, conditions are seldom favorable for extended or intensive study of the intent of a drawing, and scaling is done with a two-foot rule. Drawings should be clear, accurate and fully descriptive of the work to be done.

The natural tendency of the draftsman to make drawings which are pictures of what will be visible where the work is done, sometimes results in neglect of the intent that a working drawing should be a means and not an end.

Make your drawings to a uniform size where possible and always to an economical blueprint size

Don't overembellish the drawings—keep them as clean as possible. Bear them on your pencil—let's have some good dense prints.

Materials indications are a necessary (if sometimes tedious) part of working drawings. This "poché" is used to make the extent and relationships among various materials readily discernible.

Drawings associated with design and construction communicate in two different ways:

1. As general indication to show what a building will look like, or what being in spaces might feel like: experiential presentation drawings.

2. As a detailed explanation of how the building's parts are arranged and constructed: scaled working drawings.

Use blocks as much as possible. Make sure to draw the block's contents on layer 0 only.

208

5 — 8 DRAWINGS

MODELING

Building Information Modeling (BIM) is fundamentally different from its precursor Computer Aided Design (CAD, which here refers to both 2D drafting and 3D modeling). In CAD, a designer forms representational geometry from unbiased lines, polygons, NURBS, etc. In BIM, designers assemble highly specific components parameterized to "behave" like their real world counterparts. While CAD users are constrained only by the rules of geometry, BIM users interact with multiple constraints that differ for each object type.

PROCESS

The CAD workflow yields different products than BIM. CAD delivers geometrically rich, data poor, single purpose models. Within the larger workflow deliverables are effectively separate from and developed parallel to other deliverables. Thus, a model for renderings apart from CAD files for drawings apart from a model for solar analysis. Parallel processes tend to result in redundant labor and a lack of coordination across products.

      BIM uses an integrated process. A model (or pool of interlinked models) is the single source for visualizations, drawings, and analysis. Rather than a series of parallel efforts in separate files, all efforts occur within one place from which separate products are extracted. Integrated processes are complex (objects must meet multiple criteria) and require rigorous planning. Not coincidentally an entire discipline of systematic BIM Execution Planning (BEP) has evolved alongside BIM.

SHARING

CAD precludes direct collaboration by limiting file-write access to one user at a time—everyone else has read-only access. BIM resolved the read/write access limitation early in its development allowing a model to have multiple writers interacting in real time. Recent advances in cloud hosting models have extended collaboration outside the office and to other disciplines.

      Now, technological barriers are down, leaving only the barriers of contracts, liability, and culture. Contracts and liability concerns can be mollified through advanced (Integrated Project Delivery) as well basic instruments (electronic data release forms). Culture is more tenacious, because radical collaboration problematizes current ideas about design ownership and designer autonomy.

NEW IDEAS FOR OLD THINGS

As a disruptive technology BIM is not really replacing established practices. Instead, BIM comes to design with clear principles that push designers to think critically about how they work. The next questions are not, "Why does BIM need this: constraints, BEP, interdisciplinary collaboration, etc.?" but "Why was I not doing this before?" and "Can I apply this to anything else?" Pierce Reynoldson

Kitchen: The kitchen is for all staff use only under the provision that anyone who turns on the stove must remain in the kitchen area (2nd floor only) until the stove is turned off.

Coffee or tea will be allowed in the office provided that any beverage be transferred into a ceramic mug. Soft drinks in non-paper containers will be allowed at any time. Provided that drawings are removed and filed away and a protective covering is placed on the desk, breakfast may be eaten at one's desk prior to 8:30 A.M. and lunch may be eaten at one's desk during the regular lunch hour.

Employee lunches, if brought in, must be taken in the lunchroom. Food, with the exception of coffee and cookies, is not permitted in the drafting room.

Deliveries arrive on Monday and Thursday mornings and are intended to provide beverages throughout the day and as snacks for late nights and weekends. Be considerate of what and how much you take. The cupboards are not bottomless. There is no excuse for hoarding food. Be considerate of the people after you as they will not be able to partake until the next scheduled FreshDirect order is delivered.

Every other Monday Lunch is provided by the office and this is when the office meeting takes place. Otherwise, you are responsible for feeding yourself. You can use available space in the fridge to store your food.

5 — 9 FOOD

Food in the workplace has often been misunderstood and seen as counterproductive. As every other aspect of office life had been measured, standardized, and calibrated, food was perceived as foreign. As such, it had to be regimented and contained within designated hours and designated mugs, framed by strict policies.

Recently, as research has questioned the efficiency of such work environments, and technological advances have made working and collaborating possible from anywhere and in any configuration, a new kind of deconstructed office typology is emerging, one structured around food and the kitchen.

Food is the software of an office. It connects or isolates its employees, stimulates them or makes them drowsy, inspires them or numbs their minds. Food can also crash, spill, damage precious hardware, and may contain viruses. Organizations and individuals alike must be mindful of what they ingest but must also make themselves occasionally vulnerable, open to new experiences and possibilities, allowing for the intermittent delay and intoxication that food can provide. In the new corporate environment, taking calculated risks is becoming key to success and innovation.

A redefinition of the very nature of the office is at the heart of its shift in appreciation of food. As employees are no longer understood as gears in a machine, but as fertile soil for cultivation, food becomes a cherished source of nutrients and inspiration. Moving away from rigid guidelines and hierarchical office layouts, the celebration of food's importance in the workplace disrupts and revitalizes it in the best possible way. Creativity, chance encounters, and fluid structures are encouraged by diverse and healthy foods in collaborative settings. The cafeteria is becoming the new lab, where exchanges of ideas take place as they germinate, are composed, get seasoned and digested. Savinien Caracostea

1977
Robert Koehler,
The American Institute
of Architects
*Personnel Practices
Handbook*

Adjustments to thermostats and dampers can be made only by authorized personnel. Indiscriminate adjustments cause the heating and air conditioning system to become inoperative.

2014

*An Architecture
Office Manual*

It is difficult to balance the temperature throughout the office and almost impossible to create a climate to satisfy everyone. If you experience great discomfort as a result of the temperature in the office, please notify the office manager.

2014

Employee Handbook

█████████████ is a fragrance-free workplace. Please refrain from wearing products with perfumes or fragrances of any kind.

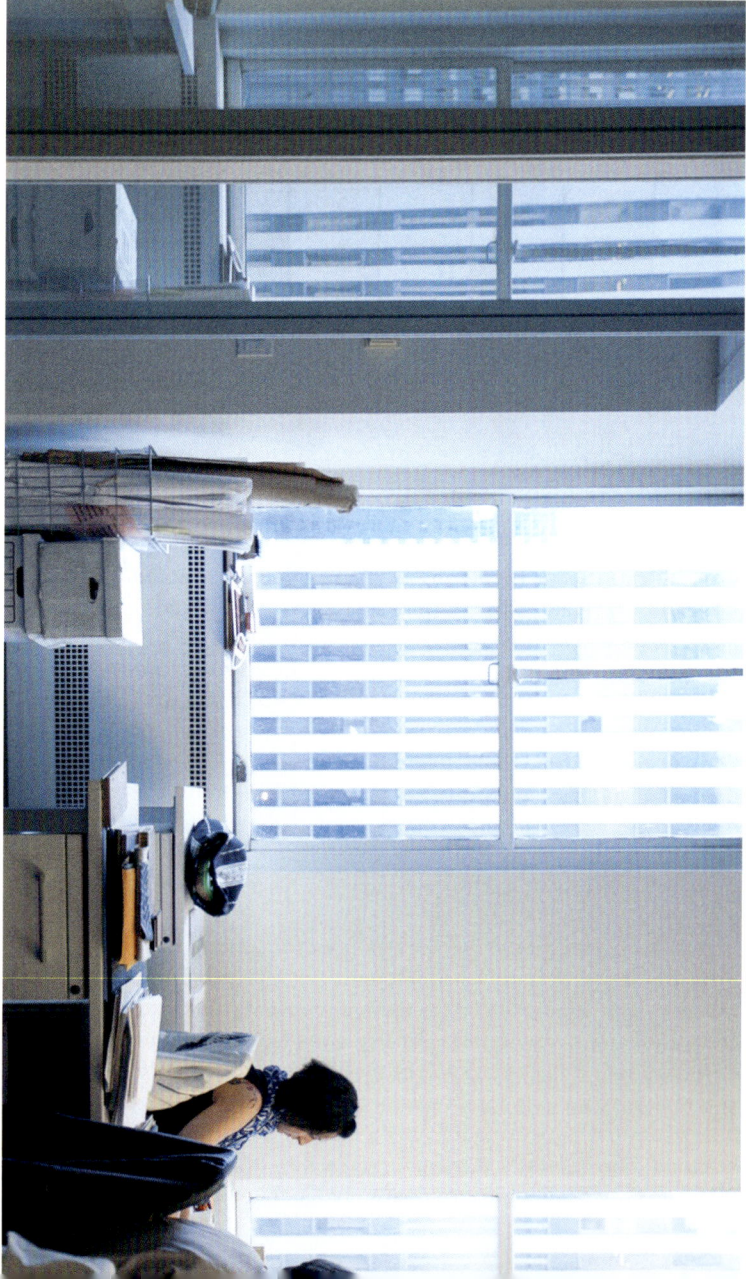

1977

2014

5 — 10 TEMPERATURE AND VENTILATION

The modern architecture office is where manufactured weather has been designed as well as implemented, serving roles as both research laboratory and project site. Over the past one hundred years—the first century of air conditioning—architecture offices have propagated and been subjected to one of the principal myths of modernism.

      The modernist myth of indoor comfort has been based on the idealized standards of temperature and ventilation. As the practice of architecture has become increasingly global, these ideals of indoor comfort have become universal. The standard of comfort in a corporate architecture office in New York City is often the same as its satellite office in Dubai, despite local differences in climate, clothing, social norms, and especially physiological differences such as gender. This ignores the subjectivity—and the need for differentiated micro-climates—which the contemporary office demands.

      The modernist myth of the universality of indoor comfort began in research experiments conducted in environmental chambers at Harvard University. In 1936, Constantin Yaglou and his associates created an environment in which two rooms of identical dimensions were built, one "clean" while the other was "dirty." Subjects would be led into the "clean" chamber, ventilated at 50 cfm, to precondition their noses before entering a "dirty" chamber. In this chamber, the subject would join varying numbers of occupants of different levels of hygiene. The ventilation air flow of this room would be between 2 to 30 cfm, to either allow for or eliminate personal odor detection. The subject would sniff the air in the "dirty" chamber and render a judgment on the strength of the odor.

      The occupants were selected to represent a range of workplace employ-ees typical in the 1930s—from office workers to laborers—each from different socioeconomic classes with various levels of personal hygiene. Yaglou, who was a professor of hygiene and not physiology, determined that lower tempera-tures would help to eliminate the detection of personal odor scents. He found that at a temperature of sixty-eight degrees Fahrenheit and 20 cfm per person, personal odors would be difficult to be detected. The relegation of thermal comfort as a product of using ventilation to eliminate odor was intrinsic to his comfort zone chart, which would eventually become ASHVE's (now ASHRAE) psychometric chart.

      Thus, the research that led to the psychometric chart did not originate with thermal comfort. Instead, it was based on modernist architects' call to design workplaces that would fit many middle class office workers close toge-ther in an odor-free environment, much like the offices that they worked in themselves. The definition of the comfort zone is inextricably linked to the sub-jectivity of olfactory response. Yaglou's experiments were based on the olfactory response of a limited sampling of 1930's middle class males that did

...

not account for the subjectivity of a different gender, social class, or ethnic group. The nameless "phantom workers" that haunt the psychometric chart have determined a century of thermal comfort in the workplace.

Architecture offices today still adopt these "phantom workers" comfort standards, despite vast social differences that are a result of the globalized workplace. For example, today's workplace involves much less odor-producing physical labor. Also, women in the contemporary workplace have different levels of personal odors, as well as metabolic rates 20 percent to 30 percent lower than men, which require less air conditioning. These are some of the differences that call for differentiated subjectivity in the definition of indoor comfort, allowing for micro-climatic zones that allow for global differences in the definition of work, climate, and physiology. Phu Hoang

1988
Emery, Roth & Sons,
P.C. Architects
Office Guidelines

There will be NO SMOKING allowed in this office at any time, day or night, other than in conference rooms #1 and #3. No one shall leave this office, during working hours, to go outside the building to have a smoke.

1990
Cannon Design
Office Protocol

A mutually comfortable environment for employees depends upon the thoughtfulness and cooperation of both smokers and nonsmokers.

The company wishes to provide and maintain a healthful and clean working environment. The company is not required to provide a "smoke free" environment and does not attempt to ban smoking entirely. Rather we hope to promote an awareness of the concerns of non-smokers among those who do smoke, asking that they be considerate of those who find proximity to smoke objectionable. Although we believe that the spirit of thoughtfulness and cooperation characteristic of our staff is normally adequate to resolve any disputes which might arise under this policy, it is part of this philosophy that where disputes cannot be so resolved, then the rights of the nonsmoker will be given precedence.

1991
SLR/Architects
Office Manual

Smoking within the office confines or in the lunchroom is strictly prohibited.

2014
███ *Employee Handbook*

To provide a healthy and productive workplace for all employees, ███ enforces a smoke-free environment. No smoking of any kind is permitted on firm premises or in the public areas of our buildings, including private offices, hallways, restrooms, elevators, conference rooms, and all service, reception and common areas.

5 — 11 SMOKING

The way policies on smoking in the workplace have recently evolved presents a clear manifestation of how subtle forms of fascism have come to define the corporate world. What was once the countenance of deep ideological battles has pervaded the office under the guise of political correctness.

I'm not a smoker, and I do not enjoy secondhand smoking. However, whenever I see a flock of smokers crowding a glass box, I can't but think that this is a new, exquisite typology of concentration camp. People whom corporations have driven to addiction are displayed as if earmarked for execution by cancer. As it was always the case, uncontained fascist instincts surface in the way the strong-willed parade their dominion over the weak.

And then there's the baby that sinks with the bath water. Without the whimsical pause created by smoking, would certain creative impulses have ever emerged? Would architects like Álvaro Siza have ever enjoyed the self-determination to reveal their genius? Pedro Gadanho

ORDER

ALBERT KAHN - 1918
13450 ft²

ice Space

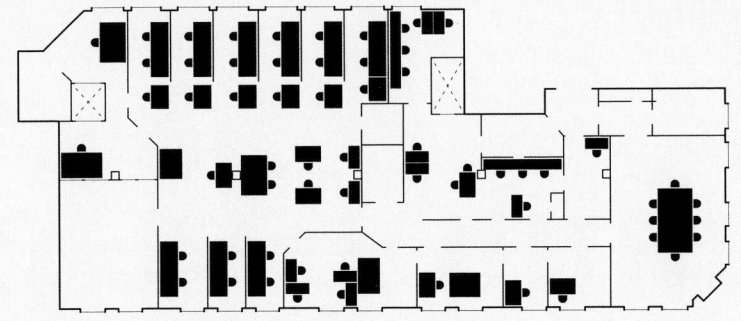

Burnham & Root
Chicago, c. 1890

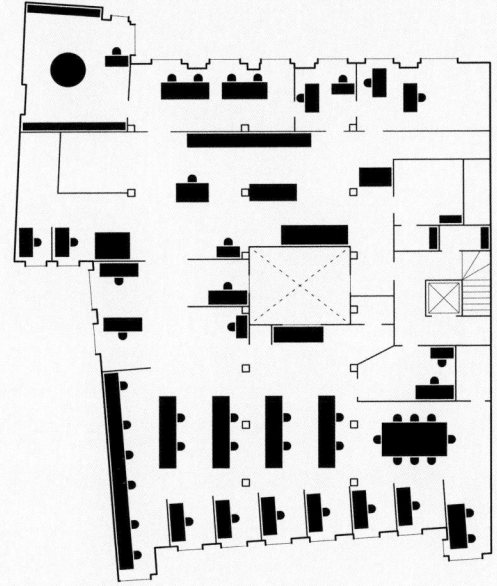

Shepley, Rutan and Coolidge
Boston, c. 1890

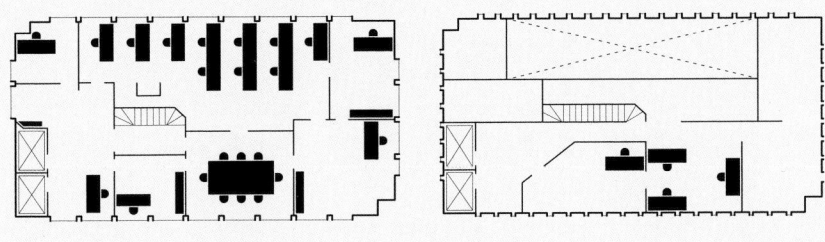

Floor 1

Floor 2

Adler & Sullivan
Chicago, c. 1890

0' 4' 8'   16'   32'

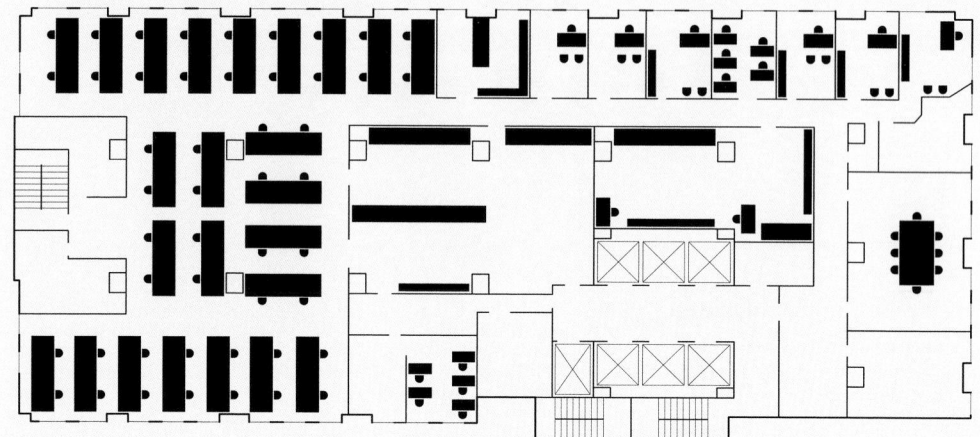

McKim, Mead & White
New York City, c. 1914

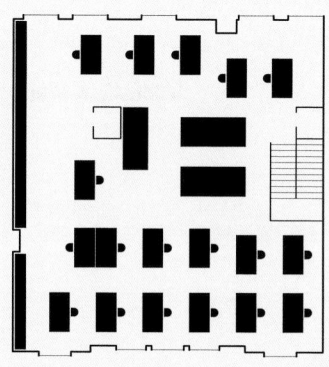

Perkins, Fellows & Hamilton
Chicago, c. 1917

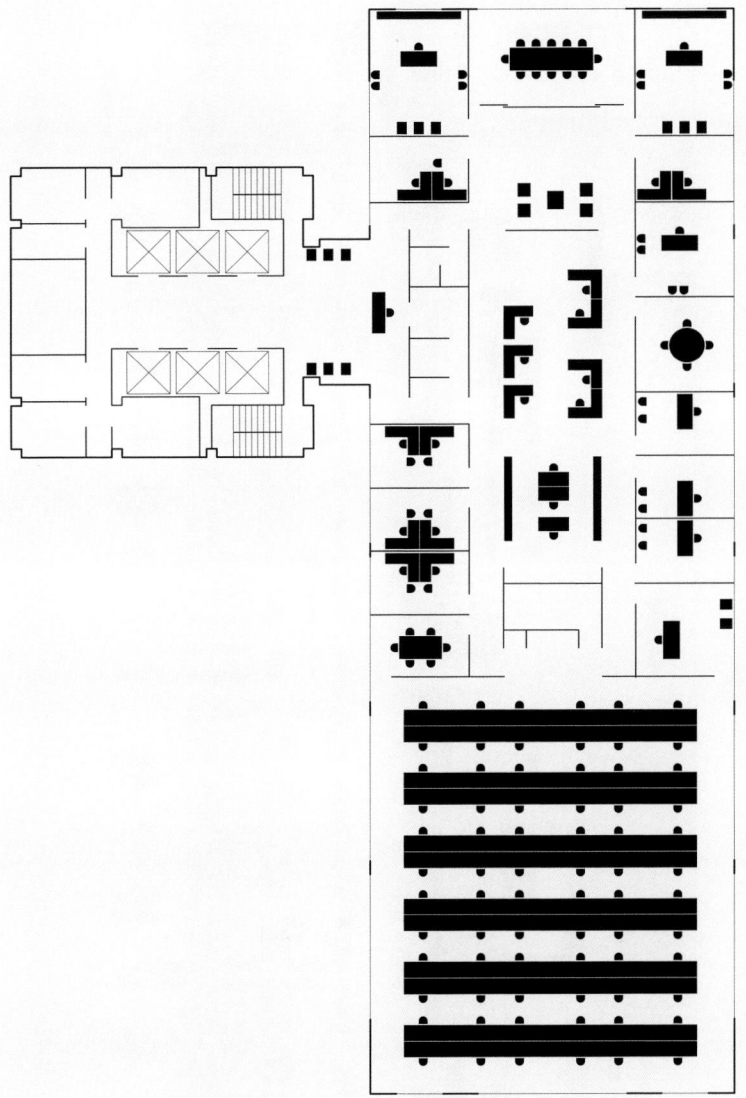

Skidmore, Owings & Merrill
Chicago, c. 1959

0' 4' 8'   16'   32'

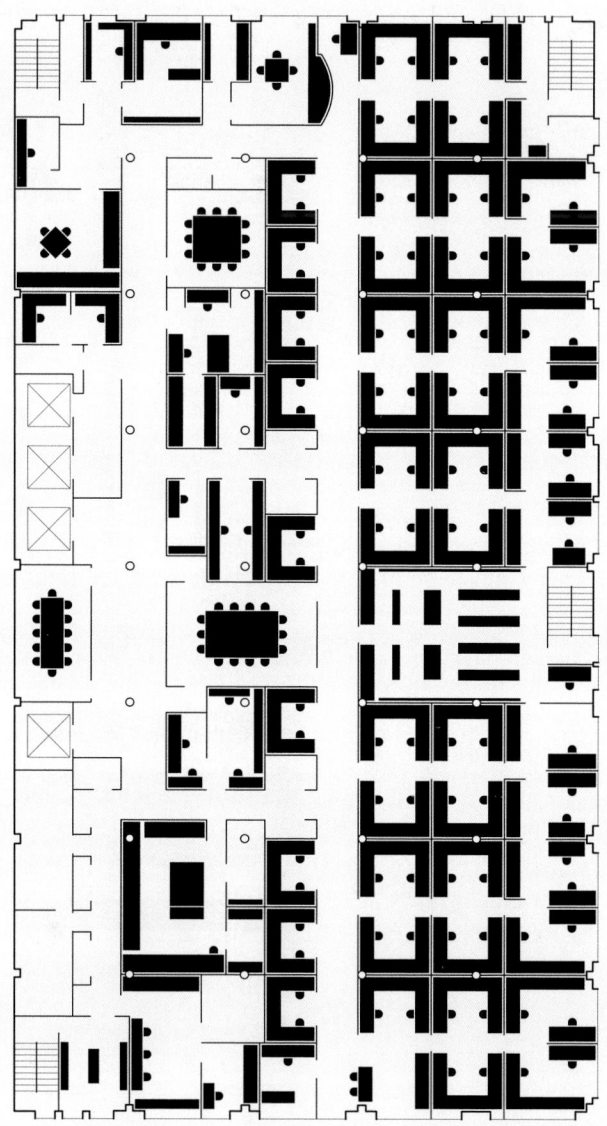

James Stewart Polshek and Partners
New York City, c. 1985

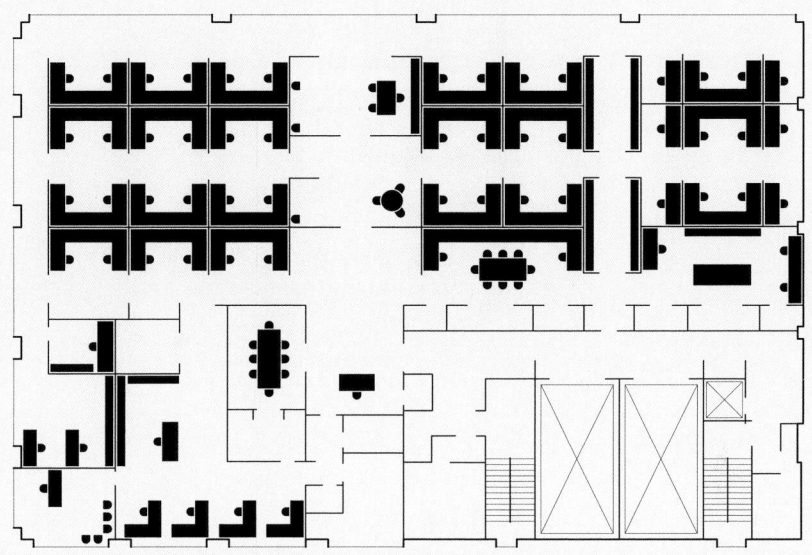

Robert A.M. Stern Architects
New York City, c. 1985

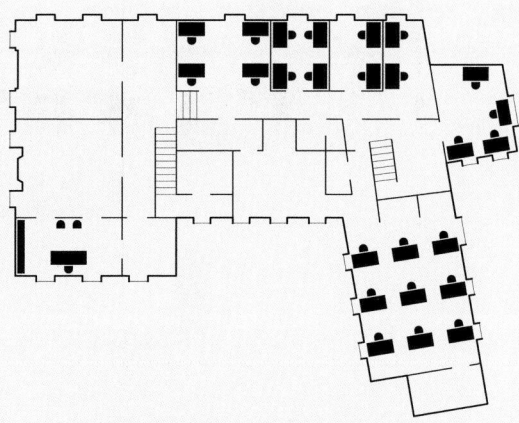

Michael Graves & Associates
Princeton, c. 1989

0' 4' 8'   16'   32'

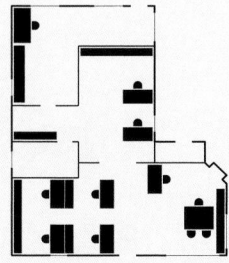

Bohlin, Cywinski Jackson
Seattle, c. 1991

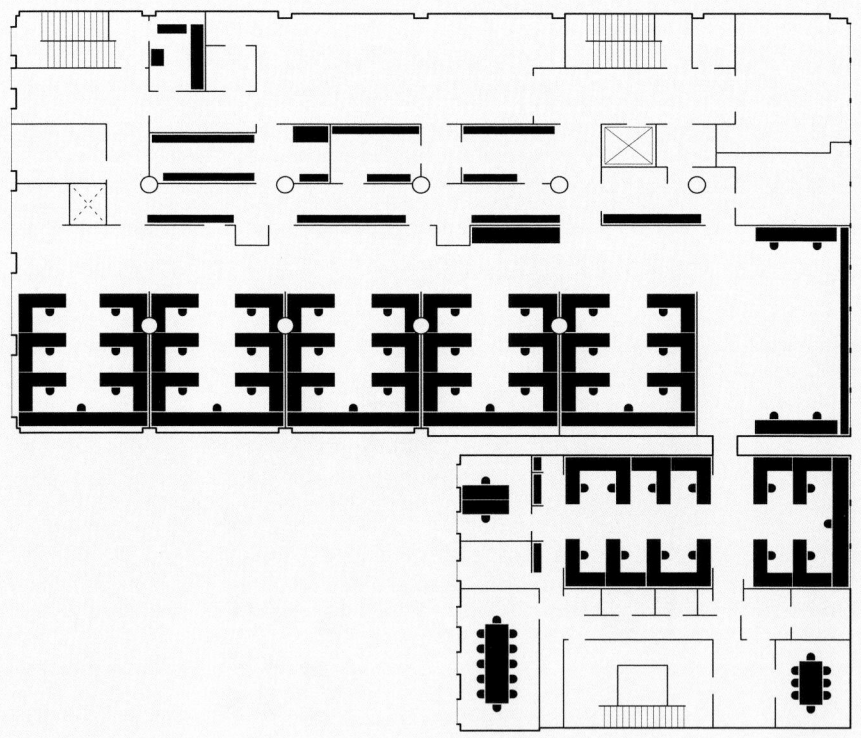

Koetter Kim & Associates
Boston, c. 2006

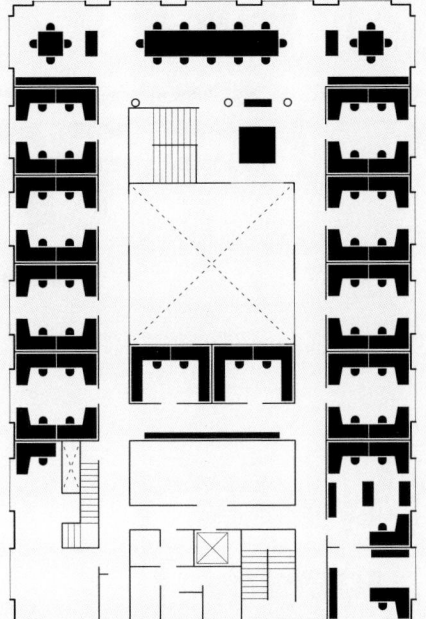

Floor 2

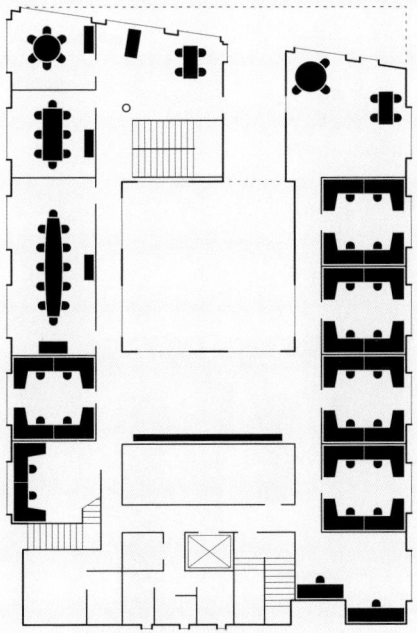

Floor 1

Arquitectonica
Miami, c. 2010

0' 4' 8'   16'   32'

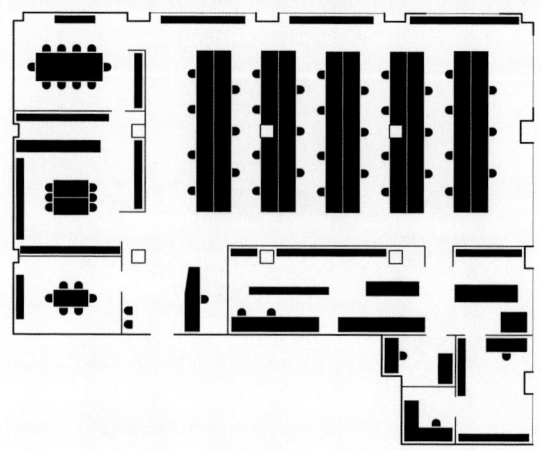

Gluckman Mayner Architects
New York City, c. 2010

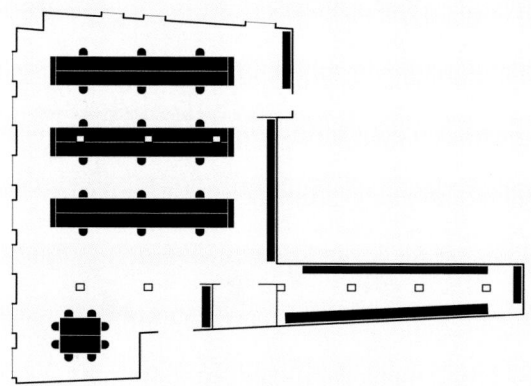

Toshiko Mori Architect
New York City, c. 2014

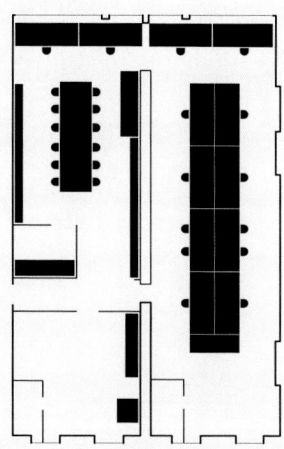

RUR
New York City, c. 2014

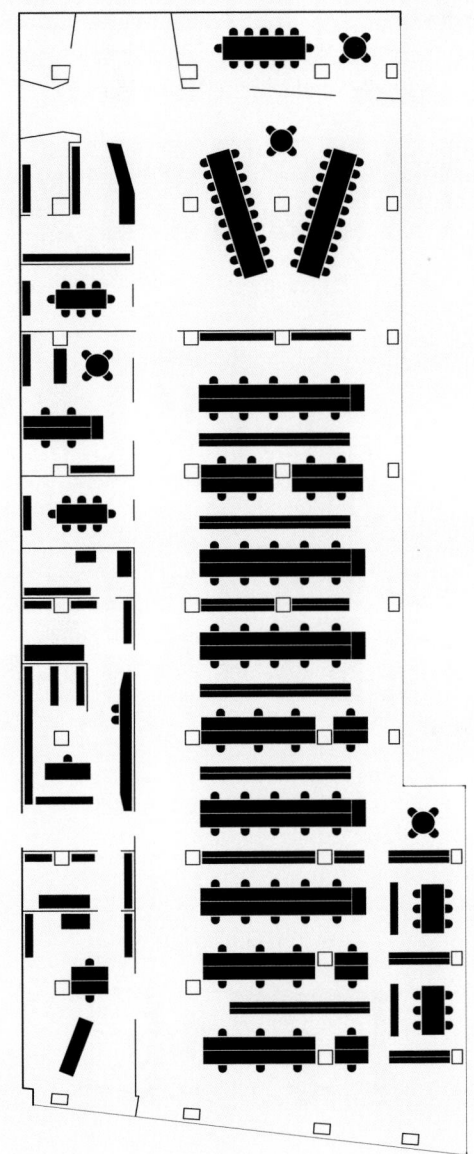

Snøhetta
New York City, c. 2014

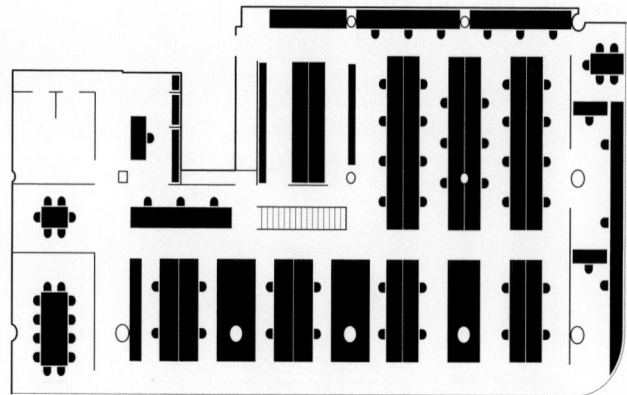

Floor 2

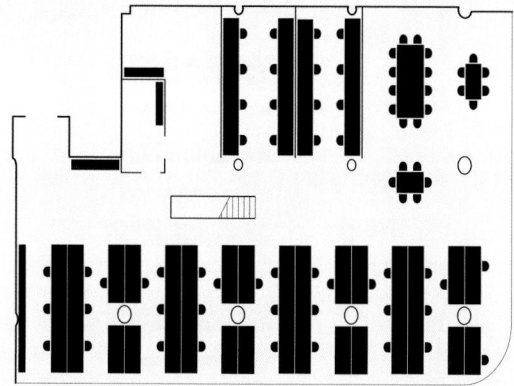

Floor 1

Diller Scofidio + Renfro
New York City, c. 2014

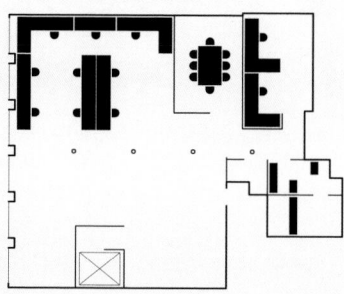

OBRA Architects
New York City, c. 2014

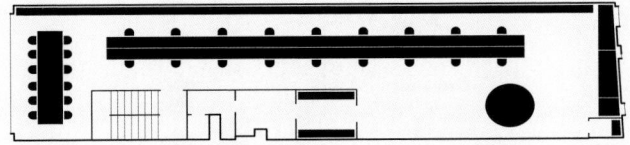

LOT-EK
New York City, c. 2014

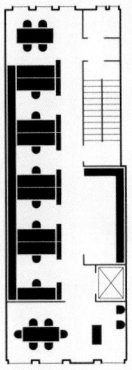

Slade Architecture
New York City, c. 2014

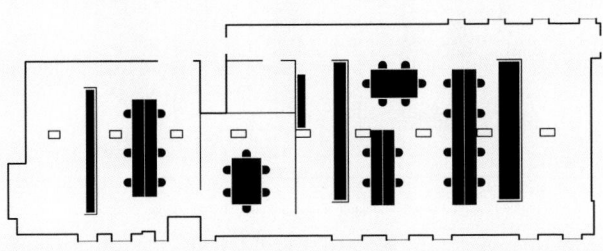

over,under
Boston, c. 2014

0' 4' 8'   16'   32'

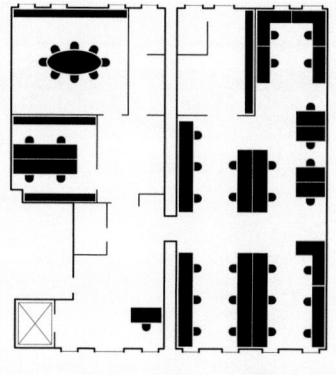

Floor 2

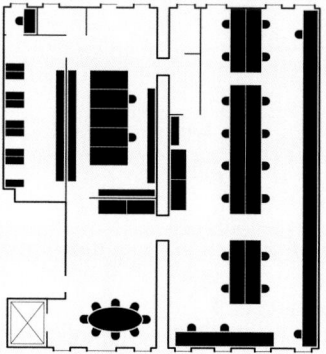

Floor 1

WORKac
New York City, c. 2014

Floor 2

Floor 1

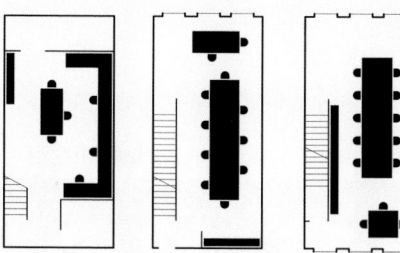

Floor 3

MOS Architects
New York City, c. 2014

0' 4' 8'   16'   32'

1939
American Institute
of Architects
"Standards of Practice
of the American
Institute of Architects"
*The Octagon, A Journal
of the American
Institute of Architects*

Architects [...] should inspire the loyal interest of their employees, providing suitable working conditions for them, requiring them to render competent and efficient services, and paying them adequate and just compensation therefore.

1972
Lewis Clarke Associates
Handbook of Office Policies

The office is a team effort composed of individuals contributing both personal and professional qualities. Each member of this team has unique qualities different from anyone else. It is the sum total of these pieces which form the office strength. Within an atmosphere of respect and give and take, we ought to be able to create such an environment that everyone looks forward to coming to work.

2009
*The Project Management
Manual*

Office design standards have been put in place by the firm. Design standards include fittings, furnishings and equipment designed by ████████████. These are promoted as part of the design excellence and range of design services provided by the firm. Offices appear consistent and familiar. Visitors to the New York office should feel like they have just been to the Hong Kong office.

2014
Employee Handbook

Architecture can be a messy process. However, personal and public spaces should be kept in orderly appearance particularly after deadlines and in preparation for meetings.

1939

1972

2009

2014

6 — 1 OFFICE ENVIRONMENT

PHYSICAL

The overall workspace needs to be conducive to communication and cross polli-
nation of ideas. An open space concept allows visibility and flexibility in
terms of interaction and sharing of information regardless of staff assignments.
Creativity is, sometimes, not related to orderliness. In fact, when a team is totally
focused on an idea and a goal anything goes and the space should promote
this. In this case, chaos is good. Individual space must also be provided, so that
one can establish boundaries while group space is needed in order to share
ideas. Teams should be flexible and never permanent. Know your neighbor.
Environments that are conducive to camaraderie are relaxed and open and allow
constructive criticism. Models, experiments, mock-ups, music, play are all part
of the process and can cause turmoil or disruption. Try not to impede the
progress of others and, while you should be guided by the process, never be
handcuffed by procedure.

HEALTH

The office must be conducive to a high quality of life. Under the greatest of
pressure and deadlines, the office should allow for spaces of rest, personal
reflection, and a balanced approach to life. Views, quality light, air quality, landscape, water are part of a positive and healthy environment in which to practice.
Creative work takes the entire body and mind commitment.

While amenities must be provided in order to maintain a level of comfort
and convenience, be aware of being trapped in the office. We do not expect you
to live in the office. If you would like, but are not able, to walk away and engage
alternative environments during the day, you may be trapped in a process that is
not allowing you to see the big picture. You do not grow wholly by sitting at your
desk staring at the computer.

Stay healthy. If you're not healthy and happy, you are not in a position to
be genuinely productive. Your family and your personal health is critical to the
office. If you need help, let someone know. Asking for help is not a sign of failure.

...

CULTURE

It's a family concept. It's not about breeding consent, but more about constructive criticism in order to excel beyond personal expectations. The culture of the office should be to create a voracious appetite for knowledge that promotes the act of sharing knowledge and experience—good and bad. Don't be afraid. Projects can be daunting and stressful but you're not alone. Seek help, give help and be supportive.

Tell the truth. Not all ideas are appropriate. Even if it's seemingly accepted, challenge the idea in a constructive and professional manner. Don't let others speak for you—speak up and build your self-confidence within the context of your colleagues. Express the idea and the team will assist to develop it to perfection. The future depends upon collaboration.

Just because it's not yours doesn't mean you don't care. We are all together and all share common goals—both personal and professional.

See the big picture. While you are focused on your tasks, be aware of why you are being asked to do certain things. If you don't know why, ask.

Look with new eyes. Push the envelope of creativity to the extreme. We are prepared to research and develop concepts which may seem, at first, unachievable. Use the resources of the office and engage senior colleagues to help you assess and solve problems. Do not accept the status quo: learn from others and then improve upon their work.

Protect your team. If you see destructive behavior, or attitudes, say something or better yet, do something about it.

Have fun. The office will demand a great deal from you and you from it. Have fun while you are creating and developing projects. It's one of the most important characteristics of work. Gordon Gill

Continuity of thought and quietude of study are essential to the preservation of thoroughness in design, and of unity in style and expression. […] Practically, it has been found advantageous to have the designer in a room where he can be comparatively alone, a room in which there may be two or three working more or less continuously, but who can give way when special study is required, or when special renderings are in progress requiring plenty of free room.

<u>Both desks are to be locked each evening without fail</u>. Keys to the desks are in top drawer of Mr. Broad's desk. Both desks are to be cleared and left in neat order each evening. Things which are not to remain on desks, pencils, note pads, carbon paper, etc. are put inside of desk.

Separate offices must be provided for the project architects or job captains. The production chief needs his own space. The checkers need lots of room where they can spread out numerous sheets of plans. This space must be isolated from the general activity of the drafting room, for theirs is a most exacting job, requiring quiet and seclusion. The specifications writer must have his own cubicle, with room for his reference files and books. Often the designer or design staff needs some form of separation from the production staff.

Each staff member is expected to keep his drafting board, side table, and the areas immediately adjacent in a neat and orderly manner. Care should be taken to maintain equipment in good working order. On Friday afternoon put away all equipment not in use, drawings and other materials, so that no accidents or losses will result from potential week-end visitors or cleaning activities.

At the end of each day, clean off materials from desk tops and place all original tracings back into the job drawer. When finished, re-file catalogs, code books, etc. at the end of the day.

Stop! Take a look at what is on the desk or around the room. Is all that "stuff" cluttering your space vital to the tasks at hand? Is it piled there because it has no place to go? Use it, file it, put it away, or throw it away!

We recognize that different workers have different physical needs. If you require an adjustment to your working environment (e.g., adjustment of position of your chair or the position of your computer), please see your Office Manager. You are responsible for keeping your work area free of hazards.

6 — 2 INDIVIDUAL WORKSTATIONS

The exterior of a company's office can send a message: a high-rise tower—status and position; an industrial shed—manufacturing roots; an individual's home—modest efficiency. But while an office's outside face helps communicate who it is, for most of history, once you moved past the front door to arrive at the individual workspace the differences faded.

Workers have often been confined by tools that define their work process. In the case of the architect, the workstation was a drafting table: a standard tool with very few options—how large, how tall, and at what angle. It was a tool created for a specific task—drawing—and represented one step in the overall design process. And because each task required a specific tool, other stations and spaces were created to complete the full act of design; meeting rooms for design review and libraries for the storage of shared reference material were essential parts to round out the whole.

Today, the individual workstation no longer defines the physical space for design and the tools have graduated from a constraint to an opportunity. More compact drafting technology and smarter shared tools have given birth to a more optimal use of desk space with far fewer functional boundaries. Mobile technology has created individual workstations that can travel with the user; an architect's desktop is no longer simply a physical space.

Architects can now design the *way* we design, and as a result design is no longer just the product of an architect's work, it is also part of the process: the composition and form of individual workstations is a considered act that represents the core values of an office and individual. And with more choices and diversity, the overall creative process is elevated. Marc Guberman

6 — 3 RECEPTION

1890
Wilson Bros & Co.
"The Organization of An
Architect's Office"
*Engineering and Building
Record*

From the lobby also opens the reception-room, used for consultation with clients and for meetings of building committees, etc. It is suitably furnished, and contains on one side a library of choice architectural books, in which, among other valuable works, may be found a complete set of Piranesi, of which there is believed to be only one other in the country.

1967
Morris Lapidus
*Architecture, a Profession
and a Business*

Make your reception room speak for you. It is like the introduction, the dust cover of a new book, the jacket on a fine phonograph record. In short, it is the opening salvo in your campaign to conquer any hesitancy a potential client might have about you or your ability. You are an architect, and therefore are expected to know how to design a functional, attractive interior.

1986
Society of Architectural
Administrators
*Handbook for
Architectural Administrators*

Callers should be received in a well designed reception area which does credit to the firm and reflects the practice's strength and success.

6 — 3 RECEPTION

At Architecture at Large, there is no reception desk or waiting room. Every visitor enters directly into the heart of the design studio, where work is pinned up, materials are laid out, and models are crafted. After being greeted by the Studio Coordinator, visitors are led through the studio to either the conference room, in the case of pin-up presentations or working sessions, or into the ante-studio for a more casual conversation on the twin sofas around the coffee table. Regardless of the visitors or nature of the visit, sparkling water (and typically a bowl of cashews) awaits them.

      A studio's collective aspirations are reflected not only in its design work, but in its dress, music, the art on the walls, the books and magazines on the tables and shelves, the quality of light in the studio. The experience of arrival should enable a visitor to comprehend these aspirations immediately and should engender a seductive quality; visitors should feel inclined to enter into your world and into any collaboration that lies ahead. Rafael de Cárdenas / Architecture at Large

...

6 — 4 CONFERENCE ROOM

1920
Frank Miles Day
The American Institute
of Architects
*The Handbook of
Architectural Practice*

In some offices the Architect holds periodic conferences with his more important assistants with a view to securing criticism of sketches or drawings, determining on the best way of conducting a given piece of work, considering improvements in the methods of the office, changes in the staff, etc. Such conferences are profitable to the participants as well as to the office. They bring about a coordination of effort and an increased *esprit de corps*.

1967
Morris Lapidus
*Architecture, a Profession
and a Business*

One or more conference rooms will have to be in the plan. As the practice grows, you will need more and more of these conference spaces for meetings with consulting engineers and materials suppliers, with contractors, and with clients. In a busy office there may be three, four or five conferences going on simultaneously. Some of these conference rooms can be small enough for four people, some large enough to accommodate twelve to fifteen. The larger rooms today have projectors for slides, as well as a built-in screen.

2014
■
Studio Manual

The Conference Room is available for everyone in the studio to use. The Conference Room space offers us the valuable possibility to "step outside" the studio for meetings, lunches, design review pin ups, and moments when we need a quiet place to concentrate on the work. If you have a project that will require use of the Conference Room for an extended period of time for large scale sewing, prototype layouts and other fabrication activities please PLAN AHEAD and announce in the weekly ■■■ office meeting.

6 — 4 CONFERENCE ROOM

Capitalism is big. But it ain't that big. Taking a page from Berger and Luckmann, let's assume there exists some variety of individual agency within the structure of capitalist society, the one begetting the other in a sort of feedback loop. In this process of cogeneration there must be a *locus originis*—a boudoir, if you will—where the system and the agents get together to make it happen, and the conference room is it. This we know from movies, as in Sidney Lumet's *Network* of 1976, where Ned Beatty looms out of the darkness—punctuated only by the ghastly glow of green-shaded table lamps—to thunder on about the power and the glory of corporate America, or in *The Big Short* (2015) where the entire global economy is deliberately and quite cavalierly kneecapped by smartly-dressed boys and girls sipping from logo-emblazoned coffee mugs. The four decades separating the two pictures mark the radical shift in the design of this most essential environment, from a mahogany-lined officer's mess to a glass-enclosed human terrarium; but what has not really changed, and what can't be overlooked, is how bizarrely indeterminate the conference room remains. The colleague in a personal crisis sneaking off to make a teary phone call, the bored intern taking in the view, the inevitable ritual of birthday cake distribution, and, as we are assured by countless other movies of admittedly lesser artistic ambition, actual sex—all of these unfold in this improbably afunctional liminal zone, this rumpus room in the heart of capital. Ian Volner

1890
Burnham & Root
"The Organization of an
Architect's Office, No. 1"
*Engineering and
Building Record*

The room is 40 by 50 feet. The most noticeable feature of the room is the division of its working space into separate compartments by partitions extending out from either side between the windows. These partitions are about 7 feet high, and serve to partially isolate each draughtsmen, so as to prevent distraction by their neighbors, and to give each one a house to himself.

1920
Howard Dwight Smith
"The 'Business' of
Architecture, The Drafting
Room, Engineering
and Inspection"
The Architectural Review

Of the one hundred to one hundred and fifty men employed there during the decade beginning with the Roosevelt administration, probably half were engaged in making quarter-scale drawings, for estimate and contract, under three or four men designated as architects, who correspond exactly to our ten "supervising architect." About a fourth of the total number were engaged in three-quarter inch scale detailing, in more or less close cooperation with the so-called "quarter-inch" squads. The remaining fourth were engaged in full-size detail work in a department as separate from the other squads as it was from the engineering or business departments.

1960
Office of Architect
Maynard Lyndon
Employee's Manual

Please clear all desks completely every night. Replace catalogs, etc. No personal files of correspondence. Keep job notes or instructions in drafting room folder marked (as) Job File. Keep drawings filed according to: Program Data, Layouts, Finish Drawings, Obsolete Material.

2014
Employee Handbook

Telecommuting is a work arrangement that allows you to work at home or at a remote location for all or some of your regularly scheduled work hours. ████ recognizes that a telecommuting arrangement can sometimes provide a mutually beneficial option for both you and the firm; however, not all jobs may be performed satisfactorily from remote locations.

6 — 5 DRAFTING ROOM

As a means of correct training, the architect's drafting room is a disciplinary space par excellence. Or so Michel Foucault might suggest. Since the rise of the modern profession, the spaces of architectural production and reproduction have been virtually one and the same. Even as architectural training was academized and outsourced to the university, drafting rooms maintained their distinctive character: one part artist's atelier, a space fostering individual and collaborative creativity; and one part factory assembly line, or military formation, accommodating specialization of tasks for optimization of production within a spatial hierarchy of ranked authorities and rank-and-filed bodies. The prevailing tenor of any drafting room even today, be that of sweatshop or convivial *esprit de corps*, issues in large part from the attitudes and ambitions of "the architect," that imaginary entity linked to some real or virtual identity in whose name, or names, or brand, the work of many minds and hands is combined to common purpose. This is the realization of the corporate ideal that underpins contemporary architectural practice.

There is another sense, however, in which the drafting room performs as an armature for architectural production. It serves as an archive of all the accrued experience that forms the collective memory of any firm—and that constitutes its collective intelligence. While information may be physically stored in adjacent reference libraries, in all the flat files on the periphery of the drafting room, on the hard drives, in the server rooms, or in the cloud, the knowledge that constitutes the distributed intelligence of any architect's office resides in the social fabric of the firm, made manifest in constructed projects. All the randomly accessible memories of those who participated in the design process, considered problems from diverse points of view, tested alternatives, balanced unexpected contingencies with unintended consequences, negotiated every uncompromising consensus, and implemented decisions within the bounded rationality of their everyday labor—those comprise the true knowledge base of any firm. The knowledge of practice resides within practices, in the minds and hands of the practitioners, interacting with others, whether working together in the drafting room or networked remotely from home or abroad. George B. Johnston

Frequently the preliminary studies have to be amplified by models, which greatly facilitate the study of mass, proportion, scale, and the relation of parts.

Models are frequently the cause of delay. Drawings required for models should be among the first details to be produced and should be placed in the modelers' hands at the earliest possible moment via the general contractor.

Many offices build a small-scale site model as soon as they get a commission—before any schemes are drawn. Block studies made on such models—even at 50 or 100 scale—are both meaningful and impressive to the client. And they photograph extremely well. Such a model, refined regularly as the design moves along, can usually serve the life of the project, not only for client presentations but also for client publicity, display and (via photographs) for the professional's own sales brochure.

███ commitment to digital fabrication as a method of design research and innovation is supported by our in-house rapid proto-typing lab, workshops and CNC router—resources which are integrated into our studio environment and its work flow. Digital fabrication is integrated with our design studio in a multi-faceted manner that can be roughly classified into three parallel processes: schematic form-finding, component mock-ups and prototypes, "design-build" where this term is defined as projects where both a design and its constructive delivery method(s) are created and completed in house.

Before starting to use all the various machines in the office and especially in the workshop please introduce yourself to Mario. Mario is a wizard with power tools and can show you how they work. Mario and Chad hold regular shop orientations where you can learn how to use each machine safely.

244

6 — 6 MODEL SHOP

At their desks, we email the person sitting next to us; perhaps to keep a record of the conversation, perhaps avoiding confrontation and interaction. In the conference room, we stare into our phones while one person mumbles on and on about backflow prevention, not exactly worth eight people's time. *When is this meeting going to end anyway?* In the kitchen, awkward gestures of hello to acquaintances prevail. *Who was that guy? Must be new.*

The most communal, social space in an architecture office is the model shop. There is no hiding behind electronics. The object of desire is there on the table, it is the focal point, and everyone has an opinion. It can't be minimized and it can't be saved and closed for someone else to work on later. Inviting conversation and criticism, it just sits there.

The model shop is where we learn about a project—how it goes together, the scale, the materiality, the connections, the infeasible, the problems, the unresolved conditions. This is where we can study options in foam before we turn them into digital lines and then concrete. This is where mistakes are fruitful and don't involve lawyers. This is where we can show off our craft. This is where the manual still has a home, where the X-Acto #11 blade still makes a perfect cut and doesn't char basswood. This is the land where spray paint can make new materials, where dried flowers are trees, and where the glossy plastic people still shimmer in their '50s apparel. Glass is always single pane, there are no weather conditions or foundations, no mechanical systems, electricity, or plumbing. It's just architecture.

The model shop is the one casual respite from the drudgery of the office and the purr of the computer. It's where we have room to spread out on large cutting mats and build our dreams for the future. Kyle May

1924
Frederick J. Adams
*Manual of Office
Practice for the Architectural
Worker, Compiled for
Use in the Office of
McKim, Mead & White*

Samples should be secured in ample time before the related work is to be begun, so that in the event of repeated rejections, the progress of the work will not be retarded by lack of approval material, except by direct default of the contractor.

1941
Royal Barry Wills
and Leon Keach
This Business of Architecture

The storage of samples is adjusted to the physical limitations of your office. It may be the spare shelves of your bookcase or a full-fledged sample room. Such is the infinite variety of materials that there seems to be nothing better than shelves, behind doors or open. Where there are many varieties of one material, as marble, it is convenient to maintain a uniform size and slip them into special racks. Be sure everything is labeled with something that really sticks, such as lithographic crayon.

1924

1967
Morris Lapidus
*Architecture, a Profession
and a Business*

Another important and separate space or room which should be provided as growth of an office takes place is a sample room. A well-planned sample room provides adequate space for all sorts of building materials. It will simplify decisions if materials are easily reached when needed.

1941

2016
Snøhetta
Snøhetta Guide

We collect all product samples in the material room and have a yearly organizing. Use the material room, but remember to clean up after yourself and to put samples back where they belong after usage.

1967

2016

6 — 7 SAMPLE ROOM

Around the turn of the twentieth century many commercial hotels began offering "Sample Rooms" to traveling salesmen as temporary storefronts. These rented rooms, which were separated from typical meeting rooms and guest rooms, served as spaces of display to set and stage merchandise for potential clients and customers. More recently we might look to the "Tasting Rooms" commonly found at most wineries and vineyards as spaces not only of display but also of consumption. Often separated from the spectacle of production to encourage and (for regulatory sake) contain the sampling, selection, and distribution of alcohol, these spaces—and the semantics attached to their labeling—mark distinctions between services, functions, and the circulation of products.

 In architecture, this distinction is repeatedly made through various contract documents and nomenclature, which amplify the separation between architects, builders, suppliers, and clients. In the contemporary architecture office the sample room is a space separated from the studio that collects, catalogs, and displays materials, hardware, and furnishings. But it is also an offshoot of the material supply chain between those who manufacture and distribute a product and those who specify it.

 If we look at the relationship between tasting, sampling, and specifying, what's perhaps most compelling is how spaces set aside for these practices complicate the relationship between manufacturing and supply, particularly through proximity. The salesman's sample room brought solicitation into close proximity with a version of hospitality. A tasting room makes the material processes of winemaking a part of the experience of the product simply by consuming the product on-site. The sample room that resides in the architect's office houses the networks that surround architecture's systems of material selection and distribution, smuggled in via product samples, material libraries, and mock-ups. Besler & Sons (Erin Besler & Ian Besler)

1901
Kaye W. Perry
Office Management;
A Handbook for Architects
and Civil Engineers

One thing that is needed to keep drawings properly is plenty of space in the drawing office, and this is not always available. It is of course essential that all drawings should be kept on the flat and not rolled up, and for that purpose a number of drawers are required. These drawers must be not less than double-elephant size, and even then they will not always be found large enough. These must be of sufficient depth to hold the drawings without risk of an overflow.

1964
Richard J. Neutra Office
Rules for Apprentice
– Students

Prints and drawings of architects and engineers will be made and placed in storage elsewhere than in the building where drawings are produced and filed.

1981
Massachusetts Committee
for the Preservation
of Architectural Records
(Mass COPAR)
Records in Architectural
Offices; Suggestions for
the Proper Organization,
Storage and Conservation of
Architectural Office Archives

Architectural records present tremendous storage problems and expense because of their bulk and their size. Although flat storage is ideal for drawings, flat files are expensive and take up floor space. Older records are usually boxed and drawings folded in with written documents or rolled into tubes.

2014
Studio Manual

The Flat File in the plotting bay is the legal safe place of deposit for all active and ongoing original project documents as well as key sketches and important surveys and site maps. The Flat File in the storage room is the place of deposit for original presentation boards, drawings and any large reprographic which must lie flat. It is the design team's shared responsibility to always return documents to the Flat File storage and to maintain the drawers in an orderly manner with updated Project Labels.

6 — 8 STORAGE

An architectural office does not make buildings, but produces material that can be translated into buildings. The totality of these stored documents, samples, and models form the final narrative of a practice. Storing this material should therefore not be considered a random depositing of scraps left over from the process of designing projects, but the single most important representation of the office's existence.

Utmost care must be taken in considering what one stores and what one moves to trash (refer to guidelines on Trash and Waste Management). Storage is to be organized in clear sections, such that future staff can easily use it as a tool for design, presentation, and press.

Always remember, the office storage is the one source left to tell the story when everyone else is gone. Florian Idenburg

RIGHTS

CLASS
NOTES
Tschumi and Mori on the
Education of Architects.

EQUAL EMPLOYMENT OPPORTUNITY
(SEE PAGE 64)

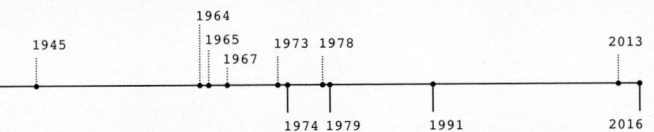

1945   1964 1965 1967   1973 1978   2013

1974 1979   1991   2016

• ···· 1945
NEW YORK STATE HUMAN RIGHTS LAW (NY)
PROHIBITS DISCRIMINATION ON THE BASIS OF
AGE, RACE, CREED, COLOR, NATIONAL ORIGIN,
SEXUAL ORIENTATION, MILITARY STATUS, SEX,
MARITAL STATUS OR DISABILITY.

• ···· 1964
CIVIL RIGHTS ACT (US)
OUTLAWS DISCRIMINATION BASED ON RACE, COLOR,
RELIGION, SEX OR NATIONAL ORIGIN.

• ···· 1965
IMMIGRATION AND NATIONALITY ACT (US)
PREFERENCE FOR IMMIGRANTS BASED ON SKILLS,
NOT BASED ON QUOTAS OF ACCEPTABLE NUMBER OF
IMMIGRANTS FROM THEIR HOME COUNTRY.

• ···· 1967
AGE DISCRIMINATION IN EMPLOYMENT ACT (US)
FORBIDS EMPLOYMENT DISCRIMINATION AGAINST
ANYONE AT LEAST 40 YEARS OF AGE IN THE US.

• ···· 1973
REHABILITATION ACT (US)
PROHIBITS EMPLOYMENT DISCRIMINATION ON THE
BASIS OF DISABILITY.

• ···· 1978
BANKRUPTCY REFORM ACT (US)
PROHIBITS EMPLOYMENT DISCRIMINATION AGAINST
ANYONE WHO HAS DECLARED BANKRUPTCY.

• ···· 2013
EMPLOYMENT NON-DISCRIMINATION ACT (ENDA)(US)
BANS DISCRIMINATION ON THE BASIS OF SEXUAL
ORIENTATION OR GENDER IDENTITY.

STANDARDS OF CONDUCT AND STANDARD OF CARE
(SEE PAGE 70)

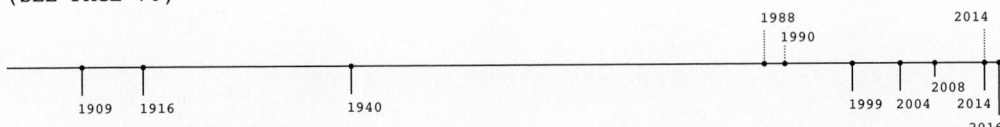

1988 1990   2014

1909 1916   1940   1999 2004 2008 2014   2016

• ···· 1988
MATTER OF CARUSO V. WARD 72 (NY)
RANDOM WORKPLACE DRUG TESTING DOES NOT
REQUIRE A WARRANT.

• ···· 1990
AMERICANS WITH DISABILITIES ACT (ADA) (US)
PROHIBITS DISCRIMINATION BASED ON REAL OR
PERCEIVED PHYSICAL OR MENTAL DISABILITIES;
EMPLOYERS MUST PROVIDE REASONABLE ACCOM-
MODATIONS FOR DISABILITY. [...] PROHIBITS
PRIVATE PLACES OF PUBLIC ACCOMMODATION FROM
DISCRIMINATING AGAINST INDIVIDUALS WITH
DISABILITIES. THIS TITLE SETS THE MINIMUM
STANDARDS FOR ACCESSIBILITY FOR ALTERATIONS
AND NEW CONSTRUCTION OF FACILITIES. IT ALSO
REQUIRES PUBLIC ACCOMMODATIONS TO REMOVE
BARRIERS IN EXISTING BUILDINGS WHERE IT IS
EASY TO DO SO WITHOUT MUCH DIFFICULTY OR
EXPENSE.

• ···· 2014
PREGNANT WORKERS FAIRNESS ACT (US)
UNLAWFUL FOR EMPLOYERS TO FAIL TO MAKE REA-
SONABLE ACCOMMODATIONS TO KNOWN LIMITATIONS
RELATED TO THE PREGNANCY, CHILDBIRTH, OR
RELATED MEDICAL CONDITIONS OF JOB APPLICANTS
OR EMPLOYEES, UNLESS THE ACCOMMODATION WOULD
IMPOSE AN UNDUE HARDSHIP ON SUCH AN ENTITY'S
BUSINESS OPERATION.

PROFESSIONAL RESPONSIBILITY
(SEE PAGE 72)

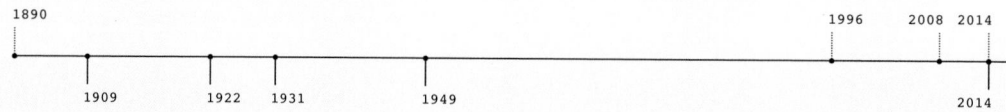

1890 · · · 1909 · 1922 1931 · 1949 · 1996 · 2008 2014 · 2014

1890
SHERMAN ANTI-TRUST ACT (US)
PROTECTS TRADE AND COMMERCE AGAINST UNLAWFUL
RESTRAINTS AND MONOPOLIES.

1996
REGENTS RULES (NY)
UNDER SOME CASES, DRAWING, PLANS, AND SPECI-
FICATIONS FURNISHED BY A THIRD PARTY MAY BE
STAMPED BY REGISTERED ARCHITECTS AND PROFES-
SIONAL ENGINEERS, BUT SUCH DOCUMENTS SHOULD
BE EVALUATED WITH WRITTEN DOCUMENTATION BY
THE LICENSED PROFESSIONAL AND PRELIMINARY
AND FINAL PLANS, DOCUMENTS, COMPUTATIONS,
AND RECORDS SHALL BE MAINTAINED FOR A MINI-
MUM OF SIX YEARS.

2008
AIA GUIDELINES: TASK QUALIFICATION (US)
IF FOR ANY REASON, THE ARCHITECT RECOGNIZES
FROM THEIR ASSESSMENT THAT THEY DO NOT HAVE
THE QUALIFICATIONS TO RESOLVE ISSUES IN
THE PROJECT, IT IS THEIR RESPONSIBILITY TO
DISCLOSE THIS INFORMATION TO THE CLIENT AND
EXPLAIN THAT THESE OTHER PARTIES NEEDED HAVE
NO OBLIGATION TO WORK PRO-BONO AND THE COM-
MUNITY CLIENT IS RESPONSIBLE FOR NEGOTIATING
TERMS OF SERVICE WITH THESE OTHER PARTIES.

2014
ARCHITECTS PRACTICE ACT (APA)(US)
PROTECTS THE USE OF THE TITLE "ARCHITECT"
AND PROHIBITS ANYONE WHO IS NOT A LICENSED
ARCHITECT FROM USING THIS TITLE IN ANY WAY.

2014
BEACON RESIDENTIAL COMMUNITY ASS'N. V.
SKIDMORE, OWINGS & MERRILL (CA)(US)
THE COURT HELD THAT ARCHITECTS OWE A DUTY OF
CARE TO FUTURE HOMEOWNERS IN THE DESIGN OF
RESIDENTIAL BUILDINGS WHERE THE ARCHITECT IS
A PRINCIPAL ARCHITECT ON THE PROJECT, MEAN-
ING THAT THE ARCHITECT IS NOT A SUBORDINATE
TO OTHER DESIGN PROFESSIONALS.

2014
CALIFORNIA BUSINESS AND PROFESSIONS CODE
(MCE)(US)
NO PERSON MAY USE AN ARCHITECT'S INSTRUMENTS
OF SERVICE WITHOUT THE CONSENT OF THE
ARCHITECT IN A WRITTEN CONTRACT, WRITTEN
AGREEMENT, OR WRITTEN LICENSE SPECIFICALLY
AUTHORIZING THAT USE. AN ARCHITECT SHALL NOT
UNREASONABLY WITHHOLD CONSENT TO USE HIS OR
HER INSTRUMENTS OF SERVICE FROM A PERSON FOR
WHOM THE ARCHITECT PROVIDED THE SERVICES. AN
ARCHITECT MAY REASONABLY WITHHOLD CONSENT TO
USE THE INSTRUMENTS OF SERVICE FOR CAUSE,
INCLUDING, BUT NOT LIMITED TO, LACK OF FULL
PAYMENT FOR SERVICES PROVIDED OR FAILURE
TO FULFILL THE CONDITIONS OF A WRITTEN
CONTRACT.

PUBLIC SERVICE
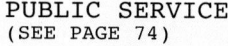
(SEE PAGE 74)

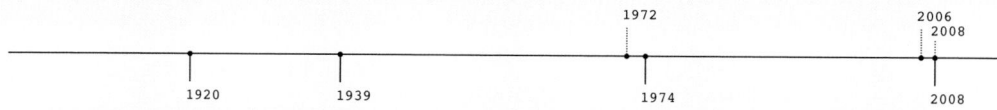

1972 · 1920 · 1939 · 1974 · 2006 2008 · 2008

1972
THE BROOKS ACT (US)
ESTABLISHES THE PROCUREMENT PROCESS BY WHICH
ARCHITECTS AND ENGINEERS (A/ES) ARE SELECTED
FOR DESIGN CONTRACTS WITH FEDERAL DESIGN
AND CONSTRUCTION AGENCIES. THE BROOKS ACT
ESTABLISHES A QUALIFICATIONS-BASED SELECTION
PROCESS, IN WHICH CONTRACTS FOR A/ES ARE
NEGOTIATED ON THE BASIS OF DEMONSTRATED
COMPETENCE AND QUALIFICATION FOR THE TYPE
OF PROFESSIONAL SERVICES REQUIRED AT A FAIR
AND REASONABLE PRICE. UNDER QBS PROCUREMENT
PROCEDURES, PRICE QUOTATIONS ARE NOT A CON-
SIDERATION IN THE SELECTION PROCESS.

2006
GOOD SAMARITAN LAW (CA)
AN ARCHITECT WHO VOLUNTARILY, WITHOUT
COMPENSATION OR EXPECTATION OF COMPENSATION,
PROVIDES STRUCTURAL INSPECTION SERVICES AT
THE SCENE OF A DECLARED NATIONAL, STATE,
OR LOCAL EMERGENCY CAUSED BY A MAJOR EARTH-
QUAKE, FLOOD, RIOT, OR FIRE AT THE REQUEST
OF A PUBLIC OFFICIAL, PUBLIC SAFETY OFFICER,
OR CITY OR COUNTY BUILDING INSPECTOR ACTING
IN AN OFFICIAL CAPACITY SHALL NOT BE LIABLE
IN NEGLIGENCE FOR ANY PERSONAL INJURY,
WRONGFUL DEATH, OR PROPERTY DAMAGE CAUSED
BY THE ARCHITECT'S GOOD FAITH BUT NEGLIGENT
INSPECTION OF A STRUCTURE USED FOR HUMAN
HABITATION OR A STRUCTURE OWNED BY A PUBLIC
ENTITY FOR STRUCTURAL INTEGRITY OR NONSTRUC-
TURAL ELEMENTS AFFECTING LIFE AND SAFETY.

2008
UNDERTAKING PRO BONO SERVICE ACTIVITIES
(AIA)(US)
WITH ANY PROJECT UNDERTAKEN BY AN ARCHITECT
OR A FIRM, IT IS CRITICAL THAT A LEGALLY
ENFORCEABLE OWNER-ARCHITECT AGREEMENT OR
LETTER OF AGREEMENT BE EXECUTED AT THE OUT-
SET OF UNDERTAKING A PRO BONO PROJECT. OFTEN
PRO BONO PROJECTS ARE THE FIRST STEP IN AN
ONGOING PROCESS INVOLVING PROGRAMMING, GRANT
WRITING, FEASIBILITY STUDIES, AND ANALYSIS
OF ALTERNATIVE SITES.

OVERTIME
(SEE PAGE 88)

- 1938
  FAIR LABOR STANDARDS ACT (FLSA)(US)
  NONEXEMPT WORKERS MUST BE PAID OVERTIME PAY
  AT A RATE OF NOT LESS THAN ONE AND ONE-HALF
  TIMES THEIR REGULAR RATES OF PAY AFTER 40
  HOURS OF WORK IN A WORKWEEK.

- 1985
  FAIR LABOR STANDARDS ACT (FLSA)(US)
  REQUIRES COMPENSATION FOR EMPLOYEES FOR
  OVERTIME HOURS WORKED WITH COMPENSATORY
  TIME OFF IN LIEU OF OVERTIME PAY, AT A RATE
  OF ONE AND A HALF HOURS FOR EACH HOUR OF
  OVERTIME WORKED.

- 2016
  FAIR LABOR STANDARDS ACT (FLSA)(US)
  EMPLOYEES EARNING A SALARY OF LESS THAN $913
  PER WEEK MUST BE PAID OVERTIME. ADJUSTMENTS
  IN THE THRESHOLD ARE EXPECTED TO OCCUR EVERY
  THREE YEARS.

BREAKS
(SEE PAGE 92)

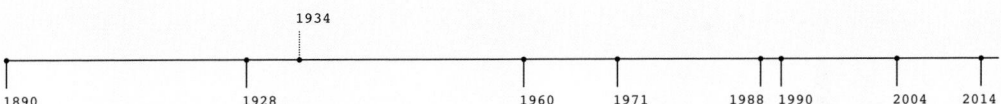

- 1934
  LABOR CODE. DIVISION 2. EMPLOYMENT
  REGULATION AND SUPERVISION (CA)
  AN EMPLOYER MAY NOT EMPLOY AN EMPLOYEE FOR A
  WORK PERIOD OF MORE THAN FIVE HOURS PER DAY
  WITHOUT PROVIDING THE EMPLOYEE WITH A MEAL
  PERIOD OF NOT LESS THAN 30 MINUTES, EXCEPT
  THAT IF THE TOTAL WORK PERIOD PER DAY OF THE
  EMPLOYEE IS NO MORE THAN SIX HOURS, THE MEAL
  PERIOD MAY BE WAIVED BY MUTUAL CONSENT OF
  BOTH THE EMPLOYER AND EMPLOYEE. AN EMPLOYER
  MAY NOT EMPLOY AN EMPLOYEE FOR A WORK PERIOD
  OF MORE THAN 10 HOURS PER DAY WITHOUT
  PROVIDING THE EMPLOYEE WITH A SECOND MEAL
  PERIOD OF NOT LESS THAN 30 MINUTES, EXCEPT
  THAT IF THE TOTAL HOURS WORKED IS NO MORE
  THAN 12 HOURS, THE SECOND MEAL PERIOD MAY BE
  WAIVED BY MUTUAL CONSENT OF THE EMPLOYER AND
  THE EMPLOYEE ONLY IF THE FIRST MEAL PERIOD
  WAS NOT WAIVED.

OFFICE ATTIRE AND DECORUM
(SEE PAGE 100)

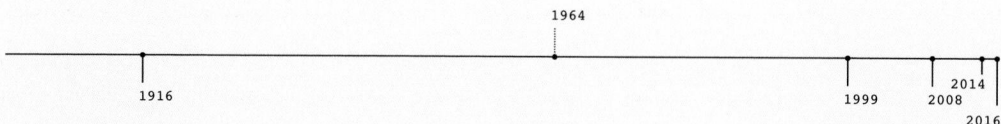

1964

1916

1999   2014
2008

2016

• ------ 1964
CIVIL RIGHTS ACT (US)
EMPLOYER CANNOT ASK AN EMPLOYEE TO REMOVE
RELIGIOUS DRESS AND GROOMING PRACTICES
INCLUDING WEARING RELIGIOUS CLOTHING OR
ARTICLES OR ADHERING TO SHAVING OR HAIR
LENGTH OBSERVANCES. HOWEVER, IF A DRESS OR
GROOMING PRACTICE IS A PERSONAL PREFERENCE
AND NOT "SINCERELY HELD", IT DOES NOT COME
UNDER TITLE VII'S RELIGION PROTECTIONS.

CONTINUING EDUCATION
(SEE PAGE 110)

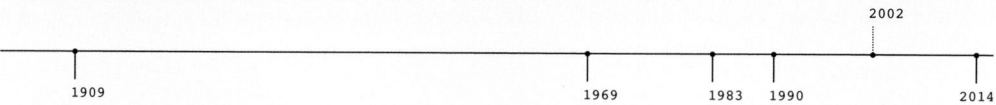

2002

1909

1969   1983 1990

2014

• ------ 2002
MANDATORY CONTINUING EDUCATION (NY)
REQUIRES ARCHITECTS TO COMPLETE 36 PROFES-
SIONALLY RELATED CONTINUING EDUCATION HOURS
EVERY THREE YEARS.

INTELLECTUAL PROPERTY
(SEE PAGE 116)

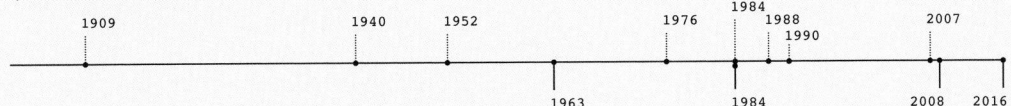

1909   1940   1952   1976   1984   1988   2007
                                             1984   1990

1963   1984   2008   2016

1909 (AMEND. 1941)
COPYRIGHT ACT (US)
GRANTS COPYRIGHT PROTECTION TO ORIGINALLY
PUBLISHED WORKS. THIS ACT GRANTED PROTECTION
FOR A WORK FOR A PERIOD OF 28 YEARS. THE
ACT GRANTS THE AUTHOR A RIGHT TO RENEW THE
PROTECTION FOR ANOTHER 28 YEARS.

1940
LANHAM ACT (US)
SETS OUT PROCEDURES FOR FEDERALLY REGIS-
TERING TRADEMARKS, STATES WHEN OWNERS OF
TRADEMARKS MAY BE ENTITLED TO FEDERAL JUDI-
CIAL PROTECTION AGAINST INFRINGEMENT, AND
ESTABLISHES OTHER GUIDELINES AND REMEDIES
FOR TRADEMARK OWNERS.

1952
JOINT OWNERS (US)
IN THE ABSENCE OF ANY AGREEMENT TO THE CON-
TRARY, EACH OF THE JOINT OWNERS OF A PATENT
MAY MAKE, USE, OFFER TO SELL, OR SELL THE
PATENTED INVENTION WITHIN THE UNITED STATES,
OR IMPORT THE PATENTED INVENTION INTO THE
UNITED STATES, WITHOUT THE CONSENT OF AND
WITHOUT ACCOUNTING TO THE OTHER OWNERS.

1976
COPYRIGHT ACT (US)
COPYRIGHT PROTECTION SUBSISTS IN ORIGINAL
WORKS OF AUTHORSHIP FIXED IN ANY TANGIBLE
MEDIUM OF EXPRESSION, NOW KNOWN OR LATER
DEVELOPED, FROM WHICH THEY CAN BE PERCEIVED,
REPRODUCED, OR OTHERWISE COMMUNICATED,
EITHER DIRECTLY OR WITH THE AID OF A MACHINE
OR DEVICE. IN NO CASE DOES COPYRIGHT PRO-
TECTION FOR AN ORIGINAL WORK OF AUTHORSHIP
EXTEND TO ANY IDEA, PROCEDURE, PROCESS,
SYSTEM, METHOD OF OPERATION, CONCEPT,
PRINCIPLE, OR DISCOVERY, REGARDLESS OF THE
FORM IN WHICH IT IS DESCRIBED, EXPLAINED,
ILLUSTRATED, OR EMBODIED IN SUCH WORK.

1984
ARTISTS AUTHORSHIP RIGHTS ACT (NY)
GIVES MEASURE OF OWNERSHIP TO THE ARTIST
EVEN AFTER PROPERTY RIGHTS OF THE OBJECT
HAVE BEEN TRANSFERRED.

1988
DIGITAL MILLENNIUM COPYRIGHTS ACT (US)
CRIMINALIZES PRODUCTION AND DISSEMINATION OF
TECHNOLOGY DEVICES, OR SERVICES INTENDED TO
CIRCUMVENT MEASURES THAT CONTROL ACCESS TO
COPYRIGHTED WORKS.

1990
COPYRIGHT ACT (SECTION 102 AMEND)(US)
THE FOLLOWING BUILDING DESIGNS CANNOT BE
REGISTERED: DESIGNS THAT WERE CONSTRUCTED,
OR WHOSE PLANS OR DRAWINGS WERE PUBLISHED,
BEFORE DECEMBER 1, 1990; DESIGNS THAT WERE
UNCONSTRUCTED AND CREATED IN UNPUBLISHED
PLANS OR DRAWINGS ON DECEMBER 1, 1990, AND
WERE NOT CONSTRUCTED ON OR BEFORE DECEMBER
31, 2002; STRUCTURES OTHER THAN BUILDINGS,
SUCH AS BRIDGES, CLOVERLEAFS, DAMS, WALK-
WAYS, TENTS, RECREATIONAL VEHICLES, MOBILE
HOMES, AND BOATS.

2007
HEALTH AND SAFETY CODE (CA)
A PUBLIC ENTITY SHOULD NOT PROVIDE COPIES OF
BUILDING PLANS WITHOUT THE WRITTEN CONSENT
OF THE ARCHITECT WHO SIGNED THE ORIGINAL
PLANS.

SEXUAL HARASSMENT
(SEE PAGE 120)

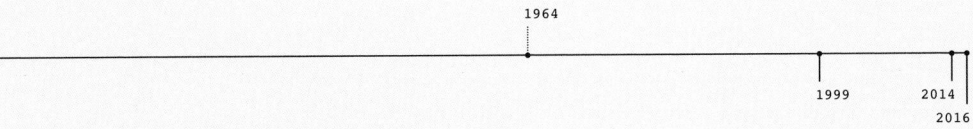

1964

1999   2014
              2016

1964
CIVIL RIGHTS ACT (US)
PROHIBITS UNWELCOME SEXUAL ADVANCES,
REQUESTS FOR SEXUAL FAVORS, AND OTHER VERBAL
OR PHYSICAL CONDUCT OF A SEXUAL NATURE.

A SAFE WORKPLACE
(SEE PAGE 122)

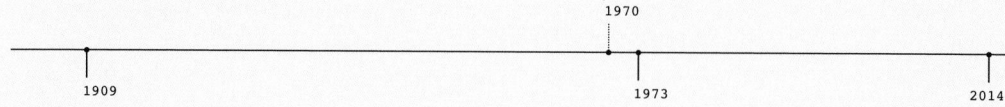

1909   1970   1973   2014

●------ 1970
        OCCUPATIONAL SAFETY AND HEALTH ACT
        (OSHA)(US)
        ASSURE SAFE AND HEALTHFUL WORKING CONDITIONS
        FOR WORKING MEN AND WOMEN.

SEPARATIONS
(SEE PAGE 130)

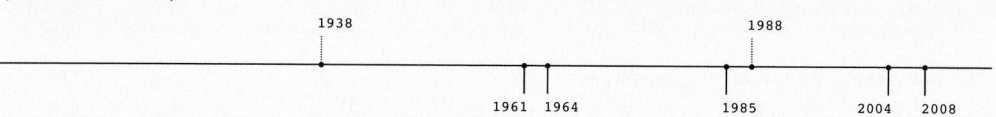

                    1938   1988

          1961 1964   1985   2004 2008

●------ 1938
        THE FAIR LABOR STANDARDS ACT (FLSA)(CA)
        EMPLOYERS MUST PROVIDE THE EMPLOYEE'S FINAL
        PAYCHECK IMMEDIATELY IF THE EMPLOYEE'S
        NOTICE TO RESIGN IS AT LEAST 72 HOURS IN
        ADVANCE.

●------ 1938
        THE FAIR LABOR STANDARDS ACT (FLSA)(NY)
        THE EMPLOYER HAS 72 HOURS TO PROCESS AND
        DISBURSE THE EMPLOYEE'S FINAL PAY.

●------ 1988
        WORKER ADJUSTMENT AND RETRAINING NOTIFICA-
        TION ACT (WARN)(US)
        OFFERS PROTECTION TO WORKERS, THEIR FAMILIES
        AND COMMUNITIES BY REQUIRING EMPLOYERS TO
        PROVIDE NOTICE 60 DAYS IN ADVANCE OF COVERED
        PLANT CLOSINGS AND COVERED MASS LAYOFFS.

TEMPERATURE AND VENTILATION
(SEE PAGE 212)

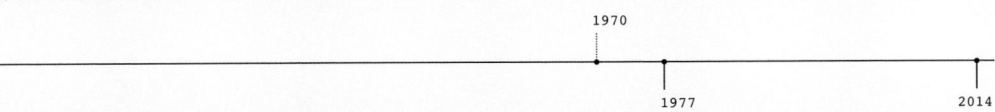

1970
OCCUPATIONAL SAFETY AND HEALTH ACT
(OSHA)(US)
RECOMMENDS TEMPERATURE CONTROL IN THE RANGE
OF 68-76° F AND HUMIDITY CONTROL IN THE
RANGE OF 20%-60%, BUT BECAUSE CLIMATE IS
USUALLY A MATTER OF PERSONAL COMFORT RATHER
THAN HAZARD, THERE ARE NO SPECIFIC MANDATES.

GENERAL BENEFITS
(SEE PAGE 260)

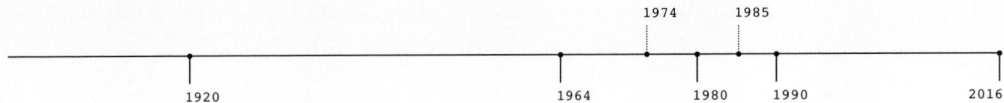

1974
EMPLOYEE RETIREMENT INCOME SECURITY ACT (US)
ESTABLISHES STANDARDS FOR THE FUNDING AND
OPERATION OF PENSION AND HEALTH CARE PLANS
PROVIDED BY EMPLOYERS TO THEIR EMPLOYEES.
[...] SETS UNIFORM MINIMUM STANDARDS TO
ENSURE THAT EMPLOYEE BENEFIT PLANS ARE
ESTABLISHED AND MAINTAINED IN A FAIR AND
FINANCIALLY SOUND MANNER.

1985
CONSOLIDATED OMNIBUS BUDGET RECONCILIATION
ACT (COBRA)(US)
OUTLINES HOW EMPLOYEES AND FAMILY MEMBERS
MAY ELECT CONTINUATION OF HEALTH COVERAGE
FOR A PERIOD OF TIME AFTER EITHER VOLUNTARY
OR INVOLUNTARY TERMINATION.

VACATION
(SEE PAGE 266)

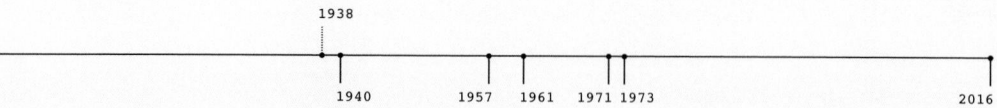

1938
1940   1957   1961   1971 1973   2016

•┈┈┈┈ 1938
FAIR LABOR STANDARDS ACT (FLSA)(US)
DOES NOT REQUIRE EMPLOYER-PROVIDED VACATION
TIME. IT DOES NOT REQUIRE PAYMENT FOR TIME
NOT WORKED, SUCH AS VACATIONS OR HOLIDAYS
(FEDERAL OR OTHERWISE). THESE BENEFITS ARE
GENERALLY A MATTER OF AGREEMENT BETWEEN AN
EMPLOYER AND AN EMPLOYEE (OR THE EMPLOYEE'S
REPRESENTATIVE).

SICK AND PERSONAL DAYS
(SEE PAGE 268)

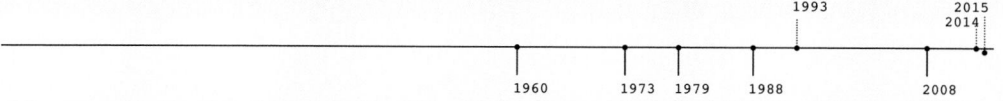

1993   2015
                             2014
1960   1973 1979   1988   2008

•┈┈┈┈ 1993
FAMILY AND MEDICAL LEAVE ACT (US)
REQUIRES EMPLOYERS TO PROVIDE EMPLOYEES
JOB-PROTECTED AND UNPAID LEAVE FOR QUALIFIED
MEDICAL AND FAMILY REASONS.

•┈┈┈┈ 2014
EARNED SICK TIME ACT (NY)
REQUIRES MOST PRIVATE EMPLOYERS TO PROVIDE
UP TO 40 HOURS OF PAID OR UNPAID SICK LEAVE
PER YEAR TO EMPLOYEES WORKING IN NEW YORK
CITY.

•┈┈┈┈ 2015
PAID SICK LEAVE LAW (CA)
PROVIDES EMPLOYEES WHO WORK IN CALIFORNIA
FOR 30 OR MORE DAYS WITHIN A YEAR FROM THE
BEGINNING OF EMPLOYMENT WITH PAID SICK
LEAVE. EMPLOYEES, INCLUDING PART-TIME AND
TEMPORARY EMPLOYEES, WILL EARN AT LEAST
ONE HOUR OF PAID LEAVE FOR EVERY 30 HOURS
WORKED. AN EMPLOYER MAY LIMIT THE AMOUNT OF
PAID SICK LEAVE AN EMPLOYEE CAN USE IN ONE
YEAR TO 24 HOURS OR THREE DAYS.

The apparent indifference on the part of so many architects to the actual working conditions of their draftsmen is greater than it should be.

A retirement plan will foresee, at least for some of the younger men, tax beneficial deferred payment of monthly pension after their 65th year of life and, above all, a life and accident insurance which will yield for widows and children another very welcome type of security.

The company provides a major medical insurance program (100% paid by the company) for all full time employees and their families. There is a 30-day waiting period before new employees become eligible and there is a provision for conversion of individual policy upon separation from the company.

The goal of Cannon's group benefits program is to meet individual requirements for your own and your family's well-being. The various plans provide a foundation for: 1. Protection—against medical/surgical/hospital expenses. 2. Security—by providing an income to you upon your retirement or for disability as well as a benefit to your survivors in the case of death. 3. Opportunity—for professional and career growth.

██████ provides full-time employees with health, dental, and short and long-term disability benefits and life insurance. Medical and Dependent Care Reimbursement accounts and the Transit Saver program allow for the setting aside of money before taxes to pay for these expenses. Employees are eligible for these benefits on the first day of employment.

1920

1964

1980

1990

2016

7 — 1 GENERAL BENEFITS

1. The output (and thus spatial and political influence) of any office is determined by the ways in which the office works internally, and the ways in which the office supports itself. In other words: the organizational and business models of the office determine its conceptual bent. This also means that certain aesthetic strategies, formal logics, or research paradigms are unattainable outside of their originating organizational structures.

    Thus, the office itself is to be treated as a site to be designed, fabricated, and experimented with, in order to research, and enact a wide variety of outcomes.

2. Experimentation arises from self-pedagogy, and does not just involve doing new things, but teaching oneself new ways to do things. In an office, a collective atmosphere of self-teaching and co-teaching manifests and originates from an atmosphere of play.

    To play is to have both a rigorous understanding of and a healthy irreverence for one's current framework of practice. Rigor without irreverence is rote, irreverence without rigor is reactionary, but rigor with irreverence is playful, flexible, and generative. At its best, play is generative, diversifying, and focused not only on performance but also on exploration. In the language of optimization, play stops you from becoming cemented in local optima; in the language of paradigms, play allows the pursuit of new frameworks, perhaps incommensurate with previous ones.

    To be playful is to potentially step outside of one's own framework and jump into another that may not exist yet. This form of play arises from a sense of freedom to discover for the sake of curiosity.

3. The degree of play (and thus experimentation) of the office's work is directly proportional to the sense of psychological safety its members feel. Psychological safety is the means for playful self-pedagogy; the means to follow ideas with a healthy and playful irreverence, the means to challenge one's own frameworks of thinking.

    Acknowledging and accommodating mental/bodily requirements are absolutely vital components for creating a healthy society capable of harboring experimentation. In the same fashion, the office should provide:

    - A clear, defined work schedule and transparent pay structure.
    - Benefits, paid sick days, health insurance, and childcare leave.
    - Pedagogical processes that actively help members learn new skills and concepts.
    - Project roles that balance experimentation and implementation.
    - A conversationally open environment where expressing risky ideas is encouraged.
    - A setting that respects a diversity of work habits and environments.
    - Processes that respect everyone's time and keeps meetings to a minimum.
    - Clear, transparent social norms for communicating difficult issues.

4. Experimentation may not be easily identified as "architectural practice." This is fine: the goal for an office is to understand experimentation as process, not as identity (e.g. "an office that experiments," not "an experimental office"). The goal for GENERAL BENEFITS is to enable its members to follow these routes for experimentation. Dan Taeyoung

1931
John Russell Pope
"Office Manual, Architect
Routine and Procedure"
The Architectural Record

New Year's Day, January 1st
Lincoln's Birthday, February 12th
Washington's Birthday, February 22nd
Memorial Day, May 30th
Independence Day, July 4th
Labor Day
Columbus Day, October 12th
Election Day
Thanksgiving Day
Christmas Day, December 25th

1957
Atlee B. and Robert M. Ayres
Office Rules

Employees will be paid in full although no work will be performed on the following days: New Year's Day, Fourth of July, Labor Day, Thanksgiving Day and Christmas Day. There will be a half-holiday on San Jacinto Day. When a holiday falls on Sunday, the following Monday will be considered a holiday.

1931

1961
Daggett, Naegele &
Associates Inc.
*A Statement Concerning
Company Policies*

This firm observes the following holidays:
New Year's Day
Memorial Day
Fourth of July
Thanksgiving
Christmas

1974
Venturi and Rauch
Venturi and Rauch Handbook

The firm observes the following as paid holidays:
New Year's Day, Memorial Day, Fourth of July, Labor Day, Thanksgiving Day (2 days) and Christmas Day

1957
1961

1985
Ibsen Nelsen
and Associates, P.S.
Office Personnel Guidelines

Full time personnel are eligible for the following 8 ½ days paid holidays:
New Year's Day
Washington's Birthday (President's Day)
Memorial Day
Independence Day
Labor Day
Thanksgiving Day and Friday following
Christmas Day and ½ day preceding

1974

2004
Davis Brody Bond, LLP
Employee Policy Manual

1985

There are nine (9) paid holidays each year, as follows:
New Year's Day
Martin Luther King's Birthday
President's Day
Memorial Day
Independence Day
Labor Day
Thanksgiving Day
Day after Thanksgiving Day
Christmas Day

2004

2016
Diller Scofidio + Renfro
Office Manual

DS+R observes the following paid holidays:
New Year's Day
Martin Luther King, Jr. Day OR Presidents' Day
Memorial Day
Independence Day
Labor Day
Columbus Day
Thanksgiving
Day after Thanksgiving
Christmas Eve
Christmas Day

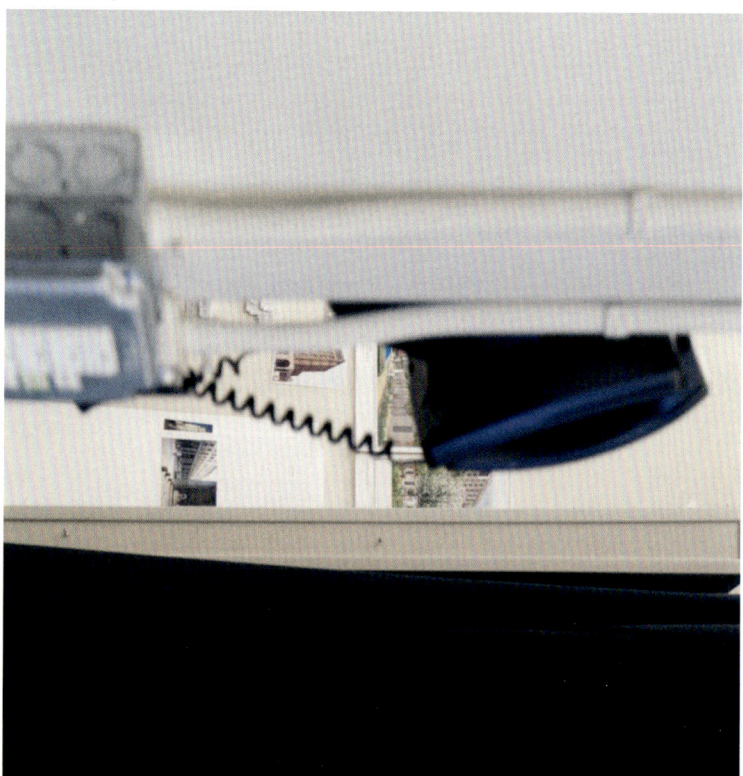

264

7 — 2 OFFICE HOLIDAYS

Holidays have a tenuous grip on history.

Since 1870, over 1,100 proposals to establish permanent holidays have been brought before the United States Congress. Only eleven of these proposals have been approved.

Moreover, national holidays, though recognized by the country's highest legislative body, have an equally tenuous grip on their future.

Pursuant to the Tenth Amendment of the United States Constitution, the federal government maintains a limited jurisdiction over official holidays. Only federal employees and residents of the District of Columbia are guaranteed the eleven official national holidays. State and local government, and ultimately private employers, hold the exclusive rights to recognize and enforce the observance of holidays, whether in terms of paid time off from work or the closing of certain businesses and government offices.

In the fluidity of the global economy, employers often elect to respect holidays of two nations when employees are embedded in a foreign job site. For example, an American employee in Italy is thankful that the tasty *sugo alla bolognese* and *vitello tonnato* he or she will eat on Assumption Day (*Ferragosto*) predate the gluttonous American barbeque on Labor Day by a mere two weeks. *Amiamo l'Italia*!

Grounded in the incipient labor movement of the 1880s, holidays were designed to ease work's toil on the body. Peter J. McGuire, a co-founder of the American Federation of Labor, invented Labor Day as an honor to those "who from rude nature have delved and carved all the grandeur we behold." As labor's focus has shifted from the stonemason of this "grandeur" to its draftsman, and finally, to its bland administrator, holidays are now couched as relief from the monotony and mental taxation of the modern office.

But as labor entangles itself more fully in life's quotidian habits and divests from employees themselves, holidays might need to find other hosts.

It's entirely feasible—and quite logical—to give architecture a holiday.

As Jean Labatut, the iconoclast architect/teacher who designed fountains, spectacles, camouflage–nearly anything but architecture, exclaimed, "architecture is a '*une maîtresse jalouse*;' (a jealous mistress) and deserves time off."

An architecture office, having given its discipline this benefit, might be free to enjoin itself to life's other experiences, pleasures, and pursuits. Perhaps the group might spend time tackling thorny social issues or volunteering for a local need. Maybe the team spends time on creating spaces and ideas that don't rely upon the stuff of architecture. They might even consider social events to foster collaboration.

It's likely, no matter how the office elects to compensate for architecture's absence, that the discipline will return with renewed vibrancy, not to mention a ruddier complexion. Matthew Clarke

7 — 3 VACATION

Those who have been in our employment over twelve (12) consecutive months shall receive 11 working days with pay for vacation.

Two-weeks paid vacation will be paid each year for those in employ over one year's time.

A new employee is entitled to two weeks of vacation after one full year of employment.

During the first year of service, an employee is entitled to one day per month vacation time, to a maximum of ten working days, and after one year's service, two weeks' paid vacation.

Vacation with pay is nine working days per calendar year.

Staff employees accrue vacation at a rate of 20 regular workdays per year on a pro-rated basis. For staff employees, on the anniversary of the 60th, 20th, and 180th months of employment, the rate of accrual will increase by an additional 5 regular workdays of vacation on a pro-rated basis.

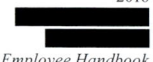

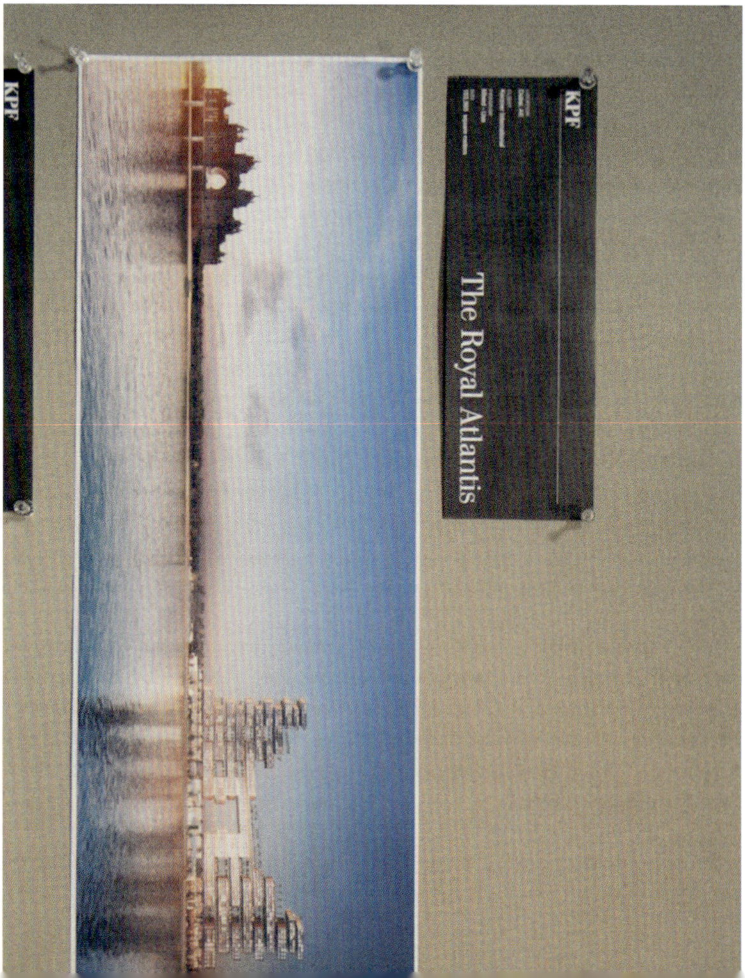

7 — 3 VACATION

The average American office worker gets ten days of paid leave annually. This means that out of the roughly 260 business days in the average calendar year, only 4 percent are available for vacation, with the remaining 96 percent reserved for work. This wildly disproportionate ratio is troubling, but perhaps even more problematic is the stark dichotomy underlying this policy: vacation is defined as the absence of work, and vice versa.

A very different ratio, along with a looser approach to the relation between work and play, is suggested by a story (perhaps apocryphal) from Google's early, most innovative days. The company's employees were supposedly directed to take 20 percent of their time off from their normal jobs, devoting it instead to personal, undirected, and experimental projects. Many of the company's most groundbreaking products, including Gmail, are said to have come from this so-called 20 percent time policy. Today, this kind of approach has become more about the atmosphere of the workplace than the structure of work itself, largely devolving into the clichés of nap pods, snack fridges, and ping pong tables. But Google's original program provides a powerful model for a kind of open-ended research that resonates far beyond the tech world.

The question of what, exactly, constitutes research in architecture is one of the most pressing questions facing the field today. On the one hand, articulating a credible model of design research is crucial to architecture's survival in an increasingly competitive global economy in which "innovation" is understood as largely synonymous with R&D and within which architects have already ceded an enormous amount of control to expert consultants from an array of research-driven fields, from engineering to ecology to urban planning. Within the academy, research is arguably even more important. As the humanities continue to be squeezed, architecture is under increasing pressure to abandon its historical position as a bridge between art and science and fall in line with the grant-funded, data-driven, revenue-generating model that dominates big research universities worldwide.

But if architecture has never quite fit into the model of open-ended creative exploration that has traditionally defined artistic practice, it is not fully compatible with the rigorous methodologies of the so-called hard sciences either. This ambiguity leaves architects in a difficult position, both confused and vulnerable to exploitation. Clients will rarely pay for any research that is not directly applicable to the project they have commissioned. Developers or manufacturers have shown a willingness to support some academic research—by underwriting design studios, for example—but the results tend to be highly self-serving, more like the "sponsored content" rapidly replacing real journalism in the online marketplace as opposed to actual disciplinary innovation.

But perhaps we could redefine architectural practice in the way that Google (at least temporarily) redefined work—building in the expectation that any architectural project or commission should by definition include a certain amount of undirected exploration. It may be that real architectural research is, in the end, simply open-ended architectural thinking and production, time to design, to play, to practice, free from specific client demands or the framework of an official academic project. The best model for architectural research may be vacation time. ^{Julian Rose}

1960
Office of Architect
Maynard Lyndon
Employee's Manual

One half day per month is credited to each employee for leave. This may be used as sick leave or vacation at employee's option. Other time off is deducted unless specific arrangements are made regarding this time.

1973
Hugh Stubbins Associates
Office Manual

Every effort should be made to restrict personal time to your Friday off. Should this not be possible, arrangements for making up time should be made with your Project Manager or Department Head.

1979
Ibsen Nelsen
and Associates, P.S.
Office Personnel Guidelines

Pregnancy is defined as an illness and individuals covered by the group health plan are eligible for benefits there to appertaining.

1988
Emery, Roth & Sons,
P.C. Architects
Office Guidelines

Sick leave is paid at the discretion of the principals. In no case is any absence paid for during the first month of employment nor is any temporary employee granted paid sick leave.

2008
Höweler + Yoon
Architecture
Policy Manual

Personal / sick days are considered "emergency time off" from a scheduled day of work. Employees should only use this on a per emergency basis. Employees are given 3 paid personal or sick days per calendar year and only after they have completed their first performance review period.

1960

1973

1979

1988

2008

7 — 4 SICK AND PERSONAL DAYS

Living under the assumption that our minds and bodies are always ready to perform at their maximum capacity, to take a sick day becomes a statement about our own fragility: I'm unable to work today.

In the assessment and quantification of the unhealthy, the politics of "normal" are mobilized. By taking sick leave I declare that I am not able—now, in the following days, or even ever again—to perform as before, or as expected from me by my employer.

The starting day of sick leave marks a moment of disruption. I'd like to prove that I could fulfill my responsibilities even if I don't feel well. After all, in a society of achievement and display, sick bodies and minds are too often sites of shame and distrust. But today, I don't feel well. I'm not fit for work. I expose myself as unable to continue what I committed and scheduled to do.

This declaration—in cases in which the employee has access to paid leave—triggers a bureaucratic protocol, an agreement between employer and employee that involves evaluation and control for health concerns, generally mediated and assessed by a qualified professional or independent agency. I am not, at least temporarily, a productive member of the social and professional group to which, by contract, I belong: I am currently on leave and will respond to your email upon my return.

To avoid becoming a potential threat to the economic and social stability of the office, I am requested to return to work as soon as my health improves. We are sorry to hear that you are not feeling well today, and we wish you a speedy recovery. Managers' annual reports highlight statistics about the relation between unscheduled absenteeism and production loss. Prevention is written in bold by those who don't support the approval of paid sick leave laws. Personal days are spent in mindfulness therapy, retreats, and coaching sessions. Every morning running crowds in sports gear render visible healthiness, the responsibility of a happier and more productive white-collar worker. Contagion—argue others who incentivize workers to stay at home when they are ill—is a public health issue. Flexible office designs, laptops, and remote communication systems, encourage and facilitate the possibility of working from home even for the sick employee. The passing of paid leave laws succeeded when sold as an investment in a healthier, less infectious work force.

Upon being declared fit to work, back at the space of maximum productivity and professionalism, I am assessed, again, as per the parameters of the healthy. Reasonable adjustments in the schedule, workload, and goals could, exceptionally, be put in place for the chronically sick or disabled. I'm sorry for the slow response, I was on leave. Please accept my sincere apologies.

Marina Otero Verzier

1941
Royal Barry Wills
and Leon Keach
This Business of Architecture

Membership in a recreational or social club has the twofold purpose of keeping the "little woman" happy and furthering one's business affairs. You cannot afford not to achieve both of those desiderata, so all or part of the club dues are properly a part of Overhead.

Professional societies quite clearly fall into the same class.

1974
Venturi and Rauch
Venturi and Rauch Handbook

Staff members are encouraged to participate in the activities of the American Institute of Architects, American Institute of Planners, Construction Specifications Institute, or the professional engineering societies of their choice. Active involvement in a professional society strengthens the individual, the firm, and the profession.

1980
Archonics
Personnel Information

Payments of dues to professional societies are paid by the firm if it is deemed to enhance the professional standing of the individual and his value to the firm. Payment of dues for service clubs and civic organizations are paid on a permission basis. Initiation fees are the responsibility of the employee.

2016

Employee Handbook

Initial and annual dues in one recognized professional organization will be paid for all full-time employees after completion of one year of continuous service. To qualify an employee must be an active participant in the organization. All memberships are to be approved by a Partner or Director in charge of the office.

1941

1974

1980

2016

270

7 — 5 PROFESSIONAL ASSOCIATIONS

In the United States, a large majority of architecture firms are very small (63 percent of the American Institute of Architects 2012 survey of firms had from one to four employees) and their young age attests to both the volatility and the entrepreneurial nature of architectural practice. Despite the continued rise of large corporate firms that account for most of the billings, the majority of small or medium firms are responsible for the bulk of architectural employment. For this reason it would be a good sign to see a policy dealing with career advancement or, more boldly, contemplating unionization.

Unionization is something that small and medium firms in the United States probably fear like the plague, although it does not seem alien to architectural practice in the United Kingdom or the Baltic countries. I am aware of one historical attempt to unionize architects in the Bay Area in the early 1970s, and it seems to have left no trace. The fledgling union won the right to represent professional employees in a medium-large office, but it lost its first election, held long enough after the first vote for employers to discourage the idea and for union supporters to be outnumbered by new hires. At the time, I was struck that so many poorly paid architects, who had neither job security nor health insurance, should consider that forming a union was "unprofessional."

Needless to say, the American Institute of Architects, which mostly represents the smaller firms, does not mention unions or even architectural employees on its site. In 2009, when the revenues of architectural firms were plummeting and architectural unemployment had increased by 450 percent (to hover between 12 percent and 9 percent depending on experience), an "Architects Union" launched a Facebook site "to test the level of interest among architects in creating an Architects Union." It had gathered seventy-one "likes" by 2012, when it disappeared. One exception is the large (4,500 members) Engineers and Architects Association of Los Angeles, "formed in 1894 as a professional association to represent and promote the interests of professionals in the City of Los Angeles." But it now includes all sorts of technical and administrative personnel and functions as a full service labor union.

The production of architecture takes place in firms of vastly different characteristics. All have problems securing commissions and, presumably, finding the employees they need. Sociologists have repeatedly noted the absence of career advancement in the architectural firms they studied and the acute problem this posed for professional employees, who were highly educated, often licensed, and frequently held advanced or specialized degrees.

As the tendency to outsource technical work proceeds apace, unionization may seem more interesting to the younger employees threatened by the loss of low level work. A 2012 survey, however, found that both firms with more than fifty employees and firms with less than ten anticipated some kind of shortage of architects in 2014 "resulting from a combination of designers exiting the profession, baby boomers retiring, a lack of skills among architects looking for work, and less talent in the pipeline as job prospects discourage students from entering the field." Both kinds of firms, especially the smaller ones, were having great difficulties finding architects skilled in sustainable design. Clearly, for growing firms, the problem of career paths and employee participation should acquire overriding and growing importance. Magali Sarfatti-Larson

The Architects
Amie Siegel

Commissioned by Storefront for Art and Architecture as part of *OfficeUS* (the project of the US Pavilion at the 2014 International Architecture Biennale), artist Amie Siegel's *The Architects* cuts transversally through the city of New York, producing a continuous image of the global architecture office today. Moving through ten architecture studios—from Fifth Avenue to Downtown to Brooklyn—the film depicts the operational territories and landscapes of worldwide architectural production from New York.

As a singular unfolding visual, the film deploys silent conversations among the architectures, locations, objects, and characters that inhabit its frames, raising questions of scale, agency, and power.

Parallel tracking shots through the working offices chart their typologies of sameness and difference, revealing reappearing elements of the spaces of architectural production: long horizontal desks, screens, renderings, and models. The film frames a wide spectrum of practices, from large firms to smaller studios, in a collective new whole. It positions itself from a vantage point that places the lens of the camera between the spaces of production and the world, which is always (and only) just outside the window.

The Architects was first presented at the Arsenale in Venice during the closing week of *OfficeUS*, the US Pavilion at the International Architecture Biennale (La Biennale di Venezia) in November 2014.

This film was made possible by Storefront for Art and Architecture with the generous support of Elise Jaffe + Jeffrey Brown.

Film Credits

Amie Siegel, *The Architects*, 2014
HD video, 33 minutes, color/sound
Commissioned by Storefront for Art and Architecture for *OfficeUS*.

Producer: Andrew Fierberg
Co-Producer: Martina Klich
Production Manager: Tina Piccari
Cinematographer: Christine A. Maier
1st Assistant Camera: Bayley Sweitzer
Digital/Tech: Henry Prince

Sound Recordist: Timothy Wong
Key Grip: Mark Solomon
Grip: Dan Stenzel and Wil Hamlin
PA: Nir Bitton and Matthew Town
Color Correct and Conform: Post Republic, Berlin
Sound Mixer: Gisberg Smialek

SOURCES

Manuals
(Not Including Confidential Sources)

McKim, Mead & White. *Manual of Office Practice*, 1922. McKim, Mead & White Collection. Avery Drawings & Archives. Avery Architectural & Fine Arts Library, Columbia University.

Ayres, Atlee B., and Robert M. Ayers. *Office Rules of Atlee B. and Robert M. Ayers*, 1923. Architectural drawings, photographs and records 1894–1977. Alexander Architectural Archive. University of Texas Libraries, University of Texas at Austin.

Adams, Frederick J. *Manual of Office Practice for the Architectural Worker, Compiled for Use in the Office of McKim, Mead & White.* (New York: Charles Scribner's Sons, 1924).

Trimble, Robert Maurice. *Office and Drafting Room Practice*, 1928. Arthur Brown, Jr. Papers. The Bancroft Library, University of California, Berkeley.

Brown, Arthur, Jr. *Office Reorganization Memo*, 1929. Arthur Brown, Jr. Papers. The Bancroft Library, University of California, Berkeley.

Ayres, Atlee B., and Robert M. Ayers. *Office Rules*, 1940. Architectural drawings, photographs and records 1894–1977. Alexander Architectural Archive. University of Texas Libraries, University of Texas at Austin.

Bonn, W. J., and J. J. Sullivan. *Manual of Instructions for Junior Architects*, 1942. Ryerson & Burnham Libraries, The Art Institute of Chicago.

Frederick G. Frost Architects. *Office Manual*, 1948. The Firm of Frederick G. Frost Architects.

Cliff May Associates. *Drafting Room Manual*, 1956. Architecture and Design Collection. Museum University of California, Santa Barbara.

Office of Architect Maynard Lyndon. *Employee's Manual*, 1960. Architecture and Design Collection. Museum University of California, Santa Barbara.

Daggett, Naegele & Associates. *A Statement Concerning Company Policies*, 1961. The Daggett Collection, Ball State Archive, Muncie, IN.

Broad and Nelson. *Office Manual: Dictation & Typing*, 1963. Donald S. Nelson Collection, University of Texas at Austin.

Richard J. Neutra Office. *A Tentative Outline, Summed Up from Various Suggestions*, 1964. Richard and Dion Neutra Papers, 1925–1970. Charles E. Young Research Library, University of California, Los Angeles.

Richard J. Neutra Office. *Rules for Apprentice – Students*, 1964. Richard and Dion Neutra Papers, 1925–1970. Charles E. Young Research Library, University of California, Los Angeles.

Richard J. Neutra Office. *Office Reorganization*, 1964. Richard and Dion Neutra Papers, 1925–1970. Charles E. Young Research Library, University of California, Los Angeles.

Victor Gruen International. *Articles of Incorporation*, 1966. Wyoming Collection, Wyoming State Archives, Cheyenne, WY.

Harry Weese and Associates. *Design Standards/Organization and Design – HWA Office and Draft Memorandum*, 1968. Harry Weese and Associates Collection. Ryerson & Burnham Libraries, The Art Institute of Chicago.

Ernest J. Kump Associates Architects. *Organization for Architectural Practice*, 1969. Ernest J. Kump Collection. Environmental Design Archives, University of California, Berkeley.

Neutra, Richard J. *Excerpts of Ideas of Possible Use in the Neutra Office*, 1969. Richard and Dion Neutra Papers, 1925–1970. Charles E. Young Research Library, University of California, Los Angeles.

Abbott, Merkt & Company. *Accounting Department Procedure Manual*, 1969. Abbott, Merkt & Company Collection. Avery Drawings & Archives. Avery Architectural & Fine Arts Library, Columbia University.

Abbott, Merkt & Company. *Procedural Manual Office Memorandum*, 1971. Abbott, Merkt & Company Collection. Avery Drawings & Archives. Avery Architectural & Fine Arts Library, Columbia University.

Abbott, Merkt & Company. *Central File and Drawing Office Memorandum*, 1971. Abbott, Merkt & Company Collection. Avery Drawings & Archives. Avery Architectural & Fine Arts Library, Columbia University.

Lewis Clarke Associates. *Handbook of Office Policies*, 1972. Lewis Clarke Collection. North Carolina State University Libraries.

Hugh Stubbins Associates. *Office Manual*, 1973. Hugh Stubbins Archives. Frances Loeb Library, Harvard University.

Abbott, Merkt & Company. *Responsibilities and Authorities of Architectural Job Captain*, 1974. Abbott, Merkt & Company Collection. Avery Drawings & Archives. Avery Architectural & Fine Arts Library, Columbia University.

Venturi and Rauch. *Venturi and Rauch Handbook*, (1974).

Ibsen Nelsen and Associates. *Office Personnel Guidelines*, 1979. Nelsen Papers. Center for Pacific Northwest Studies, Heritage Resources, Western Washington University.

Archronics. *"Information" Archronics Corporation Policies and Practices*, 1980. Johnson & Miller Architectural Records, Drawings and Documents Archive. Ball State University Libraries.

Ibsen Nelsen and Associates. *Book Keeping Procedures*, 1983. Nelsen Papers. Center for Pacific Northwest Studies, Heritage Resources, Western Washington University.

Smithey & Boynton Architects & Engineers. *Operating Manual*, 1983. Virginia Polytechnic Institute and State University.

Ibsen Nelsen and Associates. *Memorandum on 23rd March*, 1985. Nelsen Papers. Center for Pacific Northwest Studies, Heritage Resources, Western Washington University.

Ibsen Nelsen and Associates. *Office Personnel Guidelines*, 1985. Nelsen Papers. Center for Pacific Northwest Studies, Heritage Resources, Western Washington University.

Bertrand Goldberg Associates. *Interoffice Memo*, 1986. Henry B. Boynton Papers. Ryerson & Burnham Libraries, The Art Institute of Chicago.

Emery, Roth & Sons. *Office Guidelines*, 1988. Avery Drawings & Archives. Avery Architectural & Fine Arts Library, Columbia University.

Killingsworth, Stricker, Lindgren, Wilson and Associates. *Office Manual*, 1988. Architecture and Design Collection. Museum University of California, Santa Barbara.

Cannon Design. *Office Protocol*, (1990).

SLR/Architects. *Office Manual*, 1991. Sigrid L. Rupp Architectural Collection. Virginia Polytechnic Institute and State University.

Baden-Powell, Francis. *Building Overseas*: Butterworth Architecture Management Guide. (Oxford: Redwood Press, 1993).

Davis Brody Bond. *Employee Policy Manual*, (2004).

Höweler + Yoon Architecture. *Policy Manual*, (2008).

Arquitectonica. *The Project Management Manual*, (2009).

Kallmann, McKinnell & Wood Architects. *Employee Handbook*, (2010).

SsD. *Employee Handbook*, (2012).

Adrian Smith+Gordon Hill Architecture. *Employee Handbook*, (2014).

Hodgetts + Fung Design and Architecture. *Personnel Policy Manual*, (2014).

Slade Architecture. *The Slade Architecture Employee Handbook: Forms, Benefits, Policies & Information*, (2014).

Diller Scofidio + Renfro. *Office Manual*, (2014).

Snøhetta. *Snøhetta Guide*, (2016).

Essays and Articles

"The Organization of an Architect's Office, No. 1." *Engineering and Building Record* (January 1890): 83.

"The Organization of an Architect's Office, No. 3." *Engineering and Building Record* (February 1890): 181.

Higgins, Daniel Paul. "The 'Business' of Architecture, Part 1." *The Architectural Review* (September 1916): 167–8.

Higgins, Daniel Paul. "The 'Business' of Architecture, Part 4, Section 1." *The Architectural Review* (September 1918): 4.

Smith, Howard Dwight. "The Function of the Designer in the 'Business' of Architecture, Part 1." *The Architectural Review* (May 1918): 78.

Smith, Howard Dwight. "The 'Business' of Architecture, The Position of the Supervising Architect in the Organization." *The Architectural Review* (October 1920): 118.

Smith, Howard Dwight. "The 'Business' of Architecture, The Drafting Room, Engineering and Inspection." *The Architectural Review* (June 1920): 78.

Bannister, Williams P. "The Practice of Architecture." *The American Architect: Golden Anniversary Number* (January 1926): 40–48.

American Institute of Architects. "Advising the Client to Build Now." *The Octagon, A Journal of the American Institute of Architects* (November 1930): 3.

Wright, Frank Lloyd. "Architecture as a Profession is All Wrong." *The American Architect* (December 1930): 22–34.

Garfield, Abram. "Personal Publicity." *The Octagon, A Journal of the American Institute of Architects* (December 1930): 7–9.

Pope, John Russell. "Office Manual of John Russell Pope, Architect Routine and Procedure." *The Architectural Record* (February 1931): 177.

Bergstrom, Edwin. "The Architects' Responsibility." *The Octagon, A Journal of the American Institute of Architects* (February 1931): 3–6.

"The Architect in Civic Affairs." *The Octagon, A Journal of the American Institute of Architects* (August 1931): 9–10.

American Institute of Architects. "Standards of Practice of the American Institute of Architects, Part 1." *The Octagon, A Journal of the American Institute of Architects* (October 1939): 28–29.

Lorimer, Gordon. "The Bureau in Architecture." *The Octagon, A Journal of the American Institute of Architects* (April 1944): 135–140.

Stanton, Henry. "Architecture — A Profession or a Business?" *The Octagon, A Journal of the American Institute of Architects* (February 1949): 53–56.

Clarke, Gilmore D. "The Salaried Practitioner, The Ethics of Independent Practice 'On The Side'." *Landscape Architecture* (July 1951): 152.

Guidebooks and AIA Publications

Parry, Kaye W. *Office Management: A Handbook for Architects and Civil Engineers.* (London: E. & F. N. Spon; New York: Spon & Chamberlain, 1901).

American Institute of Architects, *A Circular of Advice Related to Principles of Professional Practice and The Canons of Ethics.* (American Institute of Architects' Archive, 1909).

Day, Frank Miles, and American Institute of Architects, *The Handbook of Architectural Practice.* (Washington D.C.: American Institute of Architects Press, 1920).

Wills, Royal Barry, and Leon Keach, *This Business of Architecture.* (New York: Reinhold Publishing Corporation, 1941).

American Institute of Architects. *The Handbook of Architectural Practice.* (Washington D.C.: American Institute of Architects Press, 1943).

Green, Ronald. *The Architect's Guide to Running a Job.* (Oxford: Architectural Press, 1962).

Lapidus, Morris. *Architecture: A Profession and a Business.* (New York: Van Nostrand Reinhold, 1967).

Case and Company Management Consultants. *The Economics of Architectural Practice.* (Washington

D.C.: American Institute of Architects Press, 1968).

Caudill, William Wayne. *Architecture by Team: A New Concept for the Practice of Architecture*. (New York: Van Nostrand Reinhold, 1971).

Coxe, Weld. *Marketing Architectural and Engineering Services*. (New York: Van Nostrand Reinhold, 1971).

Koehler, Robert, and American Institute of Architects. *Personnel Practices Handbook*. (Washington D.C.: American Institute of Architects Press, 1978).

Massachusetts Committee for the Preservation of Architectural. Records (Mass COPAR), *Records in Architectural Offices; Suggestions for the Proper Organization, Storage and Conservation of Architectural Office Archives*. (Cambridge: Stone Reprographics, 1981).

Greenstreet, Bob, and Karen Greenstreet. *The Architect's Guide to Law and Practice*. (New York: Van Nostrand Reinhold, 1984).

Sharp, Derek. *The Business of Architectural Practice*. (London: Collins, 1986).

Society of Architectural Administrators. *Handbook for Architectural Administrators*. (Washington D.C.: The Society, 1986).

Kaderlan, Norman. *Designing Your Practice*. (R. R. Donnelley & Sons, 1991).

Schrock, Nancy Carlson, and Mary Campbell Cooper. *Records in Architectural Offices: Suggestions for the Organization, Storage and Conservation of Architectural Office Archives*, 1992. Massachusetts Committee for the Preservation of Architectural Records, Cambridge, MA.

Jenks, Larry D. *Architectural Office Standards and Practices: A Practical User's Guide*. (New York: McGraw-Hill, 1995).

American Institute of Architects, *The Architect's Handbook of Professional Practice*, 12th ed. (Washington D.C.: American Institute of Architects Press, 1996).

Getz, Lowell. *An Architect's Guide to Financial Management*. (Washington D.C.: American Institute of Architects Press, 1997).

Society of Design Administration. *Handbook of Design Office Administration*. (New York: John Willey & Sons,1999).

Tunstall, Gavin. *Managing the Building Design Process*. (Oxford: Butterworth-Heinemann, 2000).

American Institute of Architects. *The Architect's Handbook of Professional Practice*. 13th ed. (New York: Wiley & Sons, 2001).

American Institute of Architects. "Legal Structure of Architecture Firms." In *2005 AIA Compensation Report*. (AIA, 2006). Accessed March 15, 2016. http://www.aia.org/aiaucmp/groups/secure/documents/pdf/aiap016464.pdf.

American Institute of Architects. *The Architect's Handbook of Professional Practice*. 14th ed. (New Jersey: Wiley & Sons, 2008).

American Institute of Architects. "Definition of Architects Positions." In 2005 *AIA Compensation Report: A Survey of U. S. Architecture Firms*. (AIA, 2007). Accessed March 15, 2016. http://www.aia.org/aiaucmp/groups/secure/documents/pdf/aiap016522.pdf.

Contemporary Statements

Contributors

RAMI ABOU-KHALIL is a Lebanese and Canadian architect currently based in New York, where he is a Senior Designer for Skidmore, Owings and Merrill. He leads the New York chapter of Afikra, a salon on Arab culture and history, and dreams of one day amassing a collection of columns.

SEAN ANDERSON is Associate Curator in the Department of Architecture and Design at the Museum of Modern Art. He has practiced as an architect and taught in Afghanistan, India, Italy, Morocco, Sri Lanka, and the UAE His book, *Modern Architecture and Its Representation in Colonial Eritrea,* was published in 2015.

ANDREW ATWOOD is a partner in First Office in Los Angeles, CA. He teaches architecture at UC Berkeley.

PHIL BERNSTEIN is an architect, technologist, and educator. He teaches professional practice at the Yale School of Architecture and was formerly a vice president at Autodesk, a provider of digital tools for the building industry.

BESLER & SONS is a Los Angeles based practice that works across multiple sites of production. Erin Besler is faculty at UCLA in the Department of Architecture & Urban Design. Ian Besler is a lecturer of design at the University of Southern California and adjunct faculty at Art Center College of Design.

ALEKSANDR BIERIG is a PhD student at the Harvard Graduate School of Design.

GABRIELLE BRAINARD is a façade consultant with Heintges & Associates and a Visiting Associate Professor at Pratt Institute. Previously, she was a senior associate at SHoP Architects. She was a winner of *Metals in Construction* magazine's 2016 Design Challenge, and her writing has appeared in *SQM: The Quantified House* (Lars Müeller, 2015), *ARCH+*, and *CLOG*.

LANDON BROWN is a designer and Director of VisionArc, a New York City-based think tank. His independent and professional work leverages research and visualization tools to explore new routes for systemic change amidst challenges affecting ecologies, the built environment, and social cohesion in our communities.

FELIX BURRICHTER is a German-born, New York-based creative director and writer. He studied architecture at the Ecole Spéciale d'Architecture in Paris and Columbia University in New York before founding *PIN—UP* magazine in 2006 of which he is the editor and creative director. In addition to curating exhibitions (*Haus der Kunst*, Swiss Institute) Felix Burrichter consults on artists' projects and is a regular contributor to *W Magazine*, *Fantastic Man*, *The Gentlewoman*, and *Girls Like Us*.

SAVINIEN CARACOSTEA is an architect, pastry chef, and cultural entrepreneur, with interests in retail, cinema, publications, and in the intersection between food, cities, art, and social phenomena. He directed the innovation program of the USA Pavilion at Milan EXPO 2015, and guest-edited the "Food Issue" of the journal *Log*.

RAFAEL DE CÁRDENAS is founder of SoHo-based design firm Rafael de Cárdenas / Architecture at Large, which creates artful, imaginative concepts for diverse projects spanning commercial and residential interiors, art advisory, objects and furniture, and temporary and pop-up spaces.

CHOON CHOI leads CCA (Choon Choi Architects), a Seoul-based design practice. Recently completed projects include the Sangha Farm, in collaboration with artist Kim Beom, and the Maeil Innovation Center. Choon often collaborates with curators to design exhibition spaces, and has exhibited at ArtSonje and Ilmin Museum. He is currently preparing a new performance/exhibition at the National Museum of Modern and Contemporary Art in Seoul.

MATTHEW CLARKE, an architect, planner, and writer, is the Director of Creative Placemaking at The Trust for Public Land. He has previously worked for SHoP Architects, the NYC Department of Cultural Affairs, Stan Allen Architects, and LTL Architects.

PEGGY DEAMER is Professor of Architecture at Yale University. She is the editor of *Architecture and Capitalism: 1845 to the Present* and *The Architect as Worker: Immaterial Labor, the Creative Class, and the Politics of Design*. She is the founding member of the Architecture Lobby.

DESIGNERS ASSEMBLY works to provide a forum for young designers to come together, where they build financial and strategic literacy for a better world by design. Through the building blocks of workshops, panel discussions, lectures, and information sharing events, Designers Assembly aims to construct the base for a new and improved way to practice as designers.

CAROLINE O'DONNELL is principal of the design office CODA, and the Edgar A. Tafel Assistant Professor and director of the Master of Architecture program at Cornell University. She is the editor-in-chief of the *Cornell Journal of Architecture* and recently published her first book: *Niche Tactics: Generative Relationships between Architecture and Site*.

CRAIG EDWARD DYKERS is one of the Founding Partners of Snøhetta. Craig has led many of the office's prominent projects, including the Norwegian National Opera and Ballet in Norway, the National September 11 Memorial Museum Pavilion, the Redesign of Times Square, and the SFMOMA Expansion in San Francisco. His interest in design as a promoter of social and physical well-being is supported by ongoing observation and development of an innovative design process.

KELLER EASTERLING is an architect, writer, and professor at Yale. Her most recent book, *Extrastatecraft: The Power of Infrastructure Space* (Verso, 2014), examines global infrastructure as a medium of polity. Another recent book, *Subtraction* (Sternberg, 2014), considers building removal or how to put the development machine into reverse. Other books include *Enduring Innocence: Global Architecture and its Political Masquerades* (MIT, 2005) and *Organization Space: Landscapes, Highways and Houses in America* (MIT, 1999).

FAMILY is a studio in New York that designs buildings. It's led by Dong, who's from California, and Oana, who's from Romania.

PEDRO GADANHO is a curator, a writer, and an architect. He is the Director of MAAT, the new Museum of Art, Architecture and Technology, in Lisbon. Previously he was a curator of contemporary architecture at the Museum of Modern Art, New York. He was the editor of *BEYOND* bookazine and the *Shrapnel Contemporary* blog, contributes regularly to international publications, and is the author of *Arquitetura em Público*, a recipient of the FAD Prize for Thought and Criticism in 2012.

GORDON GILL, FAIA is a founding partner of Adrian Smith + Gordon Gill Architecture, which is defining cities of the future. Gill's designs share a keen awareness of local environmental conditions, capitalizing on site-specific features that maximize building performance. His recent designs include Astana Expo City 2017 and its sustainable legacy community.

LIAM GILLICK deploys multiple forms to expose the new ideological control systems that emerged at the beginning of the 1990s. He lives and works in New York City.

MARC GUBERMAN is a Partner at Foster + Partners. He lives in San Francisco and is currently working on the design and construction of Apple's new campus.

ADAM HAYES founded Openshop, which for the last fourteen years has been based in New York City, and along with academic work at Pratt Institute and Parsons School of Strategic Design, has served as a laboratory for expanding and developing ideas about how to help companies and individuals optimize the world around them. More recently he also became a founding member of The Collective, an international consulting concern.

JUAN HERREROS is an architect, researcher, and educator. Herreros is the founder of estudio Herreros, Chair Professor at ETSAM-Madrid, and Full Professor at Columbia University's GSAPP. His latest book, *Dialogue Architecture*, contains the texts, drawings, and diagrams about contemporary practice shown in his solo room of the Venice Biennale 2012.

SARAH M. HIRSCHMAN is an architect and lecturer at UC Berkeley. She was founding director of the Keller Gallery at MIT's Department of Architecture and co-curator of *Un/Fair Use*, an exhibition about architectural copyright, at the Center for Architecture in New York in 2015.

PHU HOANG co-directs (with Rachely Rotem) the interdisciplinary architecture practice MODU based in New York City. He is a recipient of the Rome Prize in Architecture, the American Institute of Architect's New Practices New York award and the Architectural League Prize. He also teaches in the Graduate School of Architecture, Planning and Preservation at Columbia University.

FLORIAN IDENBURG is a Dutch architect and co-founder with Jing Liu of SO–IL. SO–IL is a New York based design firm, which envisions spaces for culture, learning, and innovation. Idenburg is Associate Professor of Practice at Harvard, where he teaches design and lectures on workspace design and the changing nature of practice.

MICHAEL JEFFERSON is a principle of the design office JeLe, and a Visiting Critic in the Department of Architecture at Cornell University.

GEORGE BARNETT JOHNSTON is an architect, cultural historian, Professor of Architecture at Georgia Institute of Technology, and author of *Drafting Culture: A Social History of Architectural Graphic Standards* (MIT Press, 2008). His work traces the ongoing transformation of US architectural practice in the light of social and technological contingencies.

JAMES VON KLEMPERER is President of Kohn Pedersen Fox, focusing mainly on the role that large buildings play in making urban space. His designs include Jing An Kerry Center in Shanghai, the 123-story Lotte World Tower in Seoul, and One Vanderbilt which will link midtown New York's tallest tower directly to Grand Central Terminal.

KEITH KRUMWIEDE is a writer, designer and, professor, whose work explores the use, and misuse, of found forms, materials, and words to examine the world and imagine other ways it might have been and may still be. He is the author of *Atlas of Another America*, a work of speculative architectural fiction.

JIMENEZ LAI is the founder of Bureau Spectacular and teaches at UCLA. Previously, Lai lived and worked in a desert shelter at Taliesin and resided in a shipping container at Atelier Van Lieshout on the piers of Rotterdam. Lai designed the Taiwan Pavilion at the 14th Venice Architectural Biennale.

ANDREW LAING, PhD, is a visiting lecturer at Princeton University's School of Architecture and is the head of Workplace Strategy and Design at Bridgewater Associates, LP.

JESSE LECAVALIER is assistant professor at the New Jersey School of Architecture at NJIT. He is the author of *The Rule of Logistics: Walmart and the Architecture of Fulfillment* (University of Minnesota Press, 2016).

LEONG LEONG is focused on projects that inhabit the blurry boundary between culture and commerce, public and private, figure and field, domestic and monumental, diagram and effect. The studio's interests are not defined by a particular project type, but by the potential to create environments and artifacts with cultural resonance.

THOMAS Y. LEVIN, a media theorist at Princeton University, has also curated major international exhibitions on surveillance and the Situationist International. His most recent book is a co-edited volume of Walter Benjamin's media theoretical writings. Currently he is directing a large-scale research project on the media-archaeology of voice mail.

JOHN MAY is founding partner (with Zeina Koreitem) in *MILLIØNS*, a Los Angeles-based experimental design practice. He is Design Critic in Architecture and Director of the Master in Design Studies Postgraduate Research Program at the Harvard University Graduate School of Design.

KYLE MAY is a practicing architect in NYC (www.kylejosephmay.com) and editor-in-chief of *CLOG* (www.clog-online.com).

NICHOLAS MCDERMOTT is a co-founder of the architecture office Future Expansion in New York City. He has taught design studios at the Yale University School of Architecture and the New Jersey Institute of Technology (NJIT).

MICHAEL MEREDITH teaches at Princeton University's School of Architecture and co-founded MOS Architects.

SINA NAJAFI is editor-in-chief of *Cabinet* magazine. He recently worked, together with Simon Critchley, on a project titled "School of Death," which was presented at the Pompidou Center in October 2016.

ODA stands for Office for Design and Architecture. Between 2010 and 2016 ODA prepared over forty designs located within an area of 26 km2. ODA is an outcome of NYC's residential boom. Under a growing volume of work and no time to waste, ODA distilled an intuitive formula of decision making and consolidated a position about living in the city.

JOHN PERRY earned his PhD in philosophy in 1968 from Cornell. He is professor emeritus at UC Riverside and Stanford University. Perry has published widely in the philosophy of language, the philosophy of mind, and issues related to personal identity, including *Knowledge, Possibility and Consciousness* (MIT, 2001) and *Reference and Reflexivity* (CSLI, 2011).

DANIEL PITTMAN is Director of Design at A/D/O. Previously at OMA/AMO and SYPartners, Pittman has designed, researched, advised, curated, and taught. Pittman received his Master of Business Administration at Columbia University and Diploma at the Architectural Association.

PLAYLAB, INC. is the extremely multi-disciplinary creative office founded in 2009 in New York by Archie Lee Coates IV and Jeffrey Franklin, and run alongside Jonathan O'Brien and Ryan J. Simons. With no particular focus, they explore things that interest them by initiating and working with others on ideas.

CHARLES RENFRO has been a partner at Diller Scofidio + Renfro since 2004. He attended Rice University and received a Master of Architecture degree from Columbia University. Mr. Renfro has taught at Rice University, Parsons the New School for Design, School of Visual Arts, and Columbia University.

PIERCE REYNOLDSON is a Senior Virtual Design & Construction Manager at Skanska USA and Lecturer at the Yale School of Architecture. His projects include the World Trade Center PATH Hall, LaGuardia Airport, BIM standards for Harvard University and Boston College, and developing Yale's first Revit-enabled Building Systems Integration course.

JULIAN ROSE is a founding principle of the design studio Formlessfinder and a Senior Editor of *Artforum*.

ANDREW ROSS teaches at NYU and is the author or editor of more than twenty books, including, most recently, *Creditocracy and the Case for Debt Refusal* and *The Gulf: High-Culture/Hard Labor*.

MAGALI SARFATTI-LARSON is a sociologist, who has worked extensively on the professions and on architecture. Her 1994 book, *Behind the Postmodern Facade: Architectural Change in Late Twentieth Century America*, has received an award for excellence in theory from the American Institute of Architects, as well as a sociology of culture award.

SHoP Architects was founded twenty years ago to harness the power of diverse expertise in the design of buildings and environments that improve the quality of public life. SHoP's inclusive, open-minded process allows them to effectively address a broad range of issues in their work.

MANUEL SHVARTZBERG is an architect, writer, and PhD candidate in Architectural History & Theory at Columbia University. He is also an author and editor, most recently of *The Politics of Parametricism* (Bloomsbury Academic, 2015).

GALIA SOLOMONOFF is the principal of SAS/Solomonoff Architecture Studio in Chelsea and has a long history of working with spaces where contemporary art and architecture interact. With Robert Irwin, Ms. Solomonoff oversaw the conversion of a 1929 factory into a daylight-only museum for Dia:Beacon, in Beacon, New York. Solomonoff is an Associate Professor of Architecture at GSAPP, Columbia University. She travels regularly with students to Columbia's Studio-X Global Centers and aims to combine art and architecture, furthering their mission in the cultural and public spheres.

ERICA STOLLER is the director of Esto, an agency that represents a group of architectural photographers and manages an archive of images relating to the built environment

DAN TAEYOUNG operates at the intersection of architecture, technology, and community. He believes that radical space is achieved through applied anthropology, critical engineering, and activist real estate. He is a co-founder of Prime Produce, an intentional guild for social good, and Adjunct Assistant Professor at Columbia GSAPP, where he teaches on representational strategies and experimental design tools.

NADER TEHRANI is the Dean of the Irwin S. Chanin School of Architecture at the Cooper Union. He is also a principal of NADAAA, a multi-disciplinary practice with projects in urbanism, architecture, and fabrication. He was previously a professor of architecture at MIT, where he served as the Head of the Department from 2010-2014.

TROY CONRAD THERRIEN is the Curator of Architecture and Digital Initiatives at the Solomon R. Guggenheim Foundation and Museum, and an Adjunct Professor of Architecture at Columbia University.

NATO THOMPSON is a writer and curator. He is Artistic Director at Creative Time.

ADA TOLLA founded LOT-EK, a design studio based in New York, with Giuseppe Lignano in 1993. LOT-EK has achieved high visibility in the architecture, design, and art world for its sustainable and innovative approach to construction, materials and space through the upcycling of existing industrial objects and systems not originally intended for architecture.

MARC TSURUMAKI is principal and founding partner of Lewis.Tsurumaki. Lewis (LTL Architects), an internationally recognized architectural practice based in New York City. Tsurumaki also teaches at Columbia University's GSAPP.

JULIA VAN DEN HOUT is founder and director of Original Copy, specializing in editorial and curatorial projects within architecture, and co-founder and editor of *CLOG*. Prior to founding Original Copy, she was Director of Press and Marketing at Steven Holl Architects.

J.H. VERKERKE teaches at the University of Virginia School of Law, where he also directs the Program for Employment and Labor Law Studies. His current research interests include contract theory, comparative employment law, vicarious liability, economic analysis of law, and the scholarship of teaching and learning.

MARINA OTERO VERZIER is an architect based in Rotterdam. She is Head of Research at Het Nieuwe Instituut, and Chief Curator of the Oslo Architecture Triennale 2016, together with the After Belonging Agency. Previously, she was Director of Global Network Programming at Studio-X, and Adjunct Assistant Professor at Columbia University's GSAPP. Otero is a PhD candidate at ETSA Madrid.

IAN VOLNER is a writer and critic, and has contributed articles on design, urbanism, and architecture to *The Wall Street Journal*, *Harper's*, *The New Republic*, and *The New Yorker* online, among other publications. His third book, a biography of architect Michael Graves, will be available from Princeton Architectural Press in late 2017.

DON WEINREICH is a practicing architect and partner in Ennead Architects.

MARION WEISS is the Graham Chair Professor of Architecture at the University of Pennsylvania and has also taught at Harvard, Yale, and Cornell. Her practice, WEISS/MANFREDI, is known for the dynamic integration of architecture, art, infrastructure, and landscape. Noted projects include the Olympic Sculpture Park, Brooklyn Botanic Garden's Visitor Center, Barnard's Diana Center, Penn's Center for Nanotechnology, and the US Embassy in New Delhi, India.

SARAH WHITING is Dean and William Ward Watkin Professor of Architecture at Rice University; she is also a partner, along with Ron Witte, of WW Architecture, based in Houston.

MABEL O. WILSON is a cultural historian and designer. She is an associate professor at Columbia University's GSAPP and senior fellow at the Institute for Research in African American Studies (IRAAS).

HUMAN WU is an architect currently living and working in Hong Kong. After graduating from the Harvard Graduate School of Design, he worked at international offices in New York,

NY and Basel, Switzerland. He was one of the founding editors of *CLOG*, and has written for various other magazines including *Time+Architecture* (Shanghai), *San Rocco* (Milan), *MONU* (Rotterdam), and *C3* (Seoul).

KIM YAO, AIA, is principal, with Stephen Cassell and Adam Yarinsky, of Architecture Research Office (ARO), a twenty-five-person firm based in New York City. She holds an undergraduate degree in architecture from Columbia College: Columbia University, and a Master of Architecture from Princeton University.

MICHAEL YOUNG is an architect and educator practicing in New York City where he is a founding partner of the architectural design studio Young & Ayata. Michael is currently an Assistant Professor at the Cooper Union and a Visiting Assistant Professor at Princeton University.

MIMI ZEIGER is a Los Angeles-based critic, editor, and curator. Her work is situated at the intersection of architecture and media cultures. She's an opinion columnist for *Dezeen* and has written for *The New York Times*, *Domus*, *Architectural Review*, and *Architect*, where she is a contributing editor.

Artist

AMIE SIEGEL is an American artist whose work has been the subject of solo exhibitions at The Metropolitan Museum of Art, Kunstmuseum Stuttgart, Villa Stuck Munich, and MAK, Vienna; and featured in group exhibitions at the Whitney, MoMA/PS1, Hayward Gallery, Witte de With, and the Cannes, Berlin, Toronto, and New York Film festivals.

Editors

EVA FRANCH i GILABERT is an architect, critic, curator, educator, and lecturer of experimental forms of art and architectural practice. Franch specializes in the making of alternative architecture histories and futures. Since 2010, Franch is the Chief Curator and Executive Director of Storefront for Art and Architecture in New York. Her book *Projective Archeologies* is forthcoming in 2018.

ANA MILJAČKI is a critic, curator, and Associate Professor of Architecture at Massachusetts Institute of Technology, where she teaches history, theory, and design. Her work focuses on the relationship between politics and the products and circumstances of architectural labor. Her book *The Optimum Imperative* is forthcoming with Routledge in 2017.

CARLOS MÍNGUEZ CARRASCO is Associate Curator at Storefront for Art and Architecture and Chief Curator of the Oslo Architecture Triennale 2016 with the After Belonging Agency. Mínguez has organized a wide range of exhibitions, events, and competitions with a particular focus on how social, cultural, and pressing political issues influence contemporary architecture.

JACOB REIDEL is a practicing architect, editor, and writer based in New York City. He is committed to fostering critical dialogue across the broadest possible spectrum of architects, designers, critics, scholars, and the general public. He is a founding editor of *CLOG*, edited *Perspecta* 40 "Monster", and is a former Teach for America Corps Member. He has lectured widely and taught at schools ranging from PS 161 to Columbia University's GSAPP.

ASHLEY SCHAFER is a writer, designer, educator, and registered architect whose research lies at the intersection of contemporary architecture, urbanism, landscape, history, technology, and practice. She is co-founder and co-editor of *PRAXIS*, journal of writing + building. Schafer is Professor of Architecture at The Ohio State University, where she is Chair of Graduate Studies and is Visiting Professor at the Harvard Graduate School of Design.

OFFICE*US* CREDITS

US Pavilion, 14th International
Architecture Exhibition —
La Biennale di Venezia

Commissioner
Storefront for Art and Architecture

Curators
Eva Franch, Ana Miljački,
Ashley Schafer

Associate Curator
Michael Kubo

Assistant Curators
Carlos Mínguez Carrasco, Jacob Reidel

Co-Organizer
PRAXIS

Exhibition Design
LEONG LEONG: Dominic Leong, Chris
Leong, Gabriel Burkett; Jackie Woon
Bae, Clare Johnston, Yu-Hsiang Lin,
Jane Jonghyun Yi

Graphic Design
Pentagram: Natasha Jen, Jang Hyun
Han, Joseph Han, Maurann Stein,
Boqin Peng, Ji Park, Veronica Hoglund

Technology Architecture
CASE

Global Network Strategy
Therrien-Barley

Media Producer
Andrew Fierberg

Film
Amie Siegel

Web Design
M-A-U-S-E-R; Partner & Partners

Publishing Partner
Lars Müller Publishers

Media Partner
Architizer

Project Coordinator
Irina Chernyakova

Research Coordinator
Juan Jofre

Development, External Relations and Special Events
Kara L. Meyer

Technology and Production Coordinator
Piotr Chizinski

Outreach and Communications Manager
Zeynep Göksel

Project Assistant
Natalie Snyder

Project Team:
Austin E. Knowlton School at The Ohio
State University
Laila Ammar, Levi Bedall, Tyler
Brozovich, Joe Carifa, Nicholas
Castillo, Luke Dougal, Clay
Ellerbrook, Abdelrahman Elzamly,
Talia Friedman, Chris Mannella,
Nicholas Miller, Dustin Page, Darren
Spensiero, Alexander Stagge,
Jacqueline Stern, Jianning Zhong,
Michael Zumpano

Project Team:
MIT Department of Architecture
Kyle Barker, Christianna Bonin, Kyle
Coburn, Nathan Friedman, Sam
Ghantous, Anastasia Hiller, Jessica
Jorge, Karen Kitayama, Gabriel
Kozlowski, Jasmine Kwak, Patrick Evan
Little, Ann Lok Lui, Moojin Park,
Austin Smith, Tyler Stevermer, Evelyn
Ting, Michael Waldrep, Sarah Weir,
Natthida Wiwatwicha, Rixt Woudstra,
Wenfei Xu Support: Daniel Chang,
Kristina Eldrenkamp, Nicolo Guida,
Lee Moreau, David Oliver, Chiranit
Prateepasen, Claire Shafer, Trygve
Wastvedt

Project Team: PRAXIS
Amanda Reeser Lawrence, Margaret
Arbanas, Andrew Colopy, Megan Miller,
Fred Tang, Irina Verona

Project Team:
Storefront for Art and Architecture
Silvia Callegari, Tyrene Calvesbert,
Maria Castro, Diandra Cohen, Ian
Costello, Erica Angel Fernandez de
Soto, Ashely Kuo, Francesca Lantieri,
Itzel Lavanderos, Anu Lill, Yuma
Shinohara, Michael Signorile, Zaina
Soueid, Melody Stein, Elise Stella,
Mario Torres

Project Advisors
Laurie Beckelman, Aaron Betsky, Holly
Block, Beatriz Colomina, Keller
Easterling, Campbell Hyers, Cathy
Lang Ho, James von Klemperer, Marc
Kushner, Lars Müller, Douglass Rice,
Robert Rubin, Sylvia J. Smith, Lisa
Phillips, Artur Walther, Sarah
Whiting, Karen Wong

Special Thanks
Peter Aaron; Zahra Ali Baba; Dana
Aljoud`er; Jordan Anderson; Alan I.
Appel; Iwan Baan; Chiara Barbieri;
Cecil Barnes; Roberta Bartalone;
Cameron Blaylock; Barry Beagan; Brett
Beyer; Gary Boyd; Roy Brand; Beth
Broome; Bryan Cave LLP: Alan Appel,
Greg Galvin, Nicole Gates, Robert
Lancaster, Margery Perlmutter, and
Stefan Skulesch; Michael Cadwell;
Rebecca Chamberlain; Alan Cross;
Giacomo DiThiene; Patricia Driscoll;
Ignacio Peydro Duclos; Ellen Finnie
Duranceau; Nazareth Ekmakijan; Igor

Ekštajn; Britt Eversole; Alia Farid; Enrico Fontanari; Christine Foushee; Frener & Reifer: Thomas Geissler and Michael Purzer; Miles Fujiki; Curt Gambetta; Emil Rodriguez Garabot; Roland Halbe; Jim Harrington; Sarah Herda; Dessen Hillman; Adam Himes; Margaret Ho; Yasmina Khan; Duncan Kincaid; Ryan John King; Arianne Kouri; Naho Kubota; Ricardo Leon; Neil Levine; Nicolò Lewanski; Rungu Lin; Rob Livesey; Hannah Loomis; George Louras; Elizabeth Gill Lui; Sebastian Lux; Richard Mandelkorn; Mark Jarzombek; Sandro Marpillero; Melissa Marsh; Jack Masey; Lorrie A. McAllister; Brendan McGetrick; Cathleen McGuigan; John McLaughlin; Franco Micucci; Nicholas de Moncheaux; Antoni Muntadas; Hansrobyn van Oosten; Saverio Panata & Silvia Zini; Janet Parks; Partner & Partners: Greg Mihalko, Zach Mihalko, and David Liss; Beverly Payeff-Masey; Ivan Rašković; Bika Rebek; Karl Roarty; Julian Rose; Marco Ariso Rota; Ryan Rothman; Rami el Samahy; Joel Sanders; Adèle Naudé Santos; Kelly Schein; Ori Scialom; Neslihan Sen; Karin Šerman; Douglas Sershen; Sarah Sherman; Tarek Shuaib; Simon Preston Gallery; Amber Sinicrope; Monica Socorro; Erica Stoller; Hicks Stone; Sam Sweezy; Nader Tehrani; Wayne Thom; Dicle Uzunyayla; Gary Van Zante; Ana Cristina Vargas; Davi Weber; Ann Whiteside; Mark Wigley; Jaren Wilcoxson; Mark Young; Ines Zalduendo

Office*US* Sponsors
Austin E. Knowlton School of Architecture at the Ohio State University; Autodesk; Creative Partner Bureau of Educational and Cultural Affairs, US Department of State; Herman Miller; Massachusetts Institute of Technology Department of Architecture; Peggy Guggenheim Collection, Venice (Solomon R. Guggenheim Foundation, New York)

Office*US* Supporter
AECOM; Arup; Esto Photographics; Graham Foundation for Advanced Studies in the Fine Arts; Hewlett Packard | AMD; Kohn Pedersen Fox Associates (KPF); Reggiani S.p.A Iluminazione

Office*US* Benefactor
American Apparel; Elise Jaffe + Jeffrey Brown; FXFOWLE Architects; Frederick Iseman; MakerBot; Oldcastle Building Envelope; Robert Melvin Rubin and Stéphane Samuel; Skidmore, Owings & Merrill LLP; Walther Family Foundation

Office*US* Leader
Arthur H. Schein Memorial Fund; JAHN

Office*US* Contributor
Cornell University; Dreamair; Lanny and Sharon Martin; OTTO Archive; RTKL; The University of San Diego

Office*US* Patron
Peter Aaron; American Institute of Architects; Control Group; Iwan Baan; Harman; Michael A. Manfredi and Marion Weiss; Prolitec; Charles Renfro; RD RICE Construction Inc.

Office*US* Circle
Acción Cultural Española; Adrian Smith + Gordon Gill Architecture; Daniel and Estrellita Brodsky; Eva Ching and Jeff Small; Todd DeGarmo; Beth Rudin DeWoody; Elizabeth Gill Lui; Barbara Jakobson; Roland Halbe; Knowlton School Alumni Society; Lauren Kogod and David Smiley; Richard Mishaan Design; Toshiko Mori Architect PLLC; Frederieke Taylor; David and Jane Walentas

Office*US* Friends
American Printing Company; Holly Block; C & M Shade Corporation; Carlos Brillembourg and Karin Waisman; Belmont Freeman; Claudia Gould; The Henry Ford; Glenn Horowitz; Illy; Steven T. Incontro and David Joselit; Linda and Harry Macklowe; Vram Malek; Sara P. Meltzer; NRI (National Reprographics Inc.); Jinhee Park + John Hong, SsD; Margery Perlmutter; Soho Art Materials; Karen Wong; Mabel Wilson

Office*US* was commissioned by Storefront for Art and Architecture on behalf of the US Department of State's Bureau of Educational and Cultural Affairs.

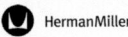

Storefront for Art and Architecture

Founded in 1982, Storefront for Art and Architecture is a nonprofit organization that advances innovative and critical ideas at the intersection of architecture, art, and design. Storefront's exhibitions, events, competitions, publications, and projects provide alternative platforms for dialogue and collaboration across disciplinary, geographic, and ideological boundaries.
www.storefrontnews.org

Further titles:
OfficeUS Agenda (Catalogue) ISBN 978-3-03778-437-2
OfficeUS Atlas (Repository) ISBN 978-3-03778-438-9